BATTLEGROUND
PACIFIC

"Close to the Flame" Sterling Mace on Peleliu, 1944. *(Courtesy Anthony Cioffi.)*

BATTLEGROUND PACIFIC

A Marine Rifleman's Combat Odyssey in K/3/5

STERLING MACE

and

NICK ALLEN

 St. Martin's Griffin ≈ New York

BATTLEGROUND PACIFIC: A MARINE RIFLEMAN'S COMBAT ODYSSEY IN K/3/5. Copyright
© 2012 by Sterling Mace and Nick Allen. All rights reserved. Printed in the United
States of America. For information, address St. Martin's Press, 175 Fifth Avenue,
New York, N.Y. 10010.

www.stmartins.com

Design by Phil Mazzone
Maps by Paul J. Pugliese

The Library of Congress has cataloged the hardcover edition as follows:

Mace, Sterling.
    Battleground Pacific : a Marine rifleman's combat odyssey in K/3/5 / Sterling
Mace and Nick Allen.—1st ed.
        p. cm.
    ISBN 978-1-250-00505-2 (hardcover)
    ISBN 978-1-250-00977-7 (e-book)
    1. Mace, Sterling.   2. World War, 1939–1945—Personal narratives,
American.   3. World War, 1939–1945—Campaigns—Pacific Area.   4. United
States. Marine Corps. Marines, Regiment 5th. Battalion, 3rd. Company K.
5. United States. Marine Corps—Biography.   6. Marines—United States—
Biography.   I. Allen, Nick, 1973–   II. Title.
    D767.9.M33 2012
    940.54'5973092—dc23
    [B]
                                                                2012004382

ISBN 978-1-250-02963-8 (trade paperback)

St. Martin's Griffin books may be purchased for educational, business, or promotional
use. For information on bulk purchases, please contact Macmillan Corporate and
Premium Sales Department at 1-800-221-7945 extension 5442 or write specialmarkets
@macmillan.com.

First St. Martin's Griffin Edition: May 2013

10 9 8 7 6 5 4 3 2 1

For Freddie Mack Allen
and
Dorothy Edna Mace

CONTENTS

ACKNOWLEDGMENTS

NOTHING CAN SURVIVE IN A VACUUM. Thanks to the countless individuals who aided us in writing this book—from its inception through the long hours of research to its life online, where hundreds of followers showed great interest and continued with their enthusiastic encouragement—we not only survived; we also thrived.

Matthew Austin, for proofreading early chapters: Offering suggestions from an outsider's point of view, you became an insider. Jody E. Powell, my daughter and my computer pro. Skip Mace, my son and golfing buddy. Stephanie, Ethan, and Penny-Lane Allen, for inspiration beyond measure. Jan Snure, Darla Bowen (you know why), Brian Leyden, and his mother, Marie Leyden, for helping us keep the *real* Billy Leyden's memory alive, along with the memories of thousands of riflemen who no longer have a voice. The Marietta, Georgia, Support Group. Lois Sellers and her five daughters. Patty Everett, from *Leatherneck* magazine—finding that photo was pure magic. James Poland—for scannin all our photos. Cheryl Rice and clan. Tommy Colonna. Dorothea Ciofi. Tray Mangum, for making me aware of a certain book (that will remain nameless—but it was valuable, outside of this writing). Harry

Raymond Mace, Harriet Mace, and Mickey. Dorothy McCarthy, our missing link to the life of Larry Mahan. Cam Finley, George M. Barrows Sr., and the marvelous Cynthia St. Claire, for all of her time, photos, and care, in giving Peleliu a new life, all these years later. Chuck Bell, for having the confidence that I could actually write something of note. Carlos, Jorge, Randy, and Reese. Alfonso Zepeda. Wally Dees. Hiroki Nakazato, for the Japanese translations (I probably didn't get it right back then, and I probably didn't get it right now). Seth Peridon, from the National WWII Museum in New Orleans. Keith Davis, for all your effort. Anthony Ciofi, for the great drawings. David Siltanaki and Nick Villarreal for your support on Facebook. In fact, the whole Facebook crowd: There are too many to name, but you know you've been great pals. Also, all the families, friends, spouses, and old marines themselves who were kind enough to let us use their photos for this book. Jerry Waldrop. Harry Bender and the rest of K/3/5 who are still living. Not to mention the guys from my platoon: Your names and what you looked like are forever etched in my mind.

Then there is Jim Hornfischer, our agent, for always pushing for bigger and better things. We are very fortunate to have you in our corner. Thank you for tapping into what we were putting out.

Marc Resnick, our editor at St. Martin's Press: Your confidence in our work was invaluable to the process as a whole. Despite all the hard work, you still managed to make this experience both fun and educating. Your taking a chance on us has been one of the most gratifying experiences of our lives. The rest of the St. Martin's crew: Sarah Johnson, Katherine Canfield, and India Cooper, our copy editor, for making us look so good in print.

Last, but not least, Monica, from New Orleans . . . where are you?

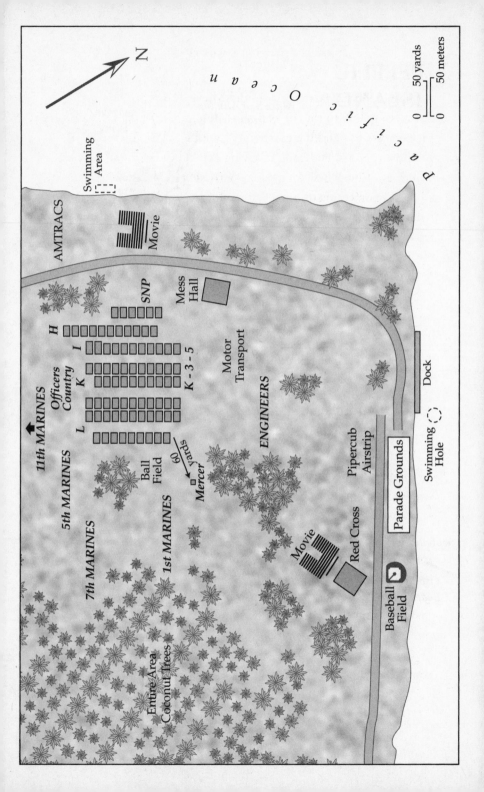

PELELIU
ISLAND

Mace and Almann
Surrounded

Kongauru
Island

Ngesebus
Island

Airstrip

P a c i f i c

O c e a n

West Road

October 1, 1944

Umurbrogol Mountains

Teskevich Killed

Five Sisters

K - 3 - 5

Air Field

Purple Beach

September 15, 1944

Orange
Beach 2

N

0	1,000	2,000 yards
0	1,000	2,000 meters

OKINAWA SHIMA

Ernie Pyle Killed

IE SHIMA

East China Sea

Nago Wan

Nago•

Pacific Ocean

Yontan Airfield

6th Marine Division

Kimmu Wan
3rd Btn.
5th Mar.

1st Marine Division

7th Army Division

Kadena Airfield

Machinato Airfield

Nakagusuku Wan

6th & 1st Marine Divisions

Naha•

Shuri Line

Philippine Sea

2nd Marine Division Fake Landing

N

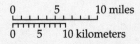

| 0 | 5 | 10 miles |
| 0 | 5 | 10 kilometers |

400 yards to
Shuri Castle

JAPANESE TERRITORY

Abandoned
Jeep

Abandoned
Tank

Sterling Mace

2nd Platoon

3rd Platoon

The Boomerang

K - Company
Command Post

1st Platoon

Machine Gun
James Allen

DANGER ZONE

Douglas Patrol

N

What we changed
Was innocence for innocence; we knew not
The doctrine of ill-doing, nor dreamed
That any did.

—WILLIAM SHAKESPEARE
(*The Winter's Tale*, Polixenes at I.ii)

BATTLEGROUND
PACIFIC

PROLOGUE

Before Carl Hubbell and Miz Muggins, before PFC Mahan and Guy Lombardo, before Harry S. dropped a "Little Boy" on 350,000 Japanese, a little girl died in South Ozone Park one day.

I didn't know much about that little girl. I knew she was my sister. Dorothy was her name. She had white skin and blond hair and a great stillness hung around her as she lay in her casket at our home in Queens. I was too young to know a whole lot more. After all, I was only four years old.

It was September 9, 1928.

My dad was there, I'm sure. Mom, too. Neighbors would arrive at the house to pay their respects to our family—and to view the little dead girl, who would never again be troubled by arms and legs, which she found unusable in her thirteen years of life. Dorothy no longer had to eat with spoons that had been bent inward at the handle, creating a ladle-like instrument, so that tiny paralytic hands could manage the utensils more easily. Those spoons would always remain in my memory, assuredly because I was viewing them at a time when my young mind was making the connection between the normal spoons I was just beginning to master and the ones my parents had to fashion for my sister out of necessity.

It was infantile paralysis that killed Mom's firstborn child. Polio to some. The same affliction that later killed a certain wheelchair-bound president—the man who stood up boldly for a grieving and angry nation, one day in late 1941, and with a "righteous might" declared that sneak attacks by little yellow bastards would not go unpunished by the United States of America.

Crippled presidents, it seems, make big decisions regarding life and death.

Crippled little girls do not.

Nobody, neither my mom nor my dad, took me by the hand and led me to see Dorothy for the final time. I led myself; and the truth is, my last look at Dorothy is a thought that also serves as my very first memory of the girl. My first memory of anything at all, in fact . . . and it was a memory of death.

So, on September 15, 1944, almost sixteen years to the day after Dorothy passed away, about two dozen other marines and I, packed like matchsticks in our amphibious tractor, found ourselves skimming the Pacific Ocean toward the beach of Peleliu Island, with the rest of the 1st Marine Division—all of us immortal young men, about to become severely mortal, courtesy of the Empire of Japan.

As we were heading in, for some reason that I will never know, my little Dorothy came to mind—just a flicker like a muzzle flash, a trace memory of something inexplicable—and I said to myself . . .

I said to myself something that I've told very few people in my life, save for my mom, upon my return from the war . . .

You see, it was my mom who explained to my middle sister, Mickey, and me that Dorothy was an angel. Mom called Dorothy an angel, and that was something she really ingrained into the minds of her living children.

Every weekend Mom would take Mickey and me to Evergreens Cemetery, in Brooklyn, to visit Dorothy's grave. We would catch the bus to Metropolitan Avenue and then take the trolley car to Bushwick Avenue. Then we'd walk the rest of the way to the cemetery, where we viewed the mound that marked Dorothy's final resting place. Every weekend, for a long, long time, we did this.

Now, as a Marine Corps rifleman, I was taking a very different journey, yet toward a place with striking similarities to the boneyard of Dorothy's eternal youth. Peleliu: The bitterest battle that the Marine Corps faced in World War II became the charnel house for many more youths, many years later.

That singular moment in time, before we hit the beach on Peleliu, ticks off the echoes of my personal past, present, and future into an amalgamation of everything that became life as I know it. It was a defining moment that transcends all the clichéd stories of old men who sit around dreaming of the days when they were young and at peril.

Understand this: The spearhead of any attack is the rifleman and his rifle.

My name is Sterling Mace. I was that rifleman.

1

SAILING THE SOUTH OZONE SEA

AT 7:13 A.M. ON THE MORNING of February 2, 1924, Punxsutaw-
ney Phil, "Seer of Seers, Sage of Sages, Prognosticator of Prognos-
ticators, and Weather Prophet Extraordinary," burrowed out of
his dirty little rodent hole and saw his dirty little rodent shadow,
signifying that another six weeks of winter was on its way. Later
that evening, I came into this world, as my mom gave birth to me
in the back of Jake Cohen's hardware store, at the corner of
135th Place and Rockaway Boulevard, Queens Borough, New
York, amid the lead piping, kerosene jars, penny nails, and post
hole diggers.

After I was born, my dad, the tall and dapper Harry Raymond
Mace, lost everything in the stock market crash of 1929. Bigwigs
were jumping out of Wall Street buildings on "Black Tuesday,"
and a fat banker leaped from the top of the Stock Exchange and
landed right on my dad's pushcart, destroying everything we
owned.

Of course, that's a little joke, but even in the biggest lies there
are still the smallest grains of truth.

In this case, the standing truths are twofold: In those days, unless you were living in the White House, to some extent or another, nobody in America remained unaffected by the Great Depression of the 1930s. Secondly, the real Pacific war did not begin on the beaches of Tarawa, Peleliu, and Iwo Jima—nor did it start with the Japanese attack on Pearl Harbor. The *real* Pacific war began with the dreams and realities, the episodes and ambitions, that beat within the hearts of the young men who would later experience it.

We youths of the era collectively and individually were molded by the Great Depression and Roosevelt's New Deal ideals, thus finding ourselves well equipped to kill the sons of Nippon and lay low their yellow nation. We didn't know it then, but the kids of the Great Depression, a deprived generation, were preparing for war—and we were becoming damned good at it, even before we laid hands on a weapon.

For me, the New York of my time was the New York of *all* time.

It is a lost New York. Lost to the years, now, but very much a product of its own time, as farmsteads and subway lines spit in the palms of their hands and shook on it as if it still meant something. Wiseguys could be seen standing on the street corners on Saturday afternoons, ogling the girls and shootin' the shit—and then later that afternoon the same bunch would hitch a truck out to the potato farms, in Suffolk County and Montauk Point, and then back again, each time seeing how far they could make it out.

So when my family moved out to Queens, before I was born, all of our relatives from Brooklyn laughed and said we were moving out to the country. Yet my dad probably took the electric train to get there!

We were the *overflow* of Queens during the Great Depression.

From our home on 123rd Street, down the back of 128th Street, was "Little Italy," where the Italians (we called them guineas back then) would throw all sorts of exotic and colorful festivities. They'd have a feast, with food stalls dotting the sidewalks, selling greasy sausages and fat cannolis. Confetti littered the streets. There were loud voices everywhere, and chirping children ran between the legs of their *padri* and *madri*.

Then me and my pals, when we got old enough, we'd swagger through the crowd, browsing for those cute little Italian girls, trying to romance them amid the spinning wheels, bright lights, and games of chance (which I swear were rigged, because those "games" would clean you out quicker than those Italian girls could heist your heart).

When I returned home for the night, empty-handed and empty-hearted, I would lie in bed, hands propped behind my head, listening to the caterwauling of the Italian opera singers as they cut loose for the last time before they closed down the show. Then the fireworks would go off.

I could hear the pops, bangs, and whizzes of the pyrotechnics as the reds, yellows, and oranges smeared lightscapes across my bedroom window.

Even after the war, I lay there, watching the sounds and listening to the sights, as they held another feast, while consciously I tried to equate those sensations to the things I had experienced in the Pacific.

The fireworks wouldn't shake me up or anything. I wouldn't become frightened. Although they were pretty close.

I was pretty close.

It was simply a unique time for all of us in Queens, from the skunk cabbage farms in South Ozone to the Aqueduct Racetrack on Rockaway to places people today never heard of, like Cornell Park and Richmond Hill Circle. Queens was popping with civilization, as one million immigrants and natives shared a commonality that not many people do today. Yet as America wore the face of tragedy in the reflection of the stock market crash of 1929, my Queens, too, was no exception. Beneath the tough lessons of meager meals and Home Relief, there was a flipside to our disposition— the mask of comedy, which diametrically opposed the Depression that assailed us: the double-sided Greek mask of classic theater.

We had to keep ourselves in clover, despite knowing better. Despite ourselves.

Then a miracle happened, when I was eleven years old—Christmas morning 1935.

It didn't change anything, yet to me it changed *everything*.

Mickey and I flew down the stairs that Christmas morning, screeching to a halt in front of the tree out on the porch. The sparkle in our eyes surely eclipsed the glamour of promises that lay beneath the traditional tree.

For traditionally, under the tree, there might be the same wooden canoe I received the year before, but this year Dad had painted it a different color, so that it looked great again. Or I had a metal dirigible, which got the same treatment a couple of times—painted up, or polished nice to give it a new shine. Rounding out our Christmas bounty, Mom and Dad put an orange, maybe an apple, and a few walnuts in the stockings that hung in front of our false-front fireplace. It didn't matter what I got for Christmas, though. It didn't matter if it was something new or a little bit of the old stuff. The happiness my family shared on Christmas had a lot to do with just being together—and also knowing that there were some children, like the kids who lived in the shantytown of Cornell Park, with their dirt roads and swamps, who were probably getting whippings on Christmas morning, just to set their minds right for the coming New Year.

Besides, we had a good roof over our heads. Our home on Panama (123rd) Street was small but comfortable. Dad had paid $2,300 for it, so that made it ours. It was a three-bedroom bungalow, with my room fairly cramped, being situated on the top floor where the roof pitched down at a slant. Mickey was upstairs also, but her bedroom was larger than mine; she got first dibs because of her age. Mom and Dad took the downstairs bedroom, coming off of the living room; then there was a small dining room and a kitchen. That was it.

We could have been a lot worse off.

Dad even had a car, a 1927 Essex, which was great, but we couldn't afford the antifreeze for it when the winter bit deep enough, so Dad would have to pour water into the radiator as a coolant. Water worked fine, until you parked the car for about three seconds. A case in point: One winter, Dad took a WPA job, building Jacob Riis Park; as he got ready to leave for the day, he went out to the Essex and tried to turn the motor over, only to find the car wouldn't start because the engine was a solid block of ice. Being the logical guy that Dad was, he built a fire under the motor with some old wood, so that after a while the water thawed and he was able to ride home again.

Even our clothes, growing up, were strictly the cheap stuff.

Mickey and I got our clothes from a handout store on 119th Street, where the uniform of the day was always brown corduroy knickers, black shoes, and black stockings. It seemed that everybody wore nothing but black in those days. And those shoes? Everyone was given a pair of size D shoes, even if they had size EEE feet. For three years I walked around with sores on my heels, trying to get into those damned lace-ups.

It was later, when I was in the Marine Corps, that I remembered those shoes, when I saw how happy the rednecks in our platoon were when they received their U.S.-issue boondockers—which, as it turned out, were the first shoes they'd ever owned in their lives.

It was funny, and we New Yorkers would crack wise at the Rebels; nevertheless, it brought back a certain thankfulness for how lucky some of us were, compared to those who had grown up in the Dust Bowl days of the Great Depression. Yet which one of us could claim we were unaffected by the hard knocks of our era? There wasn't a single marine who didn't have at least one drum to beat over the want and worry of the 1930s.

Even in 1943, as we marines took the train from Camp Lejeune to California, crossing into Georgia, the call of the Depression still knew every one of us by name. The train made frequent stops, and little black children ran up to our open windows and began dancing, performing, for any change that we'd throw out to them. They didn't know any different; they still smiled and danced, kicking up puffs of dust around their ankles. They were maybe seven or eight years old, dirty from head to toe, and living in dry wooden shacks. I even recall one such "home" being constructed out of the back end of a rusted automobile.

Those poor children probably didn't even know what a Christmas morning was.

Eight years earlier, however—before I had any notion of the Marine Corps, or of death from Japan—happiness abounded in a little corner of New York, when I saw the miracle behind our Christmas tree.

It was the greatest gift a boy could ask for.

Somehow (*gasp!*), some way (*it's the most beautifulest thing I've seen in my whole entire life!*) . . . there was a Junior Racer Flexible Flyer behind the tree—a brand-new sled! No, not just any sled, but the Cadillac of sleds! The Flexible Flyer was a work of art that might as well have been crafted by da Vinci, or God, for that matter, as far as I was concerned. The high-polished gleam-sheen of the wooden board was so glossy I could make out the shiny reflection of my huge grin, mirroring off its golden-hued surface. The fiery red runners, at the sides of the board, held their own dimensions of beauty—long and sleek, almost knifelike in their finely tooled curvature.

I wheeled around to face my parents—unbelieving, almost afraid to touch such a gift, lest it evaporate before my eyes—only to see their approving smiles as they nodded for me to go ahead and take it, love it, cherish it . . . it was mine! *Dad must've knocked over a bank to get that kinda scratch!*

"Thank you, thank you thank you!" I said, jumping up and down, hugging my parents, wetting their faces with kisses. Miz

Muggins, our old family dog, merely lay there, with her muzzle between her paws, looking up at us indifferently. It had been a long time since Muggins had been spry enough to wag and jump about anything.

It was a miracle.

I never asked my dad how he could afford it—but I never forgot that he did.

That Christmas I went sledding the whole day, coming home only once to change my wet clothes, hanging my soaked socks by the stove and putting on fresh knickers. I must have been quite a sight, going up and down Donnelly Hill with my pals, spinning snow as we went, intentionally dragging one foot behind my sled when a buddy started gaining on me. The snow would pelt him in his face, blinding him, skidding him off into a spin!

I didn't have fancy winter wear, but with my old knit cap and my rough suede workman's gloves, I was warm enough. To keep the water from getting through the holes in my shoes, I took some old burlap bags, put my feet through them, and tied them off at the ankles. I must have looked silly, though I couldn't have cared less how I appeared, just as long as my eyes watered from the speed of flying down the hill in my gold and red chariot.

Eventually some girls our age showed up, laughing and carrying on, as they are wont to do. We would speed up right behind them as we flew, and with one arm we'd take their sled and spin it! Around and around they went until they took a soft tumble in the powder. Then we'd go up and pretend we were sorry for doing it—but for some reason (a reason none of us knew at that age), we did it just to be close to them.

That evening I walked back home under the moonlight with my best pals, Tommy Colonna and Billy Boscha, none of us saying much. The only sound was the crunching snow beneath our shoes.

Presently Billy piped up and said something akin to what the rest of us were thinking.

"Ya know," Billy said, "everything was just peachy till those girls showed up."

"Ah, they were okay," I said.

"Yeah." Billy changed his mind. "They were okay."

We walked a few more yards in silence, and then Billy spoke again.

"Say, you don't think they'll be back here tomorrow, do ya?"

"Probably," Tommy said.

"Yeah, probably," I replied.

"Well . . ." You could tell Billy was deep in thought. "If they come back . . . like tomorrow, say . . . whattaya wanna do with 'em?"

I stopped walking, and everyone else did, too. "I dunno, Billy . . . spin 'em around like we did today?" I shrugged.

"Yeah, that was pretty fun." Tommy laughed.

"Funny, too!" Billy laughed also.

I was in agreement, and we resumed our walk, our gang relieved that it was finally out in the open.

"I just never had that kind of fun before!" Billy smiled.

I was eleven years old.

I'm fifteen.

At the Brooklyn Star Burlesque, my brother-in-law, Bobby Rice, gets the bright idea to sneak me into the show. Mickey got married. Bobby eventually gets the Battle of the Bulge over in Europe.

He stuffs a fedora down over my ears and turns up the collar of his long overcoat (the sleeves hang down well past my fingers); the final touch is the cigarette he puts in my mouth. *Laughter.*

"One ticket, please," I say, and I'm in. The doors open to the burlesque; my eyes are too small to hold it all in—a whole new world awaits me, and—

I'm sixteen.

Gallons of blood pour out of a strung-up horse and onto the bricks as the men from the docks slice open the animal while it dangles over the pavement. I have never seen so much blood in my life.

Van Iderstine, the offal docks, New York City. The whole place is a turd clogging the drainpipe. Tommy and I beat feet.

When the cops nabbed them, Petey Masciale and Doug Lutz must have squealed on us. Five of us had broken into a boat in Amityville. Billy claimed it was his aunt's boat, but it was no more his aunt's boat than it was his grandfather's submarine. So when Petey and Doug didn't return to our "borrowed" boat after swiping some baked goods, Billy, Tommy, and I headed for Eastport, the duck capital of the world, where all the roads are paved with duck shit. Then on to Van Iderstine, with its fat-rendering factories for dead animals.

Then home.

Mom says, "Joe Stanworth is looking for you, Brother. You better go out the back door."

Joe Stanworth, the cop who also moonlighted as the local baseball umpire. Everybody knew Joe, that great big sucker—standing six foot four, at least.

I start out the back door, but Mom calls back, "Oh no, here—he's pulling up, you might as well face him." Joe pulls up in his 1937 four-door Ford, and I know I'll be sitting in the back of it soon.

Joe rounds up the rest of the gang and says, "If I ask you a civil question, I want a civil answer!"

What the hell's a civil question? That became the gang's inside gag, until . . .

Probation.

Probation or the CMTC. I chose the Citizens' Military Training Camp, in Fort Dix, New Jersey, even though I wasn't seventeen yet. They let me slide.

The summer of 1940. The bayonet course, shooting the '03 Spring-field rifle, marching, walking through the tear-gas room, eating army chow, falling in. They even let me shoot left-handed at the range.

I am seventeen.

Spring grass and freshly squeezed sunshine, muted earth and raw calf leather—these are the sights and scents of boys playing baseball in the '30s and '40s, the golden age of a sport that became the bluster and shout for a nation that had little to cheer about. I pitched a mean game-of-my-life or two before the home team bore arms and swung for foreign fields.

The roar of the crowd.

I was Carl Hubbell on the mound, zipping the ball over the plate, really zinging it in there—*"Steeeeryk!"*

Even if there were only one hundred people in attendance, to me the crowd was deafening. The cheering crowd didn't stop when the game was over, either.

When you're a young man, athletic, in perfect health, with a gleam in your eye and a swagger in your step, the cheering crowd is always present, filling your head, lifting you to new heights. Getting up in the morning—the crowd roars with approval. Eating your breakfast—they clap with excitement. Passing an exam at school—they applaud as if you just pitched a no-hitter. Their adoration provides buoyancy. Call it confidence, call it imagination, call it youthful vigor, or even call it arrogance; no matter, the Depression-era kids needed that fighting chance to prove ourselves in any field of play, whether it was in the classroom, picking cotton, or carrying a football across the goal line.

The roar of the crowd.

While in combat, the ovation remained strong, even if it had quieted down to but a murmur. It enabled us to ride the crest to victory, unwavering, never faltering.

In glory they fell, many young lives, yet with the silver cheer of a nation's approval ringing brightly in their ears. The touchdown. The home run. In Elysian Fields they turned around and faced the crowd, streamers falling, all eyes on them, smiling in the sun, as the writers in the press box gleefully typed out the circumstances of the play: the crack of the bat, the arc of the basketball, Ace Parker and the forward pass. Laughing in the sun. Their parents would read the headlines, in the form of a telegram, yet they would never understand that there was so much more to their babies' deaths, beyond those short, clipped words. So much more.

Many years later, I could still hear the applause, the shouts, and the excitement—just as loud as it was on the day that changed our lives forever.

Football season, 1941.

"Say, Mace." The coach walked up to me. "When we use that play you made up on them today—that *one*—swinging around the left with the halfback pass . . . boy, we'll have ourselves a ball game!"

"Sure, Coach." I beamed. "It'll be great!"

"You betcha." He clapped me on the shoulder. "Go get 'em!"

Hitching my football pants up, I resumed throwing a few balls around with the guys. It was a crisp, shiny December afternoon, the field crunchy with tiny icicles in the grass, the air brisk but not frosty enough to keep the spectators away. The game was scheduled to start in twenty minutes, and the cars were just pulling up and parking along the sidelines.

Today's game was scheduled to be between my team, the Glen Morris Bonecrushers, and the City Line Leafs, in the 140-pound class, Queens/Nassau League.

There wasn't a lot of local interest. It was strictly kid stuff. Most of us didn't even have any true football gear. Our pants were simply long knickers, stuffed with towels or rags to give some padding. For a belt, I had cut up an inner tube into strips, tying one around my waist, at least creating the illusion of Red Grange or Jim Thorpe. It didn't quite wash, though, since most of us didn't own our own helmets either. Even so, we played hard and made some real games of it.

I was a pretty good ball player. On offense I played right halfback, and on defense, as skinny as I was, I was a linebacker. Good enough, at least, that when we played the Question AAs, the Questions asked me to play linebacker for their team, too. I played one game for the Questions, and we got pummeled by the Baisley Park Skulls. *Ouch!*

Suddenly something caught my attention—a sizable crowd hanging around the row of cars—so I quit tossing the ball with the fellas.

"Hey, Mace, throw the ball!"

"Wait a second," I said, inaudible to my pals, my eyes squinting at the people running up to the cars. "Here." I lobbed the ball back and trotted over toward the sidelines.

A few of the cars had their doors open, their radios synced up to the same station, and though the message became clearer the closer I got to the automobiles, still an air of confusion hung in the static. People got out, paced around, hats tilted on the backs of their heads, hands on their hips, shaking their heads—looks of concern hung on all faces.

"Hey, what's goin' on over here?"

"Shhhh!" came the reply.

The radio continued: "*. . . the attack was apparently made on all naval and military activities on the principal island of Oahu. The president's brief statement was read to reporters by Stephen Early, the president's secretary. A Japanese attack upon Pearl Harbor would naturally mean war. Such an attack would naturally bring a counterattack, and hostilities of this kind would naturally mean that the president would ask Congress for a declaration of war. There is no doubt, from the temper of Congress, that such a* *declaration would be granted. We return you back to New York, and we'll give you later information as it comes along from the White House. We return you back to New York . . ."*

A great silence hung over the crowd. I was waiting for one of the adults, maybe Coach, to come up with some words of sanity. Instead, one of the men asked the question that was on everybody's mind: "Say, where in the hell is Pearl Harbor?"

That was about the gist of it. *Where in the hell is Pearl Harbor?* Nobody had the foggiest that 108,504 U.S. servicemen would have to die in the Pacific Theater of Operation to answer that question, to make things right.

As for me, while the young men from the Bonecrushers and Leafs ran off to immediately join the navy, all I could think about was Tommy O, our Japanese classmate and batboy for the John Adams HS baseball team, and how he was such a fantastic kid— always smiling, always going out of his way to help. Surely Tommy wasn't capable of bombing anything—not even trigonometry. Neither was Sumiko Yamaguchi, a darling of a Japanese girl, a senior at school, who made straight A's and was as sweet and quiet as a field of daffodils.

Who are these Japanese people? Not anyone I knew, that's for sure.

In fact, the only thing we knew about war was from the veterans who served in the World War. They hung around the veterans' hall all day, piss drunk, yelling at us kids to get the hell away from them. "You little bastards! Get the hell away from me!"

There was something odd in their demeanor, but what it was was a complete mystery. It was something both sinister and sad, hollow and reluctant.

Perhaps they were merely living as if they really should have died.

As for me, all I knew was that life began to move a great deal faster from that moment on.

It moved faster and faster until my world grew white with blindness as the LST doors opened and deposited us on the Pacific Ocean, racing toward Peleliu, and what remained of the rest of our lives. Then it moved quicker still.

United States Marine Corps Recruiting Station, 290 Broadway, Manhattan, New York, early December 1942.

E

F P

T O Z

L P E D . . .

"Okay, son, now cover your right eye and read the chart for me, please."

A guy up the line, a few people in front of me, began reading the eye chart. I commenced to concentrate, to memorize, listening to the letters and repeating them in my head, focusing on their sequence.

I was pretty good at keeping figures and patterns in my head, but this part—the military physical—made me nervous.

"That's fine. Now cover your left eye, please," the doctor intoned at the front of the line. When the physician was satisfied with the reading, he would send the person up ahead for the next phase of enlistment, and the line lurched forward once more, the next guy filling the spot vacated by the one who just tested.

"Next!"

One more guy and then I'd be "next."

By the time I made it to the head of the line, I was finally able to peek over the shoulder of the guy in front of me to read the chart, stealing quick glances, trying not to appear too obvious.

The chart wasn't blurry. It looked perfectly clear. Even so, I knew that when it came time for me to read with my right eye alone, I'd be doomed. I didn't have any depth perception.

In fact, at the onset of the war, in 1941, I had applied for the navy, because my buddy Sonny Campbell had joined. He sent me a photo of himself dressed in his navy denims, holding a rifle to his chest, so naturally I thought I'd look pretty smart in the same getup.

Sonny was killed in the boiler room aboard the USS *Hornet* off the Solomon Islands.

I failed the navy eye test.

Amblyopia was what I was diagnosed with when I was six years old. In common parlance, they called it a "lazy eye"—even though my eye always appeared normal and never looked off toward the Joneses. It was merely a curvature in my right eye, which caused me the embarrassment of wearing eyeglasses at an early age.

The truth is, I don't think the glasses did me much good. It was sports—I excelled in just about all of them, baseball, football, basketball, and hockey—that forced my eyes to work together, so that my left eye compensated for my right eye's deficiencies. Nevertheless, sports had nothing to do with standing stationary in front of an eye chart, attempting to read off a series of letters with a bum headlight.

The U.S. Navy caught it right away.

The United States Army didn't even get the chance. I got so fed up in the waiting room that I fished my paperwork from the bottom of the incoming tray and never looked back.

So there I stood in line waiting for the Marine Corps eye exam, trying my best to get into the service any way I could before they drafted me.

This was my last chance to serve my country.

"Next!"

I walked up and gave the doctor my slip of paper. He attached it to a clipboard and then wrote something down.

Not looking up, he said, "Alright, please cover your right eye and read the chart for me. Left to right, please."

Instead, I covered my left eye, looking hazily through my right, and began spouting off the letters from memory, before I could forget them. That was the plan. To see if I could trick them up.

"E,F,P,T,O,Z,L,P,E,D,P,E,C,F,D—"

"No, no, son, you're supposed to start with your *left* eye and *then* test the right one." The doctor finally looked up.

"I'm sorry, sir. Should I do it again?"

"No. That's alright, that was fine. Just cover your right eye now, so that we can test your left."

Let me tell you, I read all the way to the bottom of the chart as quick as an auctioneer.

The next thing I knew the Marine Corps was swearing me in.

I was only eighteen years old.

I am eighteen years old.

"I'm a shitbird from Yemassee!"

"You're a *what*?" the drill instructor calls back.

"I'm a shitbird!"

"A shitbird from *where*, goddammit!"

"From Yemassee!" the new recruit says. The new "boot" staggers around the barracks with a bucket over his head, his words ringing out dull and metallic inside the pail. It's pretty comical (only if it's not you with the bucket on your head). "A shitbird from Yemassee!"

Evidently we're all shitbirds on Parris Island, South Carolina. Everywhere you go it's shitbird-this and shitbird-that. Shitbirds grow wild out in the marshes that surround the Marine Corps Recruit Depot in Jerkwater, USA. You're a shitbird when they shear

the top of your head so you look like a scalded dog. You're a shitbird for being in the front of the line, and a shitbird for standing
at the rear. You're a shitbird for not shaving your face, even though
you haven't got a hair to shave. You're a shitbird.

"Hey, shitbird, Mace! The DI wants his room cleaned, shitbird!"

Mama named us all shitbird. Even when we got off the train
at Parris Island, the new recruits who had arrived thirty minutes
prior called out, "Hey, look at them shitbirds from Yemassee!"

The tiny whistle-stop before you get to Parris Island is a place
called Yemassee, South Carolina. Everybody goes through Yemassee to get to the marines, so we're all a bunch of shitbirds from
Yemassee. Brothers all.

Strange. Nobody *ever* mentions the Japanese here.

I'm nineteen.

They built these pisspot wartime towns on Coca-Cola and swing
beats—got a dime, and you'll get yourself a draft of suds—newly
minted marines, on leave from Camp Lejeune, hands in pockets,
nicotine, laughter, beads of sweat beneath our overseas caps, our
piss-cutters, our cunt-caps, our shoes glossed up to a mirrored
shine, Kinston, Sugar Hill, Jacksonville, and Raleigh, North Carolina, thumb a ride, take a leak behind the bar, "Boogie Woogie" by
Tommy Dorsey and "Two O'Clock Jump" by Harry James—it's
got you swingin'—eyeballs on the scout for bright red lipstick,
painted on stocking seams, floral fragrances or a little vanilla ex-
tract behind the ear, *no dice,* No Coloreds Allowed—find a buddy
who's won some change in a crap game and he's the best pal you've
ever had.

They built these crap-ass wartime towns on *Ca-ching* and the
peckers of a half-million one-striped teenagers, whoresmiths all—
but only in their own minds.

It's six in the morning, and brother there's a line to get in!

"Did ya get the wood yet?"

She asks me if I've got "the wood."

"Pistol Packin' Mama" by Al Dexter and His Troopers, huh? Alright, I'll buy that.

She's asking me if I'm *ready,* is what she's saying.

After a wait in line, we saunter into a cathouse in Sugar Hill as if we really know what we're doing, but these baby-faced marines— *me,* all of us!—we don't know the business. The idea of a thing versus the genuine article has about as many similarities as the lightbulb does to the lightning bug. This joint just glows with sleaze.

Four or five hookers recline on couches and chairs in the sitting room, affecting provocative poses that almost fool you into thinking these dames are high class. That doesn't matter, though. We want the illusion, not the secret behind the trick. We're nineteen years old, and we're here to claim the rites of any passage that'll wear the sheen off of our red-cherry kid stuff. Besides, we joined the marines to see the world, and these broads look as if they've been around it enough times to chart a map on a bathroom stall.

The lights are dim—hiding the rouge in our cheeks, from timidity, from shyness, the warmth of lust going straight to our heads, as excitement swims in chemical reactions, making the very walls sweat out a fever.

I pick out a big job and follow her to a room, never looking back at my pals. As it turns out, the road less traveled has been traveled a lot more than a youngster might imagine. In fact, it's a threadbare carpet that leads to a whore's station, complete with a bed in the center of the room, a nightstand, a smoky lamp, and not much else.

"Okay," she says. "You get ready and I'll be right back." Except that when she comes back, I'm still standing in the exact same spot she left me.

"You—" she begins, then stops, looking at me as if I'm the dumbest kid on the planet. "Did ya get the wood yet?" She sighs.

I stammer around a little bit, telling her something that doesn't make sense to either of us. Exasperated, she simply carries on—a real pro—and gets the wood up, afterward throwing a towel down on the bed and climbing atop it.

"Alright. Come on, boy. Let's go." As if the war might end any second, and with it her chances of turning a buck into bullion.

So I did, and so she did.

I was only nineteen.

Pavuvu Island, Russell Island Chain, August 25, 1944.

I am twenty.

"So ya see . . . that's what I'm tryin' to tell ya, George! Ya did that whole thing on Guadalcanal, right? Where was God then, huh? I mean, what good did God do for all those saps who got hit, wearin' their crosses and Stars of Abraham around their necks? Nothin'! I'm tellin' ya, buddy! Not a fuckin' thing!"

"Yeah, sure, Larry," George said, shaking his head, "but I'm tellin' *you*—there was something *out* there, that's all, and it damn sure wasn't just the Japs. You get out there, and the shit starts comin' in on ya . . ." George paused. "Pal, you don't *know* that feeling. You're not alone out there, is all I'm sayin'."

PFC Larry Mahan grinned at me and then looked back to George. "Ya know what that's called, George? That's called your *imagination*. Hell, everyone from Queens got one of those, don't they, Mace?"

I took a drag off my cigarette. "Sure. Imagine that." I watched the smoke drift out of my mouth, floating skyward, illuminated only by the weak light emitted by gasoline lamps in the open tents lining the company street. Otherwise, it was dark.

It was late. The company street was almost void of marines. Most of them had already returned to their tents for the night. Asleep or awake, it didn't matter—the next morning we would board the LSTs

(Landing Ship, Tank) on our way to a yet-to-be-named island, to wage war against the Japanese.

As it turned out, that unknown island was Peleliu.

Larry laughed. "You bet! You've got to have an imagination if you're from Queens, otherwise you'd think you're too poor to know any better!"

That got a chuckle out of us.

Larry Mahan, from Dobbs Ferry, New York, lived only forty minutes away from where George McNevin and I grew up in Queens. He had a daddy who was some sort of big shot in the navy.

Larry was a character—a real comedian, with his impressions of Cagney and Bogart. He was a good-looking kid, intelligent, and even though everyone knew Larry was sacrilegious, you couldn't help liking the guy.

Then there was George McNevin. It was George who recommended I choose the Browning Automatic Rifle (BAR) as my weapon, as it suited a left-handed rifleman better than an M-1 rifle, and it was knowing George before the war that added some comfort to Pavuvu. In such a strange place as Pavuvu every marine drew inspiration from anything that reminded him of home.

Back in Queens, George lived on 121st Street and Hawtree Creek Road, close to Sutter Avenue and the abandoned soap factory, where we'd hold impromptu boxing matches, back when we were kids. Only three hundred yards away from my home.

George and I didn't pal around much, but we both attended John Adams High School, where George ran track and I played baseball. Sometimes we would share the walk home, just shooting the breeze, before going our separate ways. That was the extent of knowing George McNevin back in the States.

While on a work detail I saw a marine whom I thought I recognized, walking with a plank on his shoulder. As he got closer, I said, "*George? George McNevin?*" He stopped and put the plank down. "Yeah, I'll be damned!" Smiling, we shook hands, greeting each other. It had been a long time. George had served on Guadalcanal and Cape Gloucester, yet he was exactly my age.

"So," I said, pointing to the plank he had laid down. "Keeping busy, I see?"

George laughed. "Oh, that? Nah, that's just a prop. I've been carryin' that friggin' thing around all day, so they won't gripe at me for doin' nothin'."

Now, four months later, on the eve of our departure for Peleliu, the jokes had all dried up. Even Larry's wit had rolled up inside of him, among the dust clots and artifacts lost in time.

We simply stood there in the company street, quietly, looking at each other in a matter-of-fact manner—knowing that we were headed toward the same destination, only that we were moving in different directions to get there: me in K Company, 3rd Battalion, 5th Marines (K/3/5); Larry with L Company, 3rd Battalion, 5th Marines (L/3/5); and George with E Company, 2nd Battalion, 1st Marines (E/2/1). Combat was no longer a matter of *if*, but now only a matter of *when*.

"Well, gang," I said, "I guess this is it."

"Yeah," George said under his breath.

More silence.

I didn't know what to do. Times like those tend to grow awkward and slow, if you don't act on what you really want to do. The moment fades as if it never existed. So I did the only thing I could think of. Since we were roughly standing in a circle, I simply stuck my arm out and thrust it into the center of the group, with the back of my hand facing upward.

Larry caught on first, and then George, placing their hands on top of mine, one atop the other.

We had words. I don't recall who said them. It could have been any one of us, or it could have been a combination of the three. However, what was said—what was expressed beyond words— really meant something . . . if only for that moment alone.

"We're gonna get through this, guys. So let's all meet again when this is over and done with, huh?"

We all said yes. Yes was a belief that even Larry couldn't refute. We would do as we said.

"Until we meet again, fellas." Larry smiled and gave us a wink.

The only thing is, that was the last time I ever saw Larry Mahan.

I suppose dying is just another way of saying good-bye.

2

A BUNCH OF CANNIBALS

"Go get 'em, marines!"

Way above me, looking up from the inside of our amtrac toward the bow of the LST, a group of cheering sailors stands at the railing with big grins on their faces, towels around their necks, and mugs of coffee in their hands. "Give 'em hell, you guys!"

Oh Christ, I reflect. *I think I joined the wrong friggin' outfit!*

I steal a fast peek over the side of the tractor. Peleliu is a three-alarm fire. It's a real funeral pyre. You can't even see an island for all of the plumes. *We're actually going* into *that friggin' place!* For the first time it really hits me.

The smoke, the flames, the roasting sky . . .

There's just no way to take all of this in. No damn way.

The battlewagons spew blue-orange flames from hundreds of 14-inch guns—a constant blast of air-sucking power. Shimmering shock waves. Raw energy speeds its projectiles toward Peleliu, turning the distant island into clabbered smoke. Hellcats and Corsairs part the air, moving sound, in groups of threes and fours, every which direction—coming in, going out, dropping their bombs, the blue sky above us, a sense of small vertigo, circling and circling;

amtracs make whirlpools, Higgins boats skim by with little colored flags: red, green, blue, yellow—roughly eighteen of us, stuffed in a floating coffin. They even managed to squeeze a 37 mm fieldpiece into our crate. The amtrac driver gives a hand signal, gears shift, about to go in—!

September 15, 1944. Peleliu. D-day.

To my right and left are navy ships of all sizes and shapes: cruisers, destroyers, minesweepers, LCIs, dozens of other amtracs packed full of marines. The ocean around our amtrac comes all the way to the top of its hull, seeming as if the water will pour right in and sink us to the bottom. Instead, a white foam of seawater sloughs off the green painted steel sides, churning the blue water into traces of aqua, as our amtrac treads the sea.

As if I'm fanning the pages of a book with my thumb, my emotions, and my thoughts flip by quickly, separate, one right after the other: *worry wonder helpless . . . scared stressed shocked . . .*

I shade my eyes; sun flares dapple the marines in front of me—their necks, their packs, their mottled brown and tan helmet covers. We're sandwiched in, holding on, jammed right up to the prow of our tractor. I know every one of them. The marines in the front of the tractor will be the last ones out.

I'm close to the rear of the boat, so I'll be the first on the beach.

Right behind me, Sergeant Jim McEnery, the first marine by the exit ramp, cradles his shotgun, protecting it from the saltwater. Each time he grits his teeth the muscles in his jaws tighten and loosen, tighten and loosen. He's lost in his own thoughts. In fact, we all are. *Dazed distressed amazed brave miserable . . .*

The rest of my fire team is here, too. *(A group of Hellcats fly over, cracking the air, sounding like a string of firecrackers popping in their wake.)* There's Corporal Richard Van Trump, my fire team leader, PFC Donald Schwantz, our scout, and then PFC Charlie Allmann, my assistant BAR man. We're the 3rd Fire Team, in the 3rd Squad, 3rd Platoon, K Company, 3rd Battalion, 5th Marines.

How they picked us to be the first ones to hit Peleliu is anybody's guess.

The invasion of Peleliu is only the latest in a series of amphibious assaults—a chain of island-hopping maneuvers, designed to strangle the breath from Japan, one island at a time.

While we were stationed on the island of Pavuvu they passed around photos of previous amphibious assaults on Guadalcanal, Tarawa, and Saipan—all having the same things in common: Marines in open amtracs or Higgins boats leaving the safety of the navy's anchorage, circling around in groups, synchronizing the assault waves, and then heading in.

I look out to my left, and other amtracs pull parallel to us. The only thing is, they're too far behind us to suit me. Leaning in toward Allmann, I yell, nervous, "Somebody oughta talk to that driver! We're too far ahead!" I doubt Charlie hears me; the motors of the amtracs are simply too loud—too loud for us to be going so slow.

A small swell of seawater splashes in and wets my boondockers.

At any rate, what's the rush? We're the first wave going in, so we're probably dead anyway.

The air warbles once more and makes a swishing sound high above. Salvos from the battlewagons crack the sky.

In fact, the preinvasion bombardment of Peleliu has been going on for three days now.

Curious marines, we always want to see what's going on. Just this morning, for instance, right after we awoke, a group of us stood at the port side of LST 661 watching the rounds go out, wondering how there could possibly be any Japanese left on the island after such a shellacking—or even if the island would still be there by the time we arrived. The answer came soon enough, when a Hellcat flying in took a glancing hit from some type of Nip gun, sending the plane on a beeline straight for the island, crashing into her somewhere beyond the smoke.

"Hey, did you guys see that?"

"Oh, man, *did* I! Never had a chance!"

That killed whatever excitement or curiosity we had—our bravado tucking its tail between its legs and swimming back to the States. There were live Nips on that island, and they had a lot more firepower hanging over their mantel than Grandpa had in his old blunderbuss.

A marine has to wonder what kind of chance he has, hitting the beach, running up to a Nip's rifle muzzle, and sticking his head straight down the barrel. I'm sure there are better ideas. We don't know what will happen when we get in there. Imagination is a crafty creature. Perception becomes reality.

My feelings are beyond fear. It's an otherworldly sensation: I know I could be killed at any second, yet my limited life experience makes it impossible to conceptualize being alive at one moment, and then in the next instant, *poof!*—gone!

Simply stated, nonexistence grinds against the awareness of all that I know. The boom of the cannons, the vibration of the amtrac, the marine's pack in front of me bumping into my chest, the roar of the fighter planes, the smell of the ocean and the lead paint in the tractor, the heat of the sun, the weight of my equipment, the sweat in my armpits, the heft of my BAR, the herringbone of my jacket, the beat of my heart, the cloudless blue sky . . . the eagle, the anchor, and the globe in my eye . . .

fear thrill courage fright . . .

In just a few minutes I'll be on Orange Beach 2.

D-day minus 15 minutes. 8:17 A.M.

My God, how the hell did I get myself into a jam like this?

The mind takes a tumble as memories flutter back to just a few months ago, in early May 1944, when I arrived with the 43rd Replacement Battalion on Pavuvu, the home of the 1st Marine Division in the Pacific Theater of Operation. None of us had a clue, back then, about the shit we'd wade into on Peleliu—except for maybe PFC Larry Mahan.

"So this is *Pa-voo-voo*?" Mahan sneered, gazing around as we descended the gangplank from the SS *Mormachawk* onto Pavuvu's sands. "Looks more like *doo doo*, to me!" Larry laughed.

Pavuvu wasn't necessarily an eyesore, but it definitely didn't give the impression that it was an island resort, either. In fact, if you took any division camp back in the States, with its rows upon rows of tents, its bustle of activity, myriad work parties, marines moving to and fro, and sundry military vehicles, and dumped it splat in the middle of an undeveloped island, with its files of coconut trees—as straight as a die—its sandy roads, and off in the distance some of the wildest junglelike vegetation you had ever seen . . . then *that* was Pavuvu.

Originally designated to be a rest camp for the veterans of Guadalcanal and Cape Gloucester, Pavuvu turned out to be just another work party (a giant one, at that!), in the attempt to make the place hospitable for twenty thousand marines. Nothing doing. It appeared as if it would take more like twenty thousand *years* to get the place squared away, what with the constant ebb and flow of green marines coming in and old hands rotating out.

It's been said that God created the world in seven days.

On the eighth day he could've done us all a favor by sinking Pavuvu to the bottom of the sea.

It wasn't lost on us, either, that Pavuvu was only one thousand miles from Australia. Even new members of the 1st Marine Division knew that our division had saved Australia's collective ass by fending off the Nips on Guadalcanal; so, naturally, we believed the good-neighbor policy should have been extended to us as well. Or maybe the local gentry of Australia thought it was a little too much to ask, seeing that the Guadalcanal marines, who took Australia by storm, left half the local women "brokenhearted" before they set off for Cape Gloucester. That's saying it politely.

Anyway, we wanted a piece of that action. Instead, before being dropped off at Pavuvu, we made a five-day stop at New Caledonia—my first look at any overseas destination.

New Caledonia was a dump.

Our stay there started off nice enough, with its beautiful crystal blue water, and the gleaming pilot boat that met us out in the harbor, giving us the impression that better days were ahead of us after thirty days at sea. When they unloaded us on the dock, however, New Caledonia's true nature showed itself, in that the waterfront was full of filthy concrete buildings and dirty garbage-infested roads, lined with sickly coconut trees.

As they trucked us into the mountains, we were shocked by the natives—swarthy, dusky-looking characters, seemingly incapable of standing erect; all they did was squat by the sides of the roads. I don't think I ever saw one walking; if one did, he was probably the mayor of the village or a local king or something. What's more, the brass told us not to venture too far from camp, because a nearby leper colony had already infected a couple of sailors. It was said that the poor navy guys would have to spend the next several years in quarantine, their maritime careers ending on dry land, among the fine inhabitants of New Caledonia.

"Say, Bill." I smirked at PFC Billy Leyden. "If this is *New* Caledonia, I'd sure hate to see what *Old* Caledonia looks like!"

To top it off, our camp was situated in the high-altitude peaks of New Caledonia's mountains, a height that gave us flatlanders from New York a series of headaches the whole time.

In fact, our little group of four was comprised of nothing *but* New Yorkers.

When Larry Mahan and I departed San Diego for overseas duty, we became good pals with a couple of other young marines: PFC Seymour Levy, a seventeen-year-old from Brooklyn, and PFC Billy Leyden, an eighteen-year-old from Valley Stream, a little town just outside of New York City.

Sy Levy was a tall Jewish kid, well built and nice looking, with thick dark hair. Despite his age, he was a pretty tough marine. You could always find him in a white T-shirt, his pants rolled up two or three rolls since his dungarees were too long, always exposing his socks above his boondockers. He never made religion a topic. Even though Sy was a nice Jewish boy, when it came time for supper, if Spam was on the menu, Levy wouldn't put the spoon down.

Billy Leyden was another kind of guy altogether—a typical New Yorker, with the gift of gab, full of ideas, always looking for a new angle, smart on his feet. He was tall, energetic, and outspoken, with wavy hair and an infectious smile. He had a real eye for the ladies, too. There was no one like Billy. Even at eighteen, he could have sold a Cadillac to a bunch of blind Amish.

So, after the big letdown of New Caledonia, Pavuvu didn't seem so bad after all. At least we were off that horrible ship, the SS *Mormachawk*. Not only was it a piece of junk that appeared to be a holdover from the Banana Wars, but also, about a day outside of California, we hit a storm so bad that we thought we were goners before we even started.

Pavuvu? Yeah, right! Semper Fi!

We arrived at Pavuvu during the night. The next morning they walked us down the gangplank with only the clothes on our backs, helmets on our heads, and seabags over our shoulders. We didn't even have weapons. The closest I had come to a weapon in the Marine Corps was at the rifle range in basic training, and then later at the Brooklyn Naval Yard, where I was stationed for six months in 1943.

It was at the Brooklyn Naval Yard that I first met Larry Mahan.

Our job at the naval yard was the highly classified, top secret duty of guarding the dockworkers' payroll. That duty entailed carrying shotguns and Reising submachine guns. The shotguns were okay, but that Reising was so cheaply built that I was afraid to touch the damn thing—it seemed like it would go off at any second if you just looked at it funny.

Back on Pavuvu, however, the lack of weapons meant more than we knew.

We didn't know it then—as we milled around the dock, waiting for someone to tell us where to go and what to do—but if you didn't have specialized weapons training, in, say, flamethrowers or machine guns, the chances were pretty good that you'd be a rifleman. End of story. Even though I had scored high on my mental aptitude tests in basic training? Rifleman. End of story.

The Marine Corps rifleman. Every marine wanted to be like him. No marine wanted to *be* him. We were unique in our class and phylum. The lowest common denominators. Yet a whole operation—from the simplest maneuver to the grandest assault— revolved around the man and his rifle. We were the first ones in and the last ones out, viewed with a mixture of awe and pity by the other servicemen in the armed forces. Walking contradictions, paradoxical constructs—the pride we held as members of our unique fraternity was tempered solely by the maxim we whispered among ourselves: "They Don't Care About Us." They Don't Care About Us—a half-truth summed up in just a few words. Our sole potential was killing a lot of Japanese. God, we loved the Marine Corps!

After we spent a while grab-assing at Pavuvu's receiving dock, eventually some veteran NCOs came down and reined us in, escorting us to a large bivouac area—nothing more than tents, furnished only with cots on a sandy floor. Strictly the bare minimum accommodations, which told us that we wouldn't be staying there long.

The NCOs sounded muster and gave us our new assignments.

When they called Mahan and Leyden, they paired them off and marched them out in separate columns of new arrivals, leaving only Levy and me out of the original four. It didn't take them long, however, to inform Sy and me that we were now a part of

K Company, 3rd Battalion, 5th Marines. As it happened, Leyden was also assigned to K/3/5, only he was in the 1st Platoon, while Levy and I became riflemen in the 3rd Platoon. That was a nice luxury, since we all arrived together and we didn't know anybody, save for Mahan and another new arrival, PFC Eugene Holland (who we later found out was from Long Island, just north of where Levy grew up). Mahan, however, was designated to an entirely different company: L Company, which was just one street over from Company K.

It was while we were in those tents, with nothing to do, that things began to get a little bizarre. A tad uneasy. In just a short while the division vets began to trickle down to our area, in twos and threes, so they could take a gander at the newest arrivals.

It was a strange feeling to be ogled like that—almost like an auction. While some of the vets of Guadalcanal and Cape Gloucester simply came down looking for old pals, others meandered around, their sole purpose to regale the new guys with their bullshit war stories. The saltier the better.

"Hey, fellas, wanna see somethin' great?"

A short blond-haired marine sauntered up to Sy and me. The marine was shirtless, his body tanned, almost baked by the sun. One look at him and I could tell this marine had been on the island for a long time.

"Here, take a look at this." He smiled. Getting close to Sy and me, the marine took from around his neck a necklace, and at the end of the necklace was a sack, which he proceeded to open. I don't know what Sy and I expected. A magic trick or something, maybe dirty pictures, we certainly weren't anticipating what came next.

It only took half a second to register what I was seeing. The sack was full of gold bits, some of them roughly in the shape of teeth, but most of them just tiny, thin sheets of yellow, bent out of shape after being yanked from the mouths of dead Japanese.

"So, whatcha think o' these, boys? Pulled 'em out myself!" The marine ran his fingers over them so we could see every little piece, his eyes darting between Sy and me, trying to elicit a reaction from two marines fresh off the boat.

Presently Sy spoke up. "Yeah, those sure are . . . *great*. Boy, I bet there's a coupla hundred bucks' worth in there." Sy smiled, uneasy.

Suddenly the marine looked hurt. He sealed the bag up with one quick pull of the drawstring. "More like a coupla *thousand*!" he said, eyeballing us suspiciously. "But don't none of you boys be gettin' any funny ideas, ya hear? You'll get your own gold soon enough—or if ya don't, you can bet the Nips'll get you *first*!" With that he grinned again and walked away.

We all heard stories of the Japanese having gold-crowned teeth, and that much was true, but the misconception that marines were excavating whole teeth from the mouths of Nips was an exaggeration. Maybe some were, if the tooth had enough gold on it, but to rip the whole tooth out, root and all—well, a marine would have to be a real cripple to do something like that. My feeling was, if these marines who took the gold hadn't been in the service, they would've been juvenile delinquents back in the States, stealing hubcaps or swiping purses.

I pulled Levy aside by the elbow and got close enough that only he could hear me. "Jesus Christ, Sy, who'd we fall in with? A buncha friggin' cannibals?"

Maybe not quite, but after a while it became apparent that we weren't exactly tentmates with the Edisons and Einsteins, either.

Replacements grew antsy from just waiting around and cooling their heels, so a group of them started picking up coconuts, digging into them, shaking them, really yucking it up.

That's when the diarrhea parade started.

The young hero marines, hot off the *Mormachawk*, shimmied up trees or took coconuts from the ground and proceeded to demonstrate the science of unlocking their treasures. Guys argued: You had to do it this way, or that way, but the end result was the same. They really broke their necks for an hour just trying to get the husks off. Then, when they had finally managed that trick, what was left was only a little cannonball thing. Not worth a damn. Still, they'd take the hard ball between their knees and try to bore it open with a Ka-Bar for the milk inside. I didn't even bother, because as soon as you put a knife in my hand you could bet your ass I'd cut myself. These guys, though, were thrilled to get whatever meat they could from the native vegetation—most of them grinning from ear to ear, chewing on the green meat and sipping the milk.

Presently, it took everything they had to keep their smiles on, when their guts started bubbling and churning. They'd look at each other with worried eyes and . . . *zing!* Off one ran to the head, about sixty yards away.

Everybody laughed to beat the band, even some of those who'd drunk the milk but hadn't felt the effects of it yet—but eventually it caught up with the whole lot. It went on like that all night, you'd hear marines go *"hup!"* and then sprint like the wind, a steady relay of marines with the runs.

In the morning it was comical to see all the paper scattered across the field, in between the tents and the head, where the marines ran out of time and couldn't make it. Someone had found a *Life* magazine so they could wipe their asses, and from the scattered pages of the book you could make out how far each marine made it before he splattered. One poor sucker left his page right in front of the head's door. That was as close as he got, before . . . *whammo!*

Needless to say, when they ordered us out for battalion muster that morning, about half the replacements were a little the worse for wear.

"Welcome to Pavuvu, shitbirds."

All in all, though, our stay on Pavuvu wasn't that bad, despite the constant heat, the inability to bathe properly, the never-ending work parties, and the reputed suicides of homesick marines. Sure, marines complained about the land crabs. There were thousands of land crabs! Of course, if a Marine had any smarts, he would learn after the first time he found a land crab in his boondockers to check for the pests the next time he put his shoes on. The crabs were a minor nuisance.

Marines also bitched about the rats on the island. There were thousands of those, too, but the rats didn't do much of anything. A marine would probably gripe about a naked broad jumping out of a cake, if the cake was chocolate and he had his heart set on vanilla.

Marines are expert bellyachers. Real professionals.

About the rats, you heard them playing on the tops of the tents at night, jumping and gliding down the tents' slopes, like children on a playground slide. If a human came around, however, the rats would scatter. All you had to do was skirt around them. No bother. Nevertheless, the rats were cured by the hundreds when nests of them were found among the rotten coconuts. They'd call in a flame-thrower operator, and he'd torch the whole brood with a couple of sprays from his weapon. Fiery rats could be seen running every-where. Just not for very long. In a minute or two, the rats would simply run out of gas and merely lie there smoldering—the stench of burning hair and little rat claws lingering in the air.

The only Pavuvuian wildlife that really got to me was the coco-nut ants.

The ants lived in the coconut trees, so small, yet so smart, vi-ciously waiting for a marine to lean against a tree, or to scale up for a few coconuts, before they'd pounce on the poor guy. The ants wouldn't bite your arms, or legs, or your back. No, these ants were more brazen than that. They had one target and one target only—a marine's testicles! There they would cling, tighten up, and pinch the hell out of your balls, in all the spots where their little bodies lay. Down the tree you'd come—*zip!*—dropping your dungarees right where you stood, in fits of agony, pulling the ants off your nuts, one pest at a time.

That's how those tiny, itty-bitty unassuming little tree ants were analogous to the Pavuvu experience as a whole—*pulling the ants off your nuts, one pest at a time.* Every day, the same routine: Breakfast in the morning, a work party during the day—moving rocks around from one spot to the other—then lunch, then some sort of lecture, then moving some coconuts from one spot to another, and then finally we'd have the nights to ourselves. If we weren't too beat to take them in, there were movies in the evening at the battalion and regimental outdoor theaters, always the latest pictures—*Bathing Beauty,* with Esther Williams; *Going My Way,* starring Bing Crosby; *Gaslight,* with Ingrid Bergman and Charles Boyer. Those films were the highlights of our stay on Pavuvu. We whistled at Esther Williams stepping out in her radiant bathing suits (I nudged PFC McNevin—"Boy, how'd ya like to have a dame that could hold her breath for that long, George?"), and we always cheered for the villains in every picture. The more devious the villain, the better. Otherwise, Pavuvu was drudgery of epic proportions . . . *pulling the friggin' ants off . . . one at a friggin' time.*

They say adversity builds character. Pavuvu didn't build character. It built *characters.* Plural. A person's little quirks and tics that would go unnoticed in civilian life would become intensified under the South Pacific sun on Pavuvu, turning normal Joes into a menagerie of mental defectives.

The boys called it "going Asiatic," but I think it sank a little bit deeper than that.

The American serviceman in the Pacific, unlike his counterpart over in Europe, had a tremendously difficult time acclimating himself to an edge of the earth that was entirely dissimilar to anything he'd known or dreamed of. This wasn't France or Germany, and we didn't need to fight over in Europe to know the difference between a hedgerow in Holland and a jungle on Peleliu.

Simply stated, the Westerner wasn't built for those islands out there. He wasn't built for the islands in *here*. It wasn't the abject isolation or the view of the same old horizon day after day that emptied you. Nor was it the multifarious diseases: malaria, yellow fever, ringworm, dengue, dysentery, scrub typhus, jungle rot, filariasis, ad nauseam. Instead, it was the ambience of those islands that would sink into your pores, something beyond parasitic, a living vortex that tried to make the marine a part of her green and sandy world, despite his inability to sift through her jungles—a constant push and pull, within and without the battles in which we fought.

You adapt but you don't.

Like that kid Private Joe Mercer. Mercer lived the real Pacific war.

At the end of K Company's street, about sixty yards from where anybody lived, there was a rough patch of unused land, full of uneven grass and palm trees, isolated between our 3rd Regiment, the 1st Marines, and Motor Transport.

And on that lonely piece of ground was a pup tent. And in that pup tent was a Marine. Nobody spoke to him. Nobody knew him.

We could see him out there, sitting cross-legged in front of his tent, listening to the swishing breeze sighing through the palm fronds, idly gazing at the clouds through ice blue eyes, occasionally rubbing his sun-bleached reddish blond hair. His unassuming features wore a mask of utter indifference—resignation, total complacency. He was a marine with nothing. A marine with nobody.

"Boy." Levy shook his head. "I wonder what that guy did to deserve some shit like that?"

Sy and I stood at the end of the company street, looking at Private Mercer, Levy expressing the same sentiments that had been voiced a hundred times over by every marine who passed that way.

"Dunno, Sy." I took a drag from my cigarette. "Whatever it was . . . it must've been the worst."

"How do ya figure, the worst?"

"Think about it." I cocked an eyebrow. "A guy sitting out there . . . months on end, all by hisself? They ship him out here an' throw him out like *that*? So maybe prison's too good for him, they figure. He has to wait it out, they figure. Nah, this guy? They want this guy to *disappear*. Maybe he gets outta this place"—I shrugged— "maybe he don't."

Sy laughed. "Hell, Mace, I think you need to put down the Dick Tracy funny papers!"

I laughed, too. "Yeah, maybe—but it doesn't change that guy's predicament, does it?"

At that, we looked out at Mercer again. Silent. Mercer didn't bat an eye.

Like "Old Man" Haney. Haney lived the real Pacific war.

Mahan came over to our tent just to shoot the breeze. Joking. Smoking. All of a sudden Larry sees Gunny Elmo Haney coming out of his tent. "Jesus Christ!" Larry exclaimed. "What're you guys keeping over here, a Civil War relic?"

"Ah, c'mon!" Levy slapped Larry on the back. "We brought your granddad over here, and that's all the thanks we get?"

"My granddad? More like my goddamn great-*great*-granddad!"

It was true. Gunnery Sergeant Elmo Haney was a fossil. A veteran of World War I, he was scrawny; his dungarees hung off him like a scarecrow's raiment. His skin was a road map, wrinkled and leathered. In fact, Haney gave every impression that he was an animated cadaver. If you opened up his blouse, you'd probably see the Y-incision from his autopsy.

He was a real puzzle to wrap your head around, too.

If you had the misfortune to pass him in the company street and say hello, his gravelly response was "What do you mean by that?"

To us young riflemen he was a joke. At any given time you'd

find Haney talking to himself, or fighting an imaginary enemy with a bayonet affixed to the end of his rifle, looking out on the world with rheumy eyes. The world had simply grown too unfamiliar for him to comprehend it any longer.

"Who's he fightin' now, I wonder? Attila the Hun?" Everybody laughed.

On the other hand, he was a sad case—someone to be pitied.

The scuttlebutt was that the officers kept Haney around just so they could have something to laugh about over in Officers' Country. You got the distinct impression that the brass were merely mollifying him—humoring his antics, with a wink and a nod.

"Yeah," I told Mahan. "The other day, Billy and I—"

"Leyden?"

"Yeah, me and Leyden. We were over at the swimming hole, taking a dip, right? When we see Old Man Haney over there, too, having a bath. Now get *this*. This guy has this—I don't know what you'd call it—one of those horse brushes or somethin'. Real stiff bristles, and Haney is just scrubbin' an' scrubbin' hisself with this friggin' thing—back an' forth—an' he's even picking up his nuts and scrubbin' under those, too, with this goddamn brush! Never seen anything like it."

"Yeah, no foolin', huh?" Mahan asked.

"Hey." I held up a hand. "Never seen anything like it."

"Yeah, and here's one more for ya." Sy stood up. "The guys over in the mortars worship this friggin' guy."

Larry smirked. "Now I know you guys are fulla shit. The mortarmen in my company only worship themselves."

The fact is, Haney should have never been on Pavuvu in the first place; in his mind, poor Haney was still somewhere in France, scrubbing the mustard gas from his skin.

Haney was no longer a rifleman in 1944, but once upon a time . . . he lived the real Pacific war.

Semper Fidelis.

In fact, so many of us lived the real Pacific war. Right down the line. It's not as if the rifleman's war was somehow more genuine, or in some way more important, or even more terrible than any other marine's experiences. The sacrifices of the few are the sacrifices of the many.

Esprit de Corps. We were the goddamn Marine Corps.

Yet beneath all the glory rests the key that turned the lock, that enabled our boys to return home. The still silent men who took the brunt of the fighting. The silent dead who never returned.

The Marine Corps riflemen. We weren't the be-all-end-all, but if we had to do it all to end it all, we would.

Marines like PFC Orley Uhls—as we boarded LST 661 on our way to Peleliu—a nice, quiet country boy from Illinois: another blond, warm smile. If you entered a bar with Orley and a few others, he'd be the only one to come out sober. Like Lieutenant William "Bill" Bauerschmidt, USMC, from Pottstown, Pennsylvania, recipient of the Silver Star for bravery—with his high-top lace-up boots that were never tied up all the way but instead they flared out at the tops. He had a hop to his walk, and his eyes tilted in like a boxer's. Bill carried his dad's World War I .45 service revolver into combat—engraved with the initials WB on its grip—dearly wanting to make his father proud. Beyond pride, Bill had no other choice. He had to be a fine officer, in order to counteract some of the deficiencies inherent in our platoon. Like Sergeant Thomas Palmisano—his heart simply wasn't in it. Palmisano was pretty quiet for a squad leader, a dark, heavyset Italian, almost a little too fat.

There's PFC Jack Baugh, from Tennessee—you could get a smile from him every once in a while. PFC Roy Kelly, from Kansas, and Corporal John Teskevich. John was a Cape Gloucester vet, who pulled a wounded Roy Kelly to safety under intense Japanese fire. Everyone thought John should have received a medal. Nothing happened.

Then PFC Lyman Rice—5'10", broad shoulders, he'd go into combat with a ringworm-riddled back. Here's Private Frankie Ocepek, from Cleveland, Ohio, loved humor—laughed at anything, 5' 6" and wielded a nineteen-pound BAR, thirty-four years old, black hair, graying at the temples, probably never had a bad word to say about anyone. Private Henry Ryzner—just a strange kid, who might have been more in touch with reality if he and Private Mercer had been tentmates.

Like Corporal R. D. Wilson—"Blowtorch Willy"—an above-and-beyond marine, from Bozeman, Montana; you could always count on him. He got his name from bringing a small blowtorch overseas. PFC P. A. Wilson, from Des Moines, Iowa—a good marine, but as goofy as they came. There's PFC Frank Minkewitz—a tall Polack, married, thinning hair, probably a draft board decision. PFC Gene Holland—artsy, a deep thinker, like something was in his mind always wanting out. His father died when he was a child, so he was raised by his mother and sister.

They all lived the real Pacific war, like Corporal Richard Van Trump and PFC Donald Schwantz—those two were a pair in harmony. You'd walk into their tent and they'd both stop talking until you left. Schwantz could have been muscular, with a little exercise, but instead he was full of baby fat. Along with PFC Charlie Allmann—a quiet guy, almost lethargic and built wiry. The kind of guy who'd get lost in a crowd. Not too much to look at. Gunnery Sergeant Thomas Rigney—Hollywood good looks, always confident, a real poster marine; he carried his Thompson machine gun with pride. Also PFC Jesse Googe. Googe lied about his age to get into the marines and served on Guadalcanal, at maybe sixteen; he also moonlighted as a runner. Then there was PFC Thomas "Nippo" Baxter—a mystic, from Yazoo City, Mississippi. He only wore a cap, never a helmet. He had a goatee, which gave him a mysterious look. Maybe 5'9" and 155 pounds, if that. I wondered if the people back in Mississippi knew what a good marine he was.

They lined up to get on the ship: PFC Pete Candella, from San Francisco—a really good kid, always smiling. Corporal Raymond Grawet—another Hollywood type, sporting a goatee as well—and PFC Aubrey Rogers, kind of husky, nice and talkative, had a yellowed atabrine tint to his skin from the malaria pills he took; both guys were Leyden's friends. Rogers was a friend of Baxter's, too. Platoon Sergeant Harry Spiece—a great marine, who didn't like my wiseass New York ways. Here's Corporal Walter B. Stay, from Syracuse, New York, took on a big job leading his squad, despite his small stature.

Then there was Sergeant Jim McEnery.

I met him during my third day on Pavuvu (though I really wouldn't call it a "meeting"). Jim was a snappy marine with a Leo Carrillo pencil-thin mustache, coming at us with his unmistakable whiny Brooklyn accent, calling us out for a work detail.

It was lightly raining, and he had us all standing in the company street. The only things you could see of Jim were that unmistakable mustache, the inner lining of his helmet, and a rain-slick poncho.

"Alright, you marines, when I say fall out, I mean fall out! We're on a working party here, you guys, so get your shit together and follow me!"

Walking behind this McEnery guy, I looked over to Gene Holland and said, "Who the fuck is this big-shit marine?"

I would soon find out. Jim and I would see a lot of combat together.

September 15, 1944. Dawn, off the coast of Peleliu. D-day minus 2 hours.

Suddenly the LST stopped. After nearly two weeks at sea, we had reached our terminus.

The trip to Peleliu was pretty uneventful, except for our one-day stop on Guadalcanal.

There, we did a practice amphibious assault. Only, in practice, they sent us out in the front-exiting Higgins boats, instead of the back-exiting amtracs—a big difference in how we'd actually land on Peleliu, sort of defeating the purpose of a "dress rehearsal." Speaking of "dress," they had the entire company put on nice pressed khakis, as if we were on a parade ground, really uptowning it for a general or something. So when our Higgins boat stopped, about twenty yards out from the beach, and they let down the ramp? So much for clean khakis. We waded the rest of the way in, making shore on Guadalcanal with the black churned-up beach water all over our fresh parade pants.

Afterward, though, we had a nice little party on the sand. Just lounging around, or swinging from the rope that was above the local swimming hole. Every marine received two Coca-Colas, and they passed out the latest issues of *Leatherneck* magazine for our viewing pleasure.

"Say, Mace! Isn't this *you*?" Ray Grawet held up a copy of *Leatherneck*, tapping it with his finger, waving it around, showing off a photograph in the book.

Pete Candella laughed. "Hey, it sure as hell is!"

"Here, lemme see that!" I said.

It really *was* a photograph of me and a few other marines, in a train car heading from the East to the West Coast, en route to Camp Linda Vista, California, my station before shipping out overseas. It was a nice picture, despite the fact that I was stuffing my face with food in it.

"Boy." Ray beamed. "Looks like we have a regular Hollywood marine in our midst!" (This was funny, coming from a guy like Grawet.)

"Yeah, ha ha! Yuk it up, wiseguys." I grinned. The boys really gave me the business over that photo.

Not long after, however, our revelry was broken by this god-awful grating noise—almost akin to a high-pitched buzz saw, being turned off and on, off and on, repeatedly. *Haw! Haw! Haw!* this yammering went on. Except that the racket wasn't caused by a machine of any sort. No, that irritating clamor came from a single marine: PFC Merriell "Snafu" Shelton, from the mortars. It was amazing how much hubbub could come out of one so diminutive as Shelton. He was the shortest guy in the entire company, and one had to wonder how they even let him into the service in the first place.

It didn't take much of a Perry Mason, though, to figure out how he got the nickname Snafu. In common military parlance, SNAFU stood for "situation normal: all fouled up."

"Goddammit," Blowtorch Willy growled. "I wish that little shit would learn to button his lip."

"Ain't that the truth!" Frankie Ocepek agreed.

"Nah, listen, Frank," Blowtorch continued. "It was bad enough on that great big island, with his backwater nonsense, but we're about to get back on that little boat with that dumb shit, and you won't be able to get far enough from this guy to suit ya."

I interjected, "Yeah, and he's got those new mortarmen that came in after me so snowed over with his bullshit war stories, just 'cos he was on Gloucester."

"Exactly!" Blowtorch said. "Look, I'm going to cure this piece of shit, once and for all."

The mortarmen were lounging right next to us, so all Blowtorch had to do was lean over and call out, "Hey, Shelton!"

"Huh?" Snafu looked over with that stupid face of his.

You couldn't fault a guy for being short, or ugly, or even uneducated, considering the circumstances most of us came out of—but being all of those things, with a big mouth to boot? Snafu Shelton simply didn't come equipped with an off button.

"Yeah, you, Shelton," Blowtorch smirked. "Say, listen, my mother was thinkin' about joinin' the marines and she was wonderin' if she could be in the mortars."

Immediately everybody cracked up. Poor Frankie was so doubled over and red, it was a wonder he didn't pass out from laughing so hard.

Gazing over at the mortar squad, I saw that a couple of the mortarmen, PFC John Redifer and PFC Vincent Santos (our company's only guy of Spanish descent), had their heads down, smiling, really giving it everything they had to hold back their laughter.

Snafu didn't say anything for a change.

As it turned out, that was the last really fun time we had as a group, before we threw it all up on Peleliu's shore.

Weeks later, just off the coast of Peleliu, we stood on the deck of LST 661, as the dawn eased in, focusing on the ocean, barely making out the outline of the island—just a phantom hump on the horizon, no more foreboding than a cube of ice in a cup of water.

"There she is, huh?" Levy said.

I sighed. "Yeah, I guess so. Although how they find these places in the middle of the friggin' ocean, I'll never know."

About a week into our voyage the brass told us the name of the island was Peleliu. During the briefing they also informed us that Peleliu was infested with bugs and snakes, indigenous birds that made strange noises, and Japanese forces of an unknown quantity. More importantly, however, the word came to us that the island had no natural water source.

"Well, if it's so goddamn lousy, what the hell are we taking it for?" I leaned into McEnery.

Of course, there's no answer to a question like that. You just do it and shut your trap.

Standing on the deck of the LST that morning, Levy took that theorem to heart. He was pretty quiet. His eyes remained fixed on the horizon.

"Hey, c'mon, Sy." I put a hand on his shoulder. "Look, here comes Spiece and Sergeant [Kenneth] Boaz. We're gonna have to get our stuff together."

True enough, Platoon Sergeant Spiece stood in front of the 3rd Platoon. "Alright, fellas, here we go. Let's get your equipment on, double-check everything, helmets on, we're gearing up."

Just about that time every ship in the anchorage let loose with their artillery—we really jumped!—and we had a bird's-eye view of it all. First you'd see the fire shooting out from the ends of the cannons, at least twenty yards of flame really sticking out there. Then the instant squeal and the delayed boom from each salvo.

The reason we had such beautiful seats was that the 3rd Platoon was the last ones aboard as we loaded ourselves onto the LST back at Pavuvu. No room at the inn.

By the time we made ship, the ship's holds were packed to the gills with marines. So the 3rd Platoon lived like trolls under a bridge, having our cots placed underneath a Landing Craft, Mechanized that took up nearly the entire ship's foredeck. If I were sitting on my cot, beneath the LCM, I had about five inches of headroom below that monstrosity. Guys were accidentally knocking their heads on it all the time.

Sure, it was a crummy way to travel, but it had its perks, too.

It was good because we weren't smelling the farts or the sweat or breathing the used-up air in the cramped quarters below deck. Instead, we had a moderate sea breeze that cooled us off and the freedom to walk where we pleased. Yet it was bad in that all we had to drink was warm water, since the watercooler was at midship. What's more, we hit a groundswell once, and the ocean nearly washed all of our gear into the sea. We scrambled around like mad bastards to grab our stuff before it went into the drink.

So, to gear up, we had to drag our equipment from underneath our cots, putting it on in full view of the barrage.

Yet reality? There was nothing real about it. Not even the shouts from the shelling or the feel of our muscles straining under our equipment was real. It was unreal when we ate breakfast that morning, knowing good and well that I was eating steak and eggs but never tasting it, never looking up from my plate, or at any other marine for that matter. Every marine was autonomous in his actions. Thinking. Thinking.

Those of us who had never been in combat had an idea of what it would be like—but we were completely wrong. Mortally wrong. Like mechanized men, we quietly went through the motions.

Unreal. We were forced to check that we were still alive before we had the chance to die. That's a fact. Blind eyes read stories of their own.

For me, my equipment was easy to put on, although it weighed more than the average marine's gear, because of my job as a BAR gunner. My pack itself was nothing, with its poncho looped over the top and an entrenching tool fastened to its center. To secure it, the pack was affixed to a Y-strap, which ran down my spine, attaching to the rear of my cartridge belt at the waist. Therefore, putting it on was akin to donning a jacket. One arm went through one strap, and then the other, leaving only the clasp of the cartridge belt to fasten below my abdomen, securing the whole getup as one piece.

On the cartridge belt were six BAR magazine pouches, three on each side, holding two magazines apiece. That's twenty rounds a magazine, making a total of 240 rounds of .30-06 ammo, double what a marine with an M-1 rifle carried. Also I had two canteens of water and a little first-aid pouch on my belt.

Strapped across my chest and hanging to my waist was my gas-mask bag, with a gas mask inside. Add that to the contents of my pack, housing three boxes of K rations, a change of socks, a dungaree cap, and a waterproof bag with my personal effects—a pocket New Testament and my wallet, including the card I received when I crossed the equator—and that made me combat ready. I had to carry light, given that the weight of my BAR was another nineteen pounds to shoulder—and that's nineteen pounds *without* the bipod fixed to the end of the barrel. The bipod was the first thing I took off on Pavuvu; it made the BAR unbalanced and unwieldy.

My head was covered with my pisspot (helmet), unbuckled at the chinstrap, swathed with the fall motif camouflaged cover. On my legs I had a pair of tan canvas legging, enfolding my dungaree pants close to my legs.

A marine came around with a little tin of black grease. Other marines began digging their hands in the grease and striping their faces—throwing the war paint on their cheeks and beneath their eyes, looking fierce, maybe a little brave.

"Hey, Mace. You want some of this?"

"Sure, guy." I took a couple of dips in the grease with my fingers, but instead of marking my face with stripes, I naturally gave myself a Salvador Dalí mustache, complete with the curlicues on the ends.

"*Third Platoon, go below deck. Third Platoon . . . below deck.*" The ship's loudspeaker sounded.

"Well, that's us," McEnery said. "We better get a move on, guys."

Walking down the metal stairwell inside, it was difficult to keep our balance, with all the extra weight we carried; you had to watch your steps, as the staircase led farther down into the ship's lungs, eventually opening up into what amounted to a large steel belly, full of growling amtracs, reeking of exhaust fumes. It was noxious, almost gagging; I could feel the inside of my nose and the back of my throat sting with the choking vapors.

Here, the amtracs grind their treads back and forth on the steel deck, squeaking and squealing as they align themselves to load up with marines, the echoes of things banging against the metal of the corridor's sides, voices trying to be heard over other voices, worried glances, hand signals, pallid faces; we walk into the rear of what appears to be the second amtrac that'll leave the great bow doors. The driver cranes his neck and looks back at us, maybe counting heads . . . who knows what he's doing.

Sy is a few marines ahead of me as we settle into the tractor. I catch his eyes. "Three days!" I shout and give him a thumbs-up. "Three days!" I don't know if hears me or not; nevertheless, he returns my thumbs-up, affecting a wan smile as he does so.

Three days. I close my eyes and take a deep breath, not caring how foul the diesel smoke is.

Three days. Rough, but fast.

That's what they told us, anyway.

On the way over to Peleliu, Billy Leyden and I were walking topside of the LST when all of a sudden P. A. Wilson came around the corner of the LCM, almost bumping into us.

"Hey, hey! Where's the flood, Wilson? The war's that way, buddy!" Billy pointed and chuckled.

Wilson stopped. "You mean you guys haven't *heard*?"

"Heard what?" I asked.

"What Rupertus said! C'mon!"

I looked over at Billy. "Who's Rupertus, anyway? One of the Marx Brothers?"

Billy winked. "I think that's a general, Sterl."

I knew exactly who General William H. Rupertus was.

"Okay, Wilson." I crossed my arms. "What *did* Rupertus say?"

"Okay . . . Okay, he said this whole operation is only gonna last *three days*. He said rough, but fast, but only *three days,* like Tarawa."

"Hey." I beamed. "I'm beginning to like this general of yours, Wilson. What else did he say?"

"Well . . ." Wilson thought on that a moment and shrugged. "The only other thing he said was that we're gonna be in the first wave."

"Ah, see?" I threw up my hands and looked at Bill. "See? Just when ya get to know a fella, and ya start liking the guy, the next thing ya know the sonuvabitch starts stabbin' ya in the back! Now, isn't that the way it always goes?"

The doors of the LST are just beginning to open, and a thin wedge of white light slices into the dark hold . . .

Then the doors open a little wider; I slide my hand back and forth on the receiver of my BAR. Holding my BAR, I think, Is this thing all I've got to keep me alive? *My eyes are just beginning to squint at the bright light. Pupils constrict.*

Everyone's nervous; *you feel as if you're about to jump right out of your skin. The sounds grow louder as the LST doors break open wide, white as snow. Until finally the great gate opens its full width, blanching the entire corridor with the absence of all color. Full blind. This could be the last day of my life . . .*

Exiting the LST that day, on our way to Peleliu, was a new birth. Reborn.

Most men are only born once. Having never experienced war, they are never faced with the rest of their lives seen through the optic of furthest extinction. For until a man embraces the culture of death, he'll never fully live the life he's always wanted to live.

September 15, 1944. D-day minus 12 minutes. 8:20 A.M.

In just a few minutes I'll be on Orange Beach 2 . . .

"Heads down! Heads! Down!" the driver of the amtrac bawls. I really can't hear him; nevertheless, we don't need to. Everyone gets the gist when we see his outstretched arm moving in a downward motion. We're about halfway to Peleliu.

Just as my head goes down, I gaze up and see that we've pulled right alongside an LCI (Landing Craft, Infantry). Even the sailors on the deck of the LCI scramble around, taking cover. Immediately I know why.

Fhsss! Fhsss! Fhsss! Fhsss! Fhsss! Hundreds of rockets begin shooting from the LCI, from box-shaped installments on both sides of her hull and on her deck. The 4.5-inch barrage rockets launch out in an arch, sizzling, hissing, flying toward Peleliu as a last measure to pepper any Nips who still might be on the beach waiting for us to land. The rockets themselves are only blurs, but the streamers coming off of them are white-hot comets that could fry a man alive.

You just want them to do their jobs. *C'mon, babies, please do your jobs!*

Even as we pass the LCI, our journey still seems to take forever. Endless. We stay with our heads down, now blind to anything ahead of us, weapons and packs being pushed up to our chins as we crouch; the 37 mm cannon crowds us, as some of the guys in our amphib straddle the thing, attempting to stay balanced. Something large screams overhead; I place my fingers in my ears, grimacing at the din . . . when suddenly the amtrac lurches and bumps against something, losing traction. Water sprays in and guys duck, some of them with their arms folded over their helmets.

I spy the driver of the tractor frantically jerking at the gears; all the while the amtrac is protesting and moaning, grinding metal. "We're not going anywhere!" somebody shouts.

We hit the reef! I knew it. My stomach flips as I watch the driver looking back over his shoulder, parallel parking the Alligator. *We're sitting goddamn ducks out here!*

"Hey, hey, hey! What the fuck's goin' on!" marines yell at the driver.

"Get us outta here!"

The driver pulls off the coral, takes a shot at the reef again, and with one more tilt we're up and over it in a matter of seconds.

The thing is, the amtrac driver does an excellent job, but nobody ever thinks about the driver and how the poor sucker must be just as scared as we are. He goes through all of his practice runs with perfect precision, yet the reality of the situation is—like for all of us in the boat—when you do it for real, what are you going to do?

The last thing you want to do is rattle a guy any more than he already is.

We're on the water and we're going in, and my breathing comes out hot and unnatural. Quickly I swipe the sweat from my eyes. Blinking fast. We're going in and I want to take one more look.

I take my last look at Peleliu while still in the amtrac, and the only thing I'm drawn to, as I look over the side, is the white water at the beach's edge. White! It's so white and still (*as she lay in her casket at our home in Queens*), untouched by marines. It's yet to be stirred by the treads of our amtrac . . . or any other beast of war.

"One minute!" the driver yells. "One! Minute!"

That's our cue. We all turn around to face the exit ramp.

Then I say to myself something that I've told very few people in my life, save for my mom, upon my return from the war.

I say to myself, "Sister Dorothy . . . be my guide."

Be my guide.

3

HELLZAPOPPIN'

NOTHING EVER PREPARES YOU FOR the rest of your life. It's inevitable that you get there; it is a certainty that you will; yet when you do, you rarely think, *This is it*.

The split second after the U.S. steel of our amtrac grinds against the foreign sands of Orange Beach 2, and before the ramp drops, I think to myself, *This is it*. My fingers try to claw their way into the anatomy of my BAR. My groin pulls up in a knot. Knees slightly bent now, down goes the ramp!

Nobody says anything: You get out of there; you get *out* of the amtrac! Combat infantry.

McEnery is out first, and he slices off to the left, his shotgun in hand. Confusion is king of this castle, and I look to the left but don't see anybody. No marines at all, only this mongrel dog on the beach: wet, shaking from tail to muzzle, vibratory. The dog's eyes are insane. He shouldn't be here. I shouldn't be here. A machine gun opens fire and fizzes me up like a bottle of soda pop. "Jesus Christ!" Guys are spilling out of our amtrac, escapees from a madhouse.

I sprint off to the right of the tractor. *Where the hell is this fire coming from?*

Ocean spray pelts my dungarees.

Just a few steps to my right is another amtrac, and I duck behind it, sighting in, trying to get my bearings. In front of me marines dart up the beach, their footfalls fanning tufts of sand behind them. High up, black smoke fights with the Pacific blue sky. Darkness wins—God's sky no more—and this machine gun runs its steady beat; steady, steady, keeping time with my trip-hammer heart.

The only thing between the sand and the sky is a clutch of ratty trees and low scrub, whittled thin from days of bombardment, appearing like a skeleton's fingers, brittle and blistered, as anemic as I feel inside.

Then suddenly I feel naked, ass in the breeze. The amtrac I'm using for protection lurches forward, and it's gone, just as quickly as I'm moving again.

Got to get off the beach! Quick time, my legs are pumping and I'm treading coral dust where the beach begins to rise. *Move up.* Other marines are doing the same thing—scrambling, falling, a wild-eyed run—but I only catch them in my peripheral vision. They are ghosts to me. None of them are real until I jump into a shell hole holding six marines.

Who are these marines in this hole, all bunched up? They are sinning. You don't bunch up. You *never* bunch up. They grip their weapons like primitives, fetal positioned, never daring to look over the rim. If a shell lands near these marines they'll be pouring them out of their boondockers—guts, like stuffing, rolling down the beachhead. You don't think about things like that; you just move.

I jump out of the hole, running low, as echoes of gunfire suck the air and explosions wrack the earth; yet I can't tell how close or how far the lead is flying, because there's a jackhammer banging away behind my eyes, making my vision shudder. The world is having a seizure. Up, then down again, I run and then fall; I see some mangrove and I low-crawl to it. Fast! A welcome shelter; I scramble against a notch in the thick foliage and prop my back against it, trying to see who's who, or who to follow, or where everybody is.

There's sweat, stinging, blurring the eyes, as a new wave of amtracs lumbers onto the beach, but I only see them through the shimmering heat. The sun is a needle's point of light; we insect invaders sizzle and pop beneath its hateful rays.

God, it's hot. It's a heat that doesn't leave you alone. The sun is my enemy. The enemy is my enemy. The sand is my enemy—between my teeth it grits, in my ears it sits, in my boondockers it grinds. Has it fouled my weapon? I don't know. The heat is my enemy; so I dig for one of my canteens, and to my surprise half of the bastard's already been drained and I don't even recall drinking it. That's the kind of shift into chaos, phasing out of awareness, that is powerful enough to melt the hands of time.

So I take a few more draws off the canteen, but when I start to get up, I'm pulled back to earth again.

"Shit!" My gas-mask pouch hangs up in the mangrove. Of all the things the marines could have issued me, I've got a gas mask! Like bringing a wedding cake to a funeral.

Move up, move up.

Untangling myself, panting, I leave the mask behind and scooch my way into more of the thicket, being careful not to snag my BAR as I go in.

In the mangrove are several marines. All of them look around, side to side, behind them, in front of them; their cheeks are already marked by rivers of sweat making clean lines through the dirt that's powdered their faces. Faces drawn down in worry. We are a shifty, sketchy tribe. Jitterbug movements, all together like rats in a sack. *Why the hell aren't we moving?* These trees—we hide behind rows of toothpicks, the timbers are so shredded and shorn of foliage.

A marine close to me says, "They've got brown uniforms, brown helmets, wraparound leggings, and hobnail shoes." He's describing the Japanese solider. I don't know why he's telling me this. Perhaps the word has been passed down the line, but I haven't seen a Nip yet, and I probably don't care what a Jap looks like, as long as he's not looking at me.

Move up. We creep ahead maybe five feet and somebody yells, "Hold up!" Before I know it I've already gotten behind some crumpled shrubs in the mangrove.

"They're shooting low! They're trying to hit us in the legs!"

"Corpsman!" goes the call.

"Who got hit?" *Somebody got hit.* You wait, breathlessly waiting, wanting to dash away, to scamper. That's what we want to know, an immediate answer to who's bleeding out in the mangrove. Frantic seconds. Necks crane quickly, low and at strange angles, telepaths, ears to the jungle telegraph, seeking to ascertain the origins of the shots. Fat chance, though—there's gunfire, explosions, and tremors everywhere. Random shots sound like tearing paper, knifing through what few leaves remain.

A marine hustles over to us through the garbage green undergrowth. "It was Flowers," he says, skidding back into his position. PFC Leroy Flowers, the company runner. We look around nervously, gazing anywhere but into the eyes of one of your buddies. Pops of small-arms fire still flirt around the area where Flowers was hit, but we pretend to forget.

There are mumblings and typical Marine Corps bullshit as I shift my gear around on raw shoulders. Sticky scavenger bugs drown in pools of sweat on my hands. There is movement. There is only one way out of this world.

Then I hear this booming voice—a locomotive breath, coming through the scrub behind me, followed by peals of Japanese mortars perforating the marines who are still floundering on the beach.

"There's not a Jap alive on the island, let's go!" the stocky marine shouts. It's the voice of Lieutenant Colonel Austin "Shifty" Shofner. The only true marine sermon I've heard since enlisting—some gung ho muscle speech that inspires us, though it makes me wonder . . . *if there are only dead Nips on this island, then who the hell is shooting at us, Snow White and the Seven Midgets?*

Still, it's exactly what we need to get moving forward.

Half-step, whole-step, then half-step, our swaying through the mangrove is discordant music, accompanied by a flock of F4U Corsairs above us, tacking out machine-gun rhythms at some unseen objective to our front. They are beautiful gull-winged birds of war: crying blue angels, shitting out their wrath on Japanese hide. The sight of them brings with it a little bit of courage; I almost want to scream with pride, but they are way the hell up there, and here I am, a mere pimple in the armpit of the Pacific. I could be squeezed like a boil and have my eyes run out, and those fighter jocks would never see the difference from their vantage. Just another marine.

Soon, however, we're told to take ten. We stop in a half-closed-in thicket, a small clearing, and I realize that in all this time we've only come about fifty yards from the beach. The hammering on the coast is still thick and congested, but in this moment, *our* moment, marines let their helmets fall to the earth. We sit and sag; Zippos snap open, and we light our first cigarettes since landing. Men sigh, but few words are spoken. Marines squat with their rifles propped on knees, while others sit with their weapons in their laps. It's the only nervous comfort we can afford ourselves as I take a seat on a burned-out stump, still warm from the preinvasion bombardment. Pete Candella comes up and sits next to me. The front of his blouse is inked dark with a V-shaped pattern of sour sweat, just like the rest of us.

With his dark hair and freckles, Pete looks just like that kid, Alfalfa, from the Little Rascals. It seems as if Pete's about to say something, as he wipes his arm across his brow, but that's when the world erupts.

An explosion, only fifteen feet in front of me, punches me off my seat, and I hit the ground in a heap, lungs purged of breath. Eardrums go numb as all sound is bled from the air, while this sickly black wisp of smoke belches and descends on us like the soiled hand of death. Yet I'm aware of Pete yelling out. Boondockers and leggings become blurs around me as I get to my knees, my heavy pack careening to one side, then the other. I shake my head to clear it . . . and this commotion! It's the essence of confusion. I catch sight of Pete and he has a hand over one eye, dark streams of blood cutting ruby ribbons around his clawing fingers—a groping fist that's trying to hold the geyser in. *My God, Pete's hit!*

Someone hails a corpsman. Quick.

"Where's he at?"

Bandages, gauze, hemostats, morphine syrettes, tape, and tourniquets—Corpsman Chulis is a miracle because he always seems to be there whenever he's called, although he's more of a marvel because he makes so much work with what little he has.

Now he's working on Pete, and I'm looking to see if all this is real. It's amazing how you can wish all you want that something isn't true, but when you really want something to be real, it never seems to be. That's how I feel when a Nip machine gun starts chattering off to our right.

Another jolt—and then *bang!* Marines disperse and hit the deck, the brims of our helmets creasing the turf, praying this Jap gun doesn't rake across our bodies. Beside me Corporal Vincent turns to me and says, "Hey, Mace! Go in there an' find out what the hell's going on an' take care of it!" I think to myself, *Why the fuck do you pick me? How the hell does he pick me, for chrissakes?*

Nevertheless, I'm going to walk through the fire because he said to do it. That's my job. This nineteen-pound BAR weighs more than the Brooklyn Naval Yard, and I'm lifting myself off the mangrove, bent at the waist, walking as if the ground is made of precious china. Blinking rapidly, pulse racing, respiration off the chart—this Jap must be a few feet beyond the vegetation, the shots are so close. So loud.

I head into the undergrowth, and all I think about is how I'm going to react when I get through the brush. *What if this Nip's got a bead on me already?*

You've got to think, Sterling, just think and be steady.

I'm about one foot into the scrub and I've got the safety off my BAR. Always off. Putting a little pressure on the trigger, I wish I had something to wipe the perspiration dripping from my eyelashes. I'm aware of the sound the leaves make as they swish the top of my helmet, even below the racket of the machine gun's bark.

I'm two feet in and I'm about to kill a human being. To *kill* him. My facial muscles ache from the force my teeth put on my jaws. These legs of mine are crap; they are made of elastic.

Three feet in and I'm a marine. A blunt fact.

Four feet in and . . .

"Mace! Forget it, it's one of ours!" somebody yells. "Come on out o' there!"

I'm out! I went in the tortoise and come out the hare, sprinting back, relieved that it isn't a Jap gun in the undergrowth, but pissed that I had nearly shat myself in the process.

With no time to compose myself (yet steadily cursing Vincent under my breath), they tell us to move up again, into the mangrove I had just exited. Just a swift push through the tangled brush, and then out the other side into another small clearing dividing two hedges of scrubwood. We find ourselves in an open spot.

"Down!" hisses a scout who's not too far from me, sending all of us shooting for cover. Heads on swivels, it takes nothing flat to see what the scout sees. Almost in front of us, only two hundred feet, and slightly to our left, some Japs are in the mangrove, wheeling a 75 mm fieldpiece partway out of the underbrush, like the hood of a Buick halfway out of a garage. We can't see the Nips, but we damn sure feel the ominous weight of the cannon's barrel: the potential for cyclopean fury, boring at us with its lands and grooves, magnified, as if the business end of this fieldpiece can reach out and shake my hand all the way to hell.

The natural instinct is to beat feet—all assholes and elbows— but we stay put. The gun isn't firing. Gnawing on bottom lips, eyes asking what to do next; time feels heavy and soggy—seconds are syrupy. The truth is I don't think the Japanese know we're here. They are probably setting up to take more shots at the beachhead.

Beside me Sergeant Hank Boyes continues to look over his shoulder. *I wonder what Boyes got cookin'*. Then suddenly a lightbulb flicks on beneath Boyes's helmet. News flash!

"There's a tank back there somewhere, I think," Boyes says, cocking his thumb toward the beach, shooting glances to the Jap gun and back at us. "I'll see what I can do. Hold tight."

Watching Sergeant Boyes vanish into the undergrowth behind us, I peek again at the still silent gun, expecting it to erupt at any moment. Then the sight of Charlie Allmann, to my right, catches my attention instead. *Where the hell has he been?* I think.

Not long after, we hear the first rumblings of a tank approaching from behind us, steadily growing louder. A tank can be a beautiful engine of metal-on-metal, steel wheels gnashing and pig iron groaning. It crashes though the foliage only a few feet away from Charlie and me, puffing up coral dust as it grinds. The Sherman flattens the mangrove halfway to pulp and storms into the clearing with Hank Boyes riding atop the turret, Hank resembling an ancient cavalry trooper of old, General George Armstrong Custer, or the like.

I don't hear what Boyes calls down to the tanker, inside the turret, but whatever it is the Sherman digs to a halt about 150 feet from the Nip gun and lets loose with its 75 mm cannon, throwing an orange shout of fire at the Jap gun, incinerating the mangrove around it. Then another *wham*. Then another. The blast is incredible when you're so close to the tank that you smell the heavy grease inside the tank's tracks. Each time the tank fires, it rolls up a few more feet and burns up whatever life once lived on the other side of the scrub.

Just like that the deal is done.

Boyes hops off the tank. We look at him and he shrugs his shoulders. Nobody says anything and nobody has to. The fact that this is a rough moment, a rough landing, for Pete's sake, is not lost on anyone, especially on Boyes, as he merely gives us the proceed-with-caution hand signal. We start to move forward. Slowly we move, weapons at the ready. The Sherman is already out of mind. Its job is done. For now, my eyes are solely glued to where the Jap 75 had once been, though where now simply sits a charred-out divot in the foliage like a black tooth in the gum line.

Inside the scrub trees and mashed vegetation, the odor of scorched plant life is acrid and pungent. Yet above that smell of the smoky scrub is a stench I have never smelled before. I don't even see the Nip bodies before an almost sweet, evil version of cracked pork touches my nose, as I feel a sharp pull in my stomach.

They are stage props, the dead Japanese. Not real. Mannequins in a shattered shop window. One is draped over the muzzle of the fieldpiece, his uniform in tatters and split at the seams from the force of the blast. His back and head are angled toward me, flopped down and saggy—a curious pose for a stage production of *Hellzapoppin'* at the Winter Garden, back in Manhattan. I can almost hear Olsen & Johnson, the laughter bouncing through my memory, singing those revue songs, morbid on the spot, like "Blow a Balloon up to the Moon" and "It's Time to Say Aloha."

The first dead Japanese I've seen.

There are more dead Nips tossed around the cannon wheels, and a couple more are chewed up toward the rear of the big gun.

Still, you don't stop and gawk; you merely take it in and keep walking, watching the flies descend on their afternoon meal.

I look away and then move closer to the tank as I let myself become more aware of my surroundings. The din of heavy combat in the direction of the 1st Marines still comes in thick as we step high and pick our way through this mangrove crap in a ripsaw skirmish line.

It never ends.

To our right, in another clearing—the largest we've encountered so far—we find a blood clot in the artery of the island: a festering field where about twenty-five to thirty Japanese bodies are massed.

"Sonuva . . . *bitch*," a marine from the 7th mutters quietly, but I don't turn to acknowledge him. I only have eyes for disaster.

The Japanese corpses have congested this open area with open wounds, glossy red tripe boiling from naked bellies. Those arms and legs that are still attached are curiously bent akimbo. Flexed fingers, like a beggar's claws, seek in vain to snatch their departed souls from the air, as blue and black lips puff on brown faces. Eyeballs are deflated, dehydrated, collapsing in on themselves. Exposed bone shows pinkish white. While some merely appear to sleep, facedown and flyblown, they are craving for dirt—all torn asunder on the butcher's block of war.

"Are they all dead?" Levy whispers to me. I haven't seen Sy since the amtrac, and boy am I glad to see him.

"Yeah, I think so," I reply. *What the hell happened to these Japs?* My mind goes back to the Corsairs we saw flying over, tearing up something in front of them. Maybe. Who knows.

We walk gingerly, picking our way through this blood harvest. Jim McEnery turns around and says calmly, "Make sure they got flies on 'em. The suckers could be fakin'."

Flies. They are everywhere: a clogged-thick buzz of maggot

seeding, a swarm feast on Peleliu. Somewhere there's a God, but not right here.

"Hey, Sterl!" Levy breathes coarsely, excited. "I think this one's alive! No flies."

I take a few steps back from where Levy points at a corpse with his M-1. Squinting, I try to make out what he sees—but it's not much.

"C'mon, for chrissakes, Sy." I lean in toward Levy's ear. "He's got no head."

There is a splash of embarrassment on Sy's cheeks, but he needn't be ashamed. Not here. Not like this. Not with caution flashing out snapshots of mortuary creatures before our eyes.

Then the smell of these Japs—the high coppery tang of dropped blood and the low odor of feces. There is panic carved on the faces of both the living and the dead.

Another Nip catches my eye. He has no flies on him either. Lying facedown, he resembles a windmill, arms and legs splayed out. He just seems too natural with not a drop of harm on him. *Pop! Pop!* With my BAR I put two rounds in his back. Quick and anxious, I don't even think about it before I do it. I *am* my fear, and I startle myself by pulling the trigger. Whether the Jap is alive or dead, however, doesn't matter; this is the first time I've ever fired my weapon, and all I needed was to let the horror out.

"Is he dead, Mace?" McEnery asks. Right now, I could run right over Jimmy, trying to get the hell out of here.

Keep moving. That's what we do.

We move and it feels productive. We stop and it seems as if we're bathing in quicksand. Even if there's safety in numbers, it certainly does not feel like it, exposed as we are among the bony trees.

The sun is still a cigar burn in the dome of the sky when we reach the southern edge of an airfield. Rows of marines, lost and disbanded, stagger throughout the underbrush, peering wide-eyed across the expanse of flatland that makes up the airstrips. Beyond the airfield, in the close distance, are rows of ragged and cleaved cliffs, peaks, and awful ridges that look dull and irrational beneath the 100-degree heat.

Talking to one another in shaky tones, we are scared. Not scared because the airfield is imposing, but petrified because the air seems to have been gagged of sound. Near silence. The juxtaposition is stark, the cacophony of our early day's run versus this present moment of quiet.

The Japanese have quit firing in our area. Only from our far left come the scant, sporadic thumps of munitions going off—probably mortars.

"Hey, Sy," I say hoarsely between nervous puffs on my cigarette. "Why do ya think the Nips have stopped shooting at us, huh?"

Levy doesn't look at me. His eyes, instead, are focused on the flat airfield in front of us.

"I don't know," Sy says. "Maybe they're tryin' to catch us out *there*?" He motions with the end of his M-1.

When he looks back at me I know he's right. We look again, together. The airfield doesn't appear very hospitable. In fact, the flat features of the airfield seem a lot like the hardpan of the Nevada desert—the kind of no-good terrain where a would-be traveler could find all sorts of snakes, scorpions, wasps, and jackals.

Presently Schwantz and Van Trump appear.

"Where the hell have you guys been?" I ask.

Van Trump shakes his head. "Shit, tryin' to find *you* guys! This goddamn place is a mess. Had some of the boys from the 7th Marines right up our asses the whole time, all the way up here. So I don't even know if we're lost or *they* are—or who the hell knows what's goin' on! You seen Zero?"

By that he means have I seen Lieutenant Bauerschmidt.

"Nuh-uh."

"Christ! And McEnery?"

"Yeah, he's around here somewhere. Say, how about the rest of the fellas? Machine guns? Mortars? Sergeant Palmisano? You seen any of them?"

"You kiddin'?" Schwantz chimes in. "They're probably still tryin' to pick their way through this crap like the rest of us! But hey, if you hear anything about getting some water up here, you let us know, okay, Mace?"

"Yeah, sure . . . water."

After a while, Van Trump and Schwantz return with Charlie Allmann, just as the sun begins to dip a little in the sky. Evidently they've been planning something and they've come to recruit me to go along with it. I'm sure Van Trump hatched the idea, but it doesn't matter. We talk as if I have a choice in the matter.

The plan is to walk onto the airfield and take a peek at what appears to be a crashed Hellcat on one of the strips. A "curiosity mission," if you will. The Hellcat must be the plane we saw take a hit and nose-dive onto the island as we stood on the LST this morning.

Reluctantly I agree, but only because I'm a part of the fire team. Besides, most of the action seems to be coming from the north of us at the moment. I honestly expect someone to bawl us out for going out there, but as we take the first tentative steps out of the mangrove, nobody cares. All eyes merely watch as we slip out of the foliage and onto the open ground. As soon as my boon-dockers touch the concrete, the creepiest feeling sprouts wings in the depths of my stomach—moths aflutter, beating madly and try-ing to escape. Something is on the outside looking in on us, but I ignore the early warning sign inside my guts, giving in to the face of young bravado instead.

Beneath our feet, the coral pebbles crunch against the first flat-packed land we've come across since the landing. The quiet is even more disturbing as our fire team, rifles poised for use, turns and looks, side to side, swiveling around and looking some

more—halfway expecting a sneaky yellow bastard to come storming at us, jabbering his jabber, his bayonet thirsty for Yankee blood.

Maybe this is a bad idea, but it's too friggin' late: We're already
out in the open and we're not taking any fire. *So, okay, good.*

What we find, on the other hand, is not quite as bad as a Nip
high on murder—but it is a close second. The first dead American
I've seen.

Everything on the Hellcat (if you could call it a plane anymore)
is pushed up, toward the tailfin, buckled and twisted from the impact of hitting the runway nose first. Both wings are barely attached
by scraps of metal, and they're pointing at the ground, in a V, all odd
angles and scorch marks on once proud metal. The engine appears
to have bounced backward, shoving almost all the way through the
cockpit, barely leaving enough room for the pilot to repose in his
fractured coffin.

Since the crash has forced the fuselage to ground level, we're all
able to peer into the smashed cockpit, looking down into the tomb
that had once housed a gleaming American specimen, ready for
takeoff.

The pilot is scrunched forward at his middle, leaning over what
used to pass as an instrument panel. His head has an unnatural
cant to it, tilted like the RCA Victor dog's, and I can't help but
wonder if the pilot—at this very moment—is somewhere hearing
"his master's voice." *His Master's voice.*

A wide ooze of jellied blood hangs motionless from his mouth.
Deep lacerations are present on his hands, bone deep. There's no
way I dare gaze into the face below his flight helmet to see if it
looks as bad as his Hellcat. This is way too close to home. It's sick
enough as it is. In fact, to merely touch him is a deadly proposition
in itself.

The Japanese have done something bad to the pilot. Bad.

It's PFC Schwantz who sees the Nip trick first.

Attached to the pilot's flight suit is a booby trap: a string of grenades, affixed to a thin wire, which holds the grenades together like a strand of lights adorning a Christmas tree. One pluck of that string and you'd be playing the harp with St. Peter for eternity. I grit my teeth and force myself to look away. *Those sonsabitches.*

In fact, we all back off when we see the pilot rigged up for death. Everyone save for Van Trump, who's still eyeballing the cockpit for some reason. I simply can't believe any of this. None of this is real. Not this morning. Not now.

What the Christ is Van doing, for God's sake?

Van puts a leg up on one of the angled wings and tests the bent metal against his weight. The wing proves steady enough for Van to pull himself up against the fuselage. He looks as if he is about to climb into the cockpit and sit in the pilot's lap. However, Van Trump doesn't go that far. Instead, he runs one of his arms into the cockpit and fingers around in there for a few seconds.

I wince and take another step back, fully expecting the explosion that's going to tear the top of Van's head off.

When I glance around, the airfield seems somehow smaller in magnitude, closing in on all sides. Moreover, I can *feel* them—a thousand Nip eyes, glaring down on me . . . only on *me*. If it's only my imagination running wild, common sense still tells me that at least *some* Japs are watching us. That even if we're out of rifle shot, the Japanese are soldiers, too, and they'd be stupid not to have the airfield observed around the clock. The Nips must wonder what we're doing out here. Or they're anticipating the same explosion I am.

When I look back toward the plane again, Van has his arm out of the cockpit, but he's still up there examining something, as if he's a pathologist who's just discovered that the cause of death was signing up for flight school. Then, slowly, his arm goes in a second time . . . very slowly . . . but this time Van comes out with something in his hand, all without disturbing the trap the Japs had laid for us.

Dropping down from the wing, Van Trump strolls up to us, grinning, as he brandishes a .38 caliber revolver he fished out of the dead man's holster.

"A chicken in every pot, fellas," he says with a wide smile. "C'mon, let's head back before it gets dark."

I let out a long sigh. I hadn't realized that I'd been holding my breath nearly the entire time we've been out here. *Lucky sonuv-abitch, Van.*

Walking back, it is still hellishly hot, despite the sun beginning to crank down for the evening where the ocean meets the sky on the other side of the island. *This place could have been beautiful once,* I think—but there is little time to reflect.

I could have thought about how close I had come to being killed since this morning, but I don't. I could have wondered if the Nip I'd shot in the back was already dead before I pumped two rounds into him, but I don't care. If I had known at the time, I could have thought about Larry Mahan and how he was killed, taking one in the chest, as soon as he got out of the amtrac. Or how his buddy, Corporal Clement Hicks, got his hand blown off, right next to Larry, when they hit the beach together. But I am oblivious to it all . . . and I'm all the better for it.

What I think of, on the other hand, is *two more days.* If I can make it through this night—*God knows what will happen to-night*—I will only have two more days of combat, and then it'll be back to Pavuvu . . . or better yet, Australia. Anywhere but here. Only two more days and *"There's not a Jap alive on the Island, let's go!"* Just two more. *My God, Pete's hit!*

Two more.

You've got to think, Sterling, just think and be steady.

Two.

"Is he dead, Mace?"

Yet just as I'm blinded to the fate of Mahan, I'm unaware that it won't be until October 15 (D-day +30), after almost a month of constant battle exposure, that K Company will finally come off the line.

As I settle back into the mangrove, flares begin to shoot up and flutter down over the airfield, creating angular shades of dark and light against the blood hue of the sunset. The artificial light of star shells bends the sleepy glow of the sun in such a way that marines look grotesque and misshapen among the shattered screw-pine trees and crooked coral spines. The flares will go on like this all night, one right after the other, turning the air as bitter as the ground is hard—adding to our thirst in increments throughout the night.

Yet for those of us who have made it through the day, there's no guarantee that we'll make it through the night. For as the final light ebbs, and the gloom sets in, it is written on every marine's face that we are trapped here, lost here . . . and the Japanese are out there.

4

RUN!

Dawn, September 16, 1944 (D-day +1), 90 degrees Fahrenheit.

Morning brought with it the eeriest feeling, watching the low mist float and gently sway over the ground across the airfield in front of us.

When the mist arrived—as gray shifted to first light—marines began to rise in the wash of our new surroundings, slowly at first, only a few green-clad phantoms smudging the skyline with movement . . . and then a few more here and there, until finally most of us stood, becoming real once more in the morning light. Nobody had to tell us to awake. We hadn't slept all night. We are simply there—in the moment: thirsty, filthy, sunken. Not a comb touched a hair; no water washed a face.

"Say, Mace, what the hell ya think we'll be doin' today?"

"Christ if I know. C'mere, ya got any water?"

That was the whole conversation on everybody's lips. Water. The lack of it. The love of it. The thirst for it. Marines, faces toward the sky, held their canteens bottoms up, jiggling the canteens from side to side, hoping that something would finally drip into their awaiting mouths, even though they knew damned well they'd already performed the ritual all through the night, with the same conclusion time and again. Nothing.

The definition of desperation (or insanity) is to repeat the same thing over and over, expecting a different result every time. We were desperate.

Both of my canteens had been empty since late yesterday afternoon—bone dry. My tongue felt like a cut of sandpaper, swathed in cotton balls. A stale, stanched sensation clicked in my throat; my tongue snapped like a rubber band in my mouth.

We knew we were in trouble without water, yet I don't think even Corpsman Chulis knew how much danger our young bodies were in. Moreover, nobody seemed to care. The Japanese were the issue, not whether we were fit to fight or not.

Nevertheless, the facts remained: The body could lose more than sixteen ounces of sweat for every hour under the 100-degree sun. Most of us had been without water for the last twelve hours. That makes at least twelve pounds of water our bodies conceivably lost since we reached the airfield. My heart raced, my eyes were so dry it almost hurt to blink, and I no longer had the urge to urinate.

In any other place we would have been in hospitals.

"You'd think they'd get some goddamn water to us, huh?"

"What the hell is goin' on here, for chrissakes? They knew this place didn't have any water!"

"Are you shittin' me? They don't care about us."

"Hey, you think the Japs got water?"

"Why don'tja go up there and ask the Nips for some water. Tell 'em we'll bring it right back to 'em after we're done with it."

Eventually someone said, "Hey, water!"

"Water?"

"Water, where?"

We hustled over to where Billy Leyden and a few of the boys

huddled around some sort of crater in the ground, a shell hole or a natural pocket scooped out of the earth. The hole was only about eight feet wide at the top, and as it got deeper, it funneled down, an inverted cone, where the water sat in a tight pool at the bottom.

There weren't many of us there, trying to get at what water we could: Gene Holland, Billy Leyden, Orley Uhls, Frankie Ocepek, Sy Levy, Jack Baugh, and I all attempting to fill our canteens and gulping water out of our helmets. *This must be what heaven is like in hell,* I thought.

For a second I stopped short of taking a drink—but the animal in my brain told me otherwise. Though it was true that the water was a grayish puddle, the kind that was ready for a bag of Portland cement if you were laying a sidewalk. Plus some sort of jungle crap appeared slick atop the pool . . .

"Who gives a good fuck?" I said. "I'm drinking it!"

Everyone grinned from ear to ear, passing up sloshing helmets; there were sighs and thanks-be-to-gods. Oh, it tasted like nine kinds of hell—very much like swigging down chalk. Nevertheless, with each grain that went down, with each grit, I became more sure that this was the cleanest spring that had ever touched my lips.

There was never very much water in the pit to begin with, so by the time we finished, the only thing left in the bottom of the hole was a thick muddy sludge, not fit for anyone.

The ironic thing, however, was that not long after we had as much of that soupy stuff as we could take, they brought up jerry cans of water that came out of 55-gallon drums they had rolled off the LSTs.

It wasn't fresh water in those cans, though. We later found out some goldbrick marines hadn't washed the aviation fuel out of the drums when they were originally filled with water on Pavuvu. I spit the crap out before it even had a chance to splash my throat.

"What the hell is this? This ain't friggin' water!"

No, it wasn't—and a string of curses went up among the ranks, punctuating that fact.

A lot of guys drank the fuel-flavored water anyway. Most of us didn't have much of a choice. For today we may die . . .

After all, we had already made it through a night that was nearly as deadly in its own right. For just as the daylight hours of our first day on Peleliu were brimming with pandemonium, the witching hours also cradled their own chaos during the infancy of the invasion.

There had been a deep dark night of no sleep. Our eyes bulged and burned, transfixed on every stitch of inky gloom in sight. Keyed up, if a marine slept, he was either inhuman, dead, or a rear echelon shitbird. Maybe all three.

It was just that way.

There was also very little radio communication across the entire line—that is, if you could call it a line at all. We were more like the spotty growth that passes for pubescence on a young man's face. In other words, in one patch of mangrove a collection of marines was moved by Lieutenant Colonel Lewis E. "Lew" Walt's people back to their outfits; then another cluster of marines would move up to where the rest of their squad was situated in the scrub. All night it went on like this, until our lines at least had some semblance of order (although from an aerial view, our perimeter probably appeared more like the bottom half of a grin, with a few teeth missing along the way).

Had the Nips known we were so off-kilter, those gaps between the cuspids should have been soft enough spots to infiltrate our lines and do some stiff damage—but the Japs didn't know. The Japanese were probably just as frightened as we were, confused and far away in their mountainous perches. I'm sure the Nips watched the star shells blanch the skyline and drift across the airfield the same as we did. Distrustful.

"Is that K Company up there?" a voice called from the darkness, not too far from where we hunkered in the mangrove. My eyes squinted as they adjusted between the harsh artificial light of the star shells and the natural soot of night. Between the two extremes, I barely made out the soft movements of a few dull figures approaching, gently crunching the foliage as they came.

Some nearby marines answered. "Yeah, K Company! That's us, over here!"

Suddenly a lone K Company man arose, stepping between us and the converging figures, just a few yards away from Levy and me. The lone marine challenged, "Hey, hold it up! Hold up . . . who *are* these people?" I couldn't be sure, as he was just a charcoal smudge in my line of sight, but the lone marine sounded like PFC Underwood, a runner for Captain Andrew Haldane, our company CO. Whoever he was, he made a good call. "Make sure these guys identify themselves properly, okay?"

The marine was right. Somebody creeping up on us like that could have been the emperor and all his flunkies, for all we knew. Lucky for us, and them, too, that the figures were merely a few more of Lew Walt's men, making their Samaritan rounds.

Otherwise, besides some sporadic gunfire and the occasional shelling, the only action all evening was the sounds of marines trying to peck out chunks of coral rock with their spades, attempting to make crude foxholes in an unyielding surface. A fruitless and fear-induced endeavor—over three hours of whacking the coral with a shovel would produce a dent worth only about two inches of land. A size just enough to spit in, if our mouths weren't too dry to do so.

It seems that it is the marine's everlasting burden to wage war against the elements, within and without the presence of our enemies. In the case of Peleliu, even the ground detested our very presence on earth. So we did the only thing we could. We bitched and realigned ourselves in our own private pockets of hell, waiting for the mist to come, without knowing why we waited.

In fact, none of us knew what we were doing.

As for the island itself?

Peleliu is a small crap island in the Palau island chain, roughly five hundred miles east of the Philippines, five miles square, and composed almost entirely of an off-white coral rock, speckled with dense mangrove, ranging anywhere from ankle-high scrub to thick jungle marshes. Furthermore, it appeared that the Japanese garrison had used every inch of its terrain to their advantage. High in the Umurbrogol Mountains (Bloody Nose Ridge), the Japs had dug into natural pockets of ridgelines, caves, and escarpments as places of defense. What's more, the Nips had constructed pillboxes, tank traps, and artillery emplacements that covered the whole island with deadly fire.

The Japs had an airfield, too.

The rumbling among the ranks was that we had to take Peleliu because of the airfield there, as well as the other airstrips on the neighboring islands of Angaur and Ngesebus. Japanese air superiority could've put a serious dent in MacArthur's bid to retake the Philippines. In other words, if the Nips had control of the airfields, they could fly their planes into the right flank of MacArthur's Army Corps, beating the holy hell out of them. That was the scuttlebutt, anyway, but the infantry didn't know for sure.

As for me, I'm only a marine rifleman, a big nothing, and decisions to take these islands, one after the other, had very little to do with me. Nobody asked my advice about going to Peleliu. I had only two jobs: killing Nips and staying alive. Anything other than that put me on a pay scale that my BAR didn't qualify me for. Besides, those who called the shots had been soldiering longer than I'd been alive; so to think that I might have been there unnecessarily or for something less noble than winning the war didn't ever enter my mind. As in any other job, you do what you have to do and then you go home. You might not like your job, you might not like your boss; nevertheless, you signed on for it, you volunteered for it, you get paid to do it. That's the story.

That morning the Japs began shelling the airfield again, right when the sun came up, making it difficult to spot their muzzle flashes flaming off the side of the ridges, not far from the other side of the airfield. We twisted up inside: A tense pulling in the center that gives every indication that our higher level of thinking has now made peace with the more visceral aspects of our selves.

Sure, if the Nips want the airfield so badly, why are they putting friggin' holes in it?

Hoisting our gear on our backs and returning to our small groups of fire teams, squads, and platoons, we anxiously watched as our navy boys delivered in mail of their own, salvo upon salvo, against the rock face of Japanese-held soil. Great pom-poms of white smoke, with undertones of orange, absorbed into the cliffs— giving us hope that we were giving the Nips hell—yet I don't believe there was a fool among us who didn't know that it was the stones crying out for blood, instead of the Japs.

It wasn't an artillery duel, but it was a constant. As if last night's relative quiet had been only a dream, despite the total lack of sleep.

When you wake up on the other side of death, marine, will that be a dream, too?

I highly fucking doubt it.

"Alright, Third Platoon, we're gonna make a run across that airfield," Platoon Sergeant Spiece says in a flat tone, while catching the eyes of a few scattered squad leaders here and there. "Second Battalion will be on our left; we're goin' to the right. We've got the shorter run, but you never know what's gonna happen."

Now he's gone. No questions. Nothing. There certainly isn't any Marine Corps magic surrounding Spiece's briefing; he leaves the last minutes before kickoff to each marine and his own thoughts.

Me, I'm scanning the surface of the airfield, watching the intermittent Jap shells wreck hell out there.

The whole airfield is a piece of crap. Here and there you can see the detritus of war: deboned Nip planes, which appear to have been scuttled only a few weeks prior, some sort of squat concrete hut in the distance, and a smattering of cheapo Jap tanks, which look more like Model-T Fords than machines of war. Yesterday evening, the 1st Regiment gave a real spanking to the Nip tank corps on the island, and what remained was just what I was sighting in. If I had wanted to see better junkyards, I could have simply paid a visit to the Bronx, never having to cross the equator for my troubles.

Now we're in trouble. Unchained and fraught with turbulence, the Jap artillery striking the airfield gives the scene a tilted nuthouse shimmy. Warbling and swerving, a drunken fuss of coral powder, rank ash, and cordite fumes, the garden in front of us is in full bloom. The heat amplifies, the heat inflates, the heat—a dry aching thing—the heat casts upon each marine a private rainstorm of electric sweat, spreading out blanket patterns of perspiration in the pits and crotches of salty dungarees. Only 8:30 A.M. and already the oven door of Hades has broken open, set in motion, open . . . open . . .

They give us the signal and we move out of the mangrove and onto the open airfield. My first steps are horrifying. We are a barbarian horde of globes and anchors, jazzed by brutality, beginning our charge at two speeds: fast and faster!

To my left I spy the 2nd Battalion making their push, rifles at high port, much like the British going across the desert in the Middle East.

"Hey, wouldja look at those guys!" a marine remarks, gaping at the same thing I am.

"Jesus! You'd think they're real marines or somethin'!"

"Tallyho, lads! Jolly good job!"

Wham! One shell drops to my left, and bits of coral zing past and sprinkle our backs—seasoning the meat. I close my eyes and open them again, quickly, just to make sure I'm still here, as smatterings of shell fire pitch the earth at angles too steep for the eyes to rein in. We're running! For although this rain of ruin hasn't increased since the early dawn, nonetheless, trapped in the middle of it, all bets are off, as if every Jap gun on the island sees you as a little yellow duck in a shooting gallery, rusted on its track, not making very good sport of it.

Run. Then down. "Hold it!" goes the cry. When I ram the deck, I hit that sucker hard, shaving raw spots in the skin beneath my sleeves. It's all so fast. You're down as quick as you can. *C'mon, c'mon, what's the holdup? Up . . . now!*

Back on my feet, the fiery air sits low in my lungs and sags there making each (*run*) breath a little harder to (*run*) exhale. A stitch immediately cracks into my sides as I run (*run*) . . . *Wham!* Fifty yards away, another shell spins the earth off its axis; and I look to my left again, and down—just a . . . *what is that?* There's a hole in the runway; a perfectly cut hole, three feet across and four feet deep, only a few inches from my left foot. In the bottom of the hole (I see all of this in a fraction of a second) is a dead Nip, wadded up, a piece of scrap paper, thrown in the wastebasket. Crumpled. This is some man-made hole, a forward observation post or something, and this poor bastard got the rough duty the hard way.

"Get down!" *Smack!* Again, we're raw steak on the tarmac. We stop because someone's hit.

Looking, looking . . . only my immediate surroundings are clear, as straw-colored sheets of haze and heat from the earth blank out most of my vision. A marine lies flat on the strip close to me, making like a beached fish, pulling for air, his chest a squeezebox. He lolls on his pack; it's impossible for him to turn over. It's the heat. *The goddamn heat!* A sun victim. *Go!*

To my right are several more heat prostration casualties, plastered on the airfield. Running by, I see their faces. Shivering and exhausted, with mottled gray and red visages, coated with particles, and particles of particles; the pallor in their eyes stands out against the lividity of their skin. I think I see one of them cry (*or is that sweat?*)—either way, there is anguish.

Wham!

Every time we stop, Nippo Baxter goes into action.

Eagle-eyed and always alert, Nippo has a real knack for sniffing out Nips and their prized possessions.

Here we are, spread out, melted butter on the airfield, hearts pounding in the sides of our necks, hoping like hell the Japs don't light our asses up—and then there's Nippo from Yazoo, breaking off from the pack and scrounging around the airfield as if he were hunting 'coon, foraging for something to pilfer. *That dumb shit is gonna get himself killed!* Yet whether it's ignorance, bravery, or just plain *going Asiatic,* Baxter is a fine scout, who . . .

Charlie Allmann is beside me, both of us wading through the sloppy air, heads down, with bits of debris bouncing off the tops of our helmets; everything seems so . . . *Wham!*

I begin to see where we're headed; there's mangrove on the other . . .

Don't look . . .

Wham! The big stuff coming in is way behind . . .

Behind us several more shells fall, but I don't look back. I've reached the relative safety of the mangrove on the other side of the airfield. Really, the terrain is more of the same gnarled coral crap; yet even this scant vegetation is a comfort, appearing more like the place where we started, versus all that open ground.

"Who's hit? Who got hit?" I pant and take off my helmet, as other marines fall in with us, lying on their packs and sides, gulping air in great gasps. We're nearly vapor locked—spent cartridges, all in a row. Cigarettes are lit, and everyone's breathing gas fumes from guzzling that water-type-shit from the jerry cans. Some marines are

in a state of collapse, gazing over the airfield we just crossed, unbelieving, shielding their eyes from the rays of the sun, as other
marines stumble in. Nobody knows it now, but the guys on our
left, in 2/1 and 2/5, are getting flamed up by a lot hotter stuff than
what we just went through. As for us, we are two killed and about
four wounded during our jaunt. Even that is too many. Exasperat-
ing. Demoralizing. You always care for the marine next to you—
even if you don't like the bastard.

Joke: Why did the marine cross the road?

Punch line: Because the brass wouldn't let him go around it.

Funny.

We're burning up where the undergrowth becomes thicker along
the march east of the airfield. That's where we're sent. That's where
we go.

I don't know how I do it, yet just when I think I'm about to collapse, I somehow find the way to take one more step into the heat
and the unknown. You just grit your teeth at the sensation of your
blood boiling in your veins, while you hope to hell that it really isn't.

Squinting, vigilant, and painful, marines' eyes look as Oriental
as the occasional Jap corpse we come across amid the tricky mangrove. The dead Nips are black crusted, blimped, belching and
farting noxious gasses, their swollen tongues plugging their
mouths, almost taunting. Some of our guys try to pick through
their bodies, scanning for loot, yet they soon give up on these Jap
monsters—they are too far gone, too decomposed, even for the
more brazen among us.

Then.

Boom boom boom boom! In an instant some heavy Jap stuff
drops in and around us . . .

"Christ!"

We freeze. Drop. Then race for shelter—all of it in a single motion with no breaks between actions. "Ah, crap!" Levy, McEnery, Allmann, and I skate through a patch in the thicket and then collapse on the other side. Breathlessly we listen. No one calls for a corpsman, which means everyone's aces.

The Japs are using their "knee mortars" on us.

The Nips' rifles might be antiquated bolt actions, and their grenades are wonky, because they have to whack them on something to ignite their fuses, but their mortars are arguably better than what we have for close-quarter fighting. The Japanese mortars are more portable and lighter, and they pack nearly the same punch as one of our 60 mm jobs. Moreover, it takes only one Nip to use one, so they don't have to line their guys up in squads to be effective.

To add insult to injury, the story goes that when the marines on Guadalcanal confiscated the first Nip knee mortars, the marines literally tried firing them off their knees. Whether or not that's true, or whether or not the marines broke their legs doing it, is something I can't verify. Nonetheless, the Japs just stick them in the ground, fire off a few rounds, and then disappear, with very little effort wasted setting them up or tearing them down.

That makes for quick work on us. The Nips have vanished before we can sight them in.

As we regained our bearings in the small clearing, we met some boys from a JASCO unit, setting up where they could observe the Umurbrogol Mountains, about seven hundred to nine hundred yards to the north of us. The Umurbrogol Mountains were a joke as far as mountain peaks go: More like the Marine Corps making mountains out of molehills, truth be told. Those JASCO guys, however, were nothing to scoff at.

JASCO (Joint Assault Signal Company) was a unique group of assault troops, composed of marines, army, and navy men, who were responsible for directing joint artillery from the army and navy guns in support of ground troops. That meant *us*. So not only did they immediately gain our respect, but they were also one hell of a nice group of guys. In this particular unit, there were an army and a navy officer coupled with some radiomen, all of them combat armed to the teeth.

We sat and chatted with them awhile, taking any rest we could.

"So, where are you boys from?" the army officer asked.

Jim McEnery, acting like a big shit, let them know. "King Company, Third Battalion, Fifth Marines. We're headin' east of here, gonna break off the Nips across the island."

I rolled my eyes theatrically toward Levy and mouthed, "*King Company*," doing my best McEnery impression. Sy barely stifled a laugh. What Jimmy didn't know wouldn't hurt him.

"Well . . ." The navy officer put down his field glasses for a moment. "You marines have some rough goin', then." He motioned with his binoculars at all the mangrove. "All this crap. It only gets worse goin' where you're headed. I dunno about any Nips, but you've got jungle, swamp, you name it out there."

That suddenly put a damper on things. We didn't feel like joking anymore.

One of the JASCO boys saw that the mood had changed, and to his credit, he tried to cool it down—although to a man, we all had our buttholes in our throats.

"Hey, marines, take a look at these." The JASCO guy smiled, producing a fine set of glossy black-and-white photos of geisha girls, all dolled up: Dainty little darlings, fully clothed, yet enough to cause any male to salivate, even as thirsty as we were. We zealously passed the photos around, with lascivious looks and ribald remarks aplenty.

Presently Jim broke our reverie. "What the hell is that?"

Jim was focused on the distant mountains, where the muffled sounds of combat continually echoed down.

"What the hell is *what*, Jim?"

"That's a fucking Nip up there!" Jim replied.

Several of us moved up closer to Jim to see what he was pointing at. Jim then borrowed a pair of binoculars from the navy man,
saw for himself, and then passed the field glasses around for us to
confirm his hawkeyed vision.

The Jap in question was indeed a Jap, but there was something
odd about the way he was perched up on the ridge. Not only was
the Nip about nine hundred yards away and really up there, but
he was also very still, cemented to the side of the cliff and bent
strangely as if he were already a dead man. To me the Jap appeared
dead; I was about to say so when . . .

Crack! Jim cradled a borrowed M-1 rifle in his arms, shooting a
round at the faraway Nip, adjusting the elevation on the rear sight
as he prepared to take another shot. *Crack!* He popped off another round as if he had a hope in hell of hitting that Nip at such
a great distance. Target practice, I guess.

Then more.

Boom!

Boom boom!

A few Jap mortars dropped near us again, and just like before,
everyone hit the deck—it's automatic—as pretty glazed photos of
Japanese womanhood wafted into the air.

When the mortars ceased coming in, we all picked ourselves up
and dusted ourselves off, as though whatever jungle matter we'd
collected on our dungarees was coming off anytime soon.

Maybe the Japs have been zeroing us in, I thought—the same
Nips who had thrown in the heavy stuff earlier, before we met the
JASCO boys. However, before we parted company—that is to say,
before the JASCO unit could catch on that maybe we brought the
Nip mortars with us—we quickly let the JASCO troops know that
it had been great, good luck, and see ya later.

As we left the clearing, a few marines, including myself and Sy,
were amazed that such nice geisha girl photos suddenly appeared
in our dungaree pockets.

"Yeah, a nice buncha fellas, those JASCO guys, huh?" Levy smiled. We never looked back.

Wham!

Good evening.

Just before night the Nips start throwing in heavy stuff on us, real big stuff—not like the knee mortars. Shrapnel and coral debris zig and zag, splitting the very elements in the air, turning them into something else entirely. Something like panic. *Wham!* Something like *fast* panic. It's suffocating. *Wham!* The ground still offers the impossible, never quite devouring the shock of the Japanese shell fire; instead, it kicks off fragments of harsh powder in every direction imaginable. This time there's nowhere to run.

Mashing myself as low to the coral as I can, I lift my head for as long as I dare and spot Van Trump and Donald Schwantz. *Wham!* They've found cover in an eight-inch depression in the coral rock, each with his arms wrapped around his helmet. A wide shallow in the earth, not deep, yet the best I've seen so far. *Cover!* Something is better than nothing as . . . *Wham!* This is worse than the airfield.

I jump up, run, and then duck in between them, stolen bases, sliding headfirst into home plate.

"C'mon, there's no room for you here!" one of them shouts. I don't know which one said it; I wouldn't doubt it if they said it in unison.

Goddammit! The screaming in my head is louder than the artillery. *Wham!* Barbed shafts of steel fly too close; they fall red and thirsty, but I move out; no questions asked.

Dusk finds me with my back against a tangle of mangrove, curled up, my arms wrapped about my legs, knees to my chest. There's nothing tougher than waiting for what'll kill you. The only thing separating me and a bellyful of oblivion is several gnarled leaves and ropes of plant life that could never possibly grow any-where civilized—so I'm uncivilized. Who gives a damn.

This is where I'll spend the night, come death or not. Just one more day. *Wham!* One more *mother lovin'* day. *Wham!* In the morning I'll get up and two of my buddies will tell me that a two-inch-diameter shell fragment landed in the spot Van Trump and Schwantz occupied. Evidently those guys had pushed off, too, or they would have ended up sauce.

The ground shudders like hell. Many flickers of light.

There's nowhere to run.

So this is where I spend the night. About to die.

5

A BLAST FURNACE IN YOUR SOUL

September 17–25, 1944

"*Corpsman!*"

A sharp explosion and a quick burst of light,

Since we've left the airfield, the marines' objective on Peleliu has been to seal off the island into three separate pockets. The 1st Marines have taken the north and are getting chewed up in the mountain ranges. The 7th Marines are moving south and are mopping up any resistance down there. As for us, the 5th Marines, we've been in the center since landing and have been steadily pushing eastward, toward the coast, the other side of the island.

A sharp explosion and a quick burst of light as a belch of smoke blackens the green, green foliage.

The brass has no idea how many Japs lie ahead of us or what their disposition is. On the other hand, if the Japanese are thick in our area, they will be just as disadvantaged as we are. There's no waging war in a jungle so dense that it's impossible to see what you're shooting at.

. . . as a belch of smoke blackens the green foliage. "What the hell was that?"

"Corpsman, over here!"

The jungle is a vampire who sucks the pus from a pox-infested pit. We trudge through the bowels of a terrestrial leech, sick with blood, yet wanting more. Nothing describes this misery as thousands of branches pull at our equipment, beg for our weapons, and grope at our clothing. A straitjacket of greenery, tailor-made to trap all bugshit intruders.

"What was *that?"*

"Corpsman, over here!"

Nothing describes this misery, for there is one variety of heat that stings and blisters, yet there is quite another that sits on your chest, a hothouse compress, turning sweat into runnels of sludge. In the jungle there's a despair that stretches time like taffy: slow minutes, fast hours, and seconds simulating infinity. If a buddy were to tell me we had traveled twenty yards in a day, or even one hundred, I wouldn't be able to disagree with him either way.

Boom!

"What the hell was that?" I shout. Marines make odd turtle-head bobs and crouch instinctively at the sound of an explosion somewhere in the green.

"Corpsman, over here!"

We stay squatted; our rifles scan the foliage for anything that doesn't look right coming out of the shade. Waiting. Watching. All behind paranoid eyes. Drops of perspiration the size of marbles roll off my cheeks and fall to the jungle floor.

Muffled pops of branches splinter among the rustling of leaves and vines. A marine would be lucky to see three or four guys around him, the jungle is so encapsulating. The canopy of overgrowth above us only allows a few thin rays of sunlight to dapple the ground below it; so in this place there's an alien sense of both night and day, simultaneous, beneath this natural ceiling.

We wait.

Presently a marine comes jerkily through the growth behind me, trying to keep his balance.

"Hey," I call to him, "what the hell happened back there?"

"Goddamn trip wire. Must've been," he says rapidly, moving along at the same clip. "Got Levy in the chin."

"He alright?" I lean into my words, hoping they'll catch up to the marine before he's gone.

"Think so. Probably got hisself a million-dollar wound." Then the marine *is* gone. The jungle swallows him as quickly as he came.

A trip wire. *Yeah, had to be,* I think. I remember back to the Hellcat pilot, all messed up in his cockpit, Jap grenades dangling off of his flight suit. I didn't even know the pilot's name, but I know Levy's—and that's when naivety becomes more of a friend to me than any marine could ever be. Out of sight, never mind.

Back then—just three days on Peleliu—I was wise enough to know that dead meant dead (and never coming back), yet jejune enough to believe that if a marine were merely wounded, that meant that he'd be okay—on his way back to the States, drinking Coca-Cola and flirting with Red Cross girls on Banika Island.

Like yesterday, on the airfield, we passed those heat prostration guys and kept moving, because you knew a corpsman would appear out of nowhere to fix them up. Faith is faith. Whether it's a lie or not.

The truth is, however, you seldom see a marine die right in front of you. They linger. They shout. They suck air through holes in their chests as their eyes grow glassy, far-seeing, staring at something that only the soon-to-be-dead can witness, until the stretcher bearers take them away. Later you would find out they had died, but by then you had grown tougher, less susceptible to the wild imaginings of drinking anything cold, *anywhere,* let alone with girls of any sort kissing your Purple Heart.

It's the reality of the grave, like it was for Larry Mahan, who I found out later could have been saved; he could have lived, if only he hadn't gone nutty on the hospital ship and begun tearing the plasma out of his chest, trying to jump out of his hospital bed. Screaming, they said. Larry had been screaming.

He was buried at sea, where the pressure of the ocean, versus the fragility of human skin, will implode a man, once a certain depth is reached.

What kind of no-good burial is that?

Death gives meaning to life once a certain depth is reached.

When did I lose my childish way of thought?

One thing is certain: At twenty years old and in combat I see things as they truly are and not as they are viewed when men get older and convince themselves that their stories are real—that their tales have some mystical meaning to them.

So I have very few qualms about not seeing Levy off. Sy will be alright. This I know. The only thing to do now is to continue heading east, being more guarded against trip wires, until we reach the other side of the island, where a navy ship is waiting to take us back to Pavuvu.

There's nobody in front of me but the enemy.

Night has come again. If it were quiet, a marine could hear the speed-buzzing of mosquitoes circling around his ears. Or the sounds of men shifting their weight and grumbling, trying to keep their asses out of the water. We are at a place where the jungle meets up with some pisshole of a swamp.

It's not quiet, though. Instead the night is in overdrive, roaring fire from hundreds of 155 mm fieldpieces, whooshing overhead and kicking the hell out of the mountains beyond.

The ridges are far away, but we're so close to the muzzle blasts of these 155s—no more than two hundred yards from them—that the heat burns up the night. My hands begin to shake, and it's painful just attempting to compose a coherent thought. "Loud" means nothing when describing these powerhouses, commensurate to having a subway tunnel running between your ears.

They've been going on like this since midday. A blast furnace in your soul.

Beside me is PFC Dennis Hoffman, a good-looking, curly-haired blond kid from Buffalo, New York. Since knowing him, I've wondered if a pullover sweater and a job as a mail clerk back in Manhattan would suit him better than looking to get himself killed in the Marine Corps.

He's trying to keep up with the throb of the night—and he might have a chance at it, too, if not for this debilitating jungle rot gnawing at his feet.

Eating his spirit away from the bottom up, the ulcers on Dennis's feet made their intentions clear on his face, as each step he took turned his fresh schoolboy features into a rictus of agony. Step—and red bulbous cankers ground against the insoles of his boondockers. Step—and another slice of skin sloughed off his foot, America peeling slowly away, along with any hope of ever returning there.

At the edge of the swamp, stagnant water pools as high as midway up our leggings. We squat in it. There is no way this infected water is doing Hoffman any good, with his wounds sponging up the dirt, the decay, and the jungle excrement.

"Say, Mace?" Dennis turns to me in the gloom. His eyes clearly speak with primordial fear and shock. "Do you think we'll be gettin' out of here tomorrow, like they said?" He pauses. "Three days . . . right?"

I look back toward the expanse of enemy ground before us. The night booms and yells murder, yet there is a soundlessness in the near pitch of darkness: An almost detailed blindness that can morph into nearly anything if the imagination is willing.

"Don't worry about it," I say. "Everything's gonna be fine, Dennis."

Everything's gonna be fine, Sterling. Everything is going to be fine.

It's here that perception becomes serrated and ill defined. Abstract. Smeared against the hands of time. I'm awake but asleep, where the mind can only handle so much before it rocks the madman to sleep.

Sometime during the night, marine dog handlers come up through our lines. These two dogs, sleek war Dobermans—all etched musculature and regal black-diamond fur—look like better marines than us raggedy-ass riflemen.

The dogs' coal-tinted eyes stand out glossy and unfearing, in front of animal brains that know no difference between kennels and killing fields. They are out of place, despite their purpose.

"Hey, you guys, wanna see the dogs?" a handler asks, really showing off here.

"Yeah, let's see 'em. C'mere."

"I'll be a sonuvabitch. What kinda mutts are those?"

Smiles go around, and morale is cranked up a few notches. Their handlers take good care of these dogs, and it shows. I've hardly eaten three bites in the last three days, and there's still the ever-present lack of clean water, but these Doberman pinschers haven't missed a square. They're majestic.

The handlers tell us that if there are any Nips out here, the dogs will root them out. Sure as hell, they will. The Dobermans have been trained to whiff out the scent of a Jap from several yards. That's a reassuring thought—if it works, that is. Otherwise, what's going to happen when the dogs run into a Nip?

So they let one of the dogs run into the jungle. All around we detect movement as the dog sniffs and paws his way through the mangrove. I figure twenty minutes, and if the dog doesn't find a Jap, we'll feel a lot safer. Here's the rub: If the dog's only out looking for a place to take a leak, we're not going to care how beautiful these beasts are. For all we know, he could be giving our position away.

Nippo Baxter leans over to me and whispers, "Ya know . . . I heard them Nips . . . they like to *eat* a dog, is what I heard."

Some marines will believe anything they hear about the Japanese, like the Nips file their teeth down to points, they rape their enemies, and even that they eat their fish uncooked. I'm not here to judge Japan, though. I'm here to hurt him before he hurts me. The real Pacific war. Whether or not they eat domesticated animals doesn't do me one bit of good in the jungle.

Nevertheless, soon the dog comes back out, uneaten, and the handler appears pleased, giving us a matter-of-fact look.

"Okay, that clears you guys out. Good thing for you fellas this is a Nip-free area."

There's nobody in front of me but the enemy.

Looking at these dogs . . . I can't explain what I feel. I'm in the middle of a sweltering jungle and I'm thinking about 1932. The winter of 1932. I'm eight years old in one place, freezing cold, icicles hanging from Wall Street awnings—and then I'm twenty in another place, feverish and frightened.

Miz Muggins gave birth to six puppies. Yes, I remember that now.

A winter morning, the puppies are just weaned off of Muggins, and my dad puts all six of the pups in a cardboard box. He bundles me up, and Dad and I walk a mile to the Lefferts and Liberty station, catching the El for a nickel apiece, riding across the Brooklyn Bridge and into Manhattan.

At the Park Row Station we get off the train and walk downtown with the box of pups, near Wall Street, on Maiden Lane.

A lot of people work in these big office buildings in Manhattan. To have jobs out here, during the Depression, means a little something extra to most people's pocketbooks. These New Yorkers are like royalty as far as we're concerned; which also means they are rubes. Plain and simple, easy prey.

Dad and I place our box of pups down and set ourselves up in front of a tall building as the biting wind comes screaming around the sharp angles of city blocks.

As the people come out of the buildings for lunch, we have a couple of the puppies out, playing with them. I'm herding them from one place to another, on display as if we're carnival barkers or some such. If they aren't pedigrees, you wouldn't know it, they are so cute—pawing around, nipping at each other's tails and ears—and here I am, eight years old, and despite the arctic air, I'm having a good time.

Sure enough the number-crunchers and pencil-pushers make their way out, and one of them says, "Oh, that's cute. How cute! How much?"

My dad says, "Six bucks."

It's not a hard sale. All the pups are gone within an hour.

The Dobermans *are* fine specimens, yet at the edge of the swamp the dogs have the shakes so bad, it looks as if they're trying to shit out peach pits.

The next day, we see one of the same dogs crapped out from heat exhaustion, lying on his side, panting, his tongue swabbing the deck. The Doberman couldn't stand the heat.

Beasts and men are alike. They evacuated the dog and Dennis Hoffman the next day.

The next day is more of the same: a fever dream, sloshing through a mix of mangrove, jungle, and swamp. Peleliu is where God must have taken out the trash once he had created the rest of the world. It's all a joke. Our Father, the benevolent caretaker and master designer, but the shittiest comedian of all time. Instead, he gave his sense of humor to his Marine Corps children, with our rifles and grenades, bayonets and Brownings. We are here to kill the Japanese man, not to die by means of jungle taint and claustrophobia.

A deadly war within and without, without firing a single shot.

I'd give anything to know what's trying to kill me.

So by the time we reach the eastern shore, the sea and the sky greet us with a crocodile's grin: full of hospitality, yet barbed with great sharp teeth.

There will be no evacuation. There will be no Pavuvu. The "three days" gag is just a dry-hump. Blue-balled, we are now on Purple Beach, where we're ordered to keep guard against Nip infiltration and reinforcements along the eastern shore. If the Japanese wanted to, they could send in reinforcements from any one of the Nip-held islands in the Palau chain: Babelthuap, Ngaraard, or Ngesebus . . . and they would aim straight for Purple Beach as their port of call.

Code-named "Purple Beach," this is the original beach where our invasion was to take place, but it was thought by Rupertus & Co. that it was too heavily defended to make a successful landing. It ended up that they were correct in their assessment. For although we don't see pillboxes or any signs that the Japanese had ever been here, just one look at the beach—much longer and wider than Orange 2—tells us that we would have been clay pigeons to the Nip gunners had we attempted a landing. Much, much worse than the inferno of Orange 2.

Yet finally we'll have at least some semblance of respite.

After three days of brutality, human emotions have become too frayed. First it was the enemy, then the war with our environment, and lastly the straw that broke the gunny's back: There had been a ghastly slaying during a night patrol.

It had rained all night. They sent forty of us, waterlogged and soaked to the gills, out into the wild, hunting for Nips.

Buzzing through a thin radio frequency, the voice of our shepherd for the evening, Major John H. Gustafson, said something about when, where, and how to make contact with the enemy. However, I don't think the mission was very clear to anybody except for maybe First Lieutenant Edward "Hillbilly" Jones and Sergeant Hank Boyes.

The scuttlebutt had come down that there were two thousand Japanese reinforcements chopping their way west through the jungle, trying to link up with their forces in the mountain ranges. The funny thing was, the Nips on the ridges must not have needed their friends badly; otherwise the Jap commanders would have picked a better route for their reinforcements, given that the jungle we had just hacked our way through was assuredly the longest path that one could take to reach the road to hell—and it sure as shit wasn't paved with good intentions.

So it's forty marines against two thousand Japanese in an overgrown arboretum, with perhaps only a few openings in the jungle in which to fight. At night, no less. In the rain, no less. Whoever hatched this plan must have laid an egg—and a lot of marines say as much.

It's no wonder our anxiety is stuck in the red: Morse-code nerve endings, synapses crackling at thirty million pops per second; I can't make out the marine in front of me. *We're going in goddamn circles here.* Even so, I know the rest of the 3rd Platoon is somewhere up ahead, as well as a couple of other BAR men, Gene Holland and Frank Minkewitz. Also with us are some of the mortarmen and machine gunners, but unless they have somewhere to set up their weapons in this labyrinth, if we get into a row with the Nips, there will be mortar rounds bursting in the screw-pine trees, raining down stuff on us a lot more vicious and heavier than water.

So it went all evening, green-garbed mud-crunchers, noctambulist dreamwakers, numb but highly volatile, so keyed up that close to the next morning, Lieutenant Jones convinced Major Gustafson that he should reel the patrol back in.

If the Japs had been out there, they had missed us and we had missed them.

It wasn't until our patrol had returned to Purple Beach that the guys in my squad learned that one of the boys in the mortar platoon, in a fit of fright, had slain one of his own with a spade. What would provoke a marine to kill another marine was anybody's guess. Whoever the killer was, he must have been damned good at his job, committing the act so quietly that none of us heard a thing.

"Jesus H. Christ! What the hell were they doing out there?" Jack Baugh asked, lighting cigarettes and passing them around to everybody.

"Beats the fuck outta me," Billy Leyden said frowning, "but if I ever see one of those shitheads walkin' around with a shovel, I'm surrenderin' to the goddamn Japs!"

There's nobody in front of me but Marines.

Purple Beach, Peleliu, Palau Islands, 7° 1' 0" N, 134° 15' 0" E, September 20-something, 1944.

It was almost like I didn't want to tell anybody about Purple Beach, it was so good. That's why you'll hear few marines mention our stay there.

On Purple Beach, marines actually enjoyed digging, because the digging was so good. Real sand, not that jagged coral rock, provided a deep hole for each marine to cozy up in. A machine-gun section dug in right beside me, guarding, scanning the ocean from surf to tide. If the Nips decided to land on this shore, we would tear their asses up. Little slant-eyed Japs, putting us through the meat grinder for the last three days—I don't think there was a marine who wasn't trigger-happy enough to send one of those bow-legged bastards back to whatever passed for a god in their savage yellow minds.

So, despite the bitterness of not getting off the island, our new purpose was at least assuaged by the relative ease of our duty on Purple Beach.

Those of us who hadn't eaten in the last three days once again found our stomachs (for the most part). We could bathe in the ocean and not care too much about the tacky residue it left on our skin. None of us had to speak in those too-hushed voices to which we had become accustomed while clambering through the jungle. Purple Beach was almost serene.

Almost.

I dug my foxhole only ten feet from the ocean. Dozens of marines dug their foxholes close to the shore as well—as close as we dared without running the risk of water seeping into our holes. Crisp little pops of snapping breakers came in with the currents, not too far away from me, as the moon cast a bridge of light upon hypnotic waves. Gently, gently . . . For brief moments there was not a war going on at all. Only at night, when you cared to see it, could the eye make out the silhouette of a navy minesweeper, gliding up and down the coast: Faint lights aboard ship, some ensign smoking a cigarette on deck; their easy duty was our easy duty, trying hard to blank out the muffled sounds of carnage ringing out on other parts of the island.

When daylight came you could find marines playing cards on the beach, or fortifying their positions, when . . . *Crack! Foom!* Out by the minesweeper a funnel of ocean sprayed up as one of the navy guys, on deck, took out a mine with his M-1 rifle. We looked for a second but immediately resumed our game, uncaring. A novelty. A marine could get used to games like this.

"Hey, Mace, wouldja take a look at that!"

I squint out the sun and look in the direction that Orley Uhls is nodding.

"Well, I'll be a sonuvabitch!" I say. "Is that Levy?"

It *is* Levy, standing only a few yards away with some other marines, Levy sporting a clean set of dungarees (much too green and bright for a place like this). Yet his dungarees are not the only thing that sticks out; for on the bottom half of his face is a bright white swath of thick gauze, held together by liberal strips of adhesive tape. To tell the truth, my pal looks like some sort of wacko Santa Claus, his faux beard obscuring his good looks. Above the cotton, though, Seymour's eyes are smiling more than enough to make up for what we can't see below them.

It's a situation that's hard to describe, seeing Levy back.

"Levy! What the fuck are you doin' here?" I grin at Sy and he grins back.

"I was on a hospital ship, but I saw this DUKW coming back so I figured I'd just hop aboard." He shrugs.

Some of the other guys rib him good-naturedly. "What the hell's a matter with ya, you stupid ass?"

"Yeah, boy, you sure blew it this time, Sy!" says Leyden.

Levy merely beams above his wounds. "I just wanted to be back with you guys," he says, as if it were the most noble and sane thought on earth.

"Jesus, Sy, you must be friggin' nuts," I reply, shaking my head, still not fully comprehending. "Anyway, c'mon, I'll get ya squared away over here."

So we walk over to where the foxholes pock the beach at the ocean's curb, but I see that Levy's eyes have suddenly lost the sparkle they had radiated only a few seconds ago.

"What's wrong, Sy?"

"Ya know, Sterl," he says, "when I came back on this island . . . when I came back, it just stunk! It really friggin' stunk! This place is so bad that I just . . . I just felt like turning around and goin' back out, ya know?"

I don't know. I have never left the island and then come back. Desensitized, I don't realize that the whole island—even Purple Beach, maybe a mile away from the nearest fighting—holds the stench of mortal decay, fire, blood spilled on coral, aged brown by the sun, the constant odor of spent munitions, amalgamated with the rank bouquet of festering swamp water and a dying jungle collapsing in on itself.

Whatever it is that Sy discovered—what he *saw*—was the truth. *There's nobody in front of me but this crap.*

It's only now that I see what Levy sees—that the light at the end of the tunnel is just a freight train coming my way.

I will never forget our last couple of days on Purple Beach.

Some marines will tell you about the land crabs there, swarming into your foxhole—a hive mind of clipping claws and blue-black bodies. Other marines might tell you about the sand fleas on the beach and how the fleas would breed inside your dungarees, making life an itchy hell for anyone who wore the globe and anchor. Some marines will just bellyache about anything:

"You know what? I'd like these goddamn eggs better if there were any goddamn *eggs* in 'em!"

"Ah, c'mon. You know they don't care about us!"

"Ah, jeez, ah, Jesus—just take a look at my skin, willya! I look like a buck-Chink from all those atabrine tabs they've been tellin' me to take!"

"Would you guys shut the fuck up? I'm trying to take a crap over here, for God's sake! Christ!"

To me, in those last days, the sun was just as hot, yet it smiled a little cooler. I was just as filthy and unshaven, but simply gazing upon that crystal water made me feel a little sharper. Any piece of sky to hang my civility on was enough to allow me to feel normal again, and that was enough, even for the briefest of time we spent under a different sun—fooling ourselves with foolery.

So when an LST had moored up to the edge of our beach and parked itself up against the reef out there, Sy and I pulled the perfect caper. One last stunt under the banner of youth and imagination, before Peleliu tore us from the tides and sucked us into the under-tow of a river running red.

"Hey, fellas!" some navy guy called from the railing of the LST.

"Hey, yourself!" Sy shot back. We smiled at each other and shielded our eyes from the sun.

"No, hey, really, you boys got any souvenirs to trade?"

Souvenirs, souvenirs . . . my mind quickly cataloged what I had picked up along the way (which wasn't much). I had one crap Japanese "Bible" that I had found somewhere, and . . . *what else, what else? Oh yeah!* I had hung on to a couple of those photos of geisha girls we had borrowed from the JASCO unit. (*"Yeah, a nice buncha boys, those JASCO guys, huh?"*)

"Yeah, we got some souvenirs!" I said.

Levy didn't ask me what I was talking about, but the look he gave me said, *We do?*

I winked at Sy, as if to say, *Whattaya mean, Sy, sure we do!*

"Well, then," the navy guy interjected, "why don't you guys swim out here and let's see what ya got?"

"Alright, alright. Keep your girdle on, we'll be over in a sec."

It wasn't that far to swim. Just to the berm of the reef, where the big front gate of the LST was already opened about ten feet away from the other side of the coral. Another couple of navy guys stood on the reef, smoking and talking, as they gave us a hand up the ramp; from there we went topside, shaking ourselves of water, standing on the upper deck.

Showing off our bullshit souvenirs, I knew those navy guys wouldn't know hot air from a blowhole when they felt it. They looked pleased as they passed the photos among themselves. As for our presence, though, they eyeballed us almost resentfully, as if they were reading from the Navy Manual, under the subtitle "How to Resent the U.S. Marine."

The only one who did any talking was the swab who initially called us up.

"Have you guys eaten?" He looked at us, perhaps admiring Sy's battle scars, as Levy had gotten rid of his weird Santa's beard nearly as soon as he'd rejoined the platoon.

"Nah," I said. "We haven't eaten a thing." (Which was a lie.)

So there Levy and I sat in the ship's galley, gluttonous, our bellies near bursting to the tune of steak and potatoes, greasy, with thick white bread to sop it all up with.

I think I'm full now.

Full on Peleliu. Nothing lasts forever.

Suddenly they were there. The Prophets of Combat. The 1st Marines.

They were our future selves.

Eyes glazed and distant, they looked like hell, with battered dungarees salted white with sweat, unshaven and filthy from powder burns, bloodstained and near emaciated. They came to us at Purple Beach, a menagerie of funhouse mirrors, in which we saw the skewed reflections of ourselves in a host of dull likenesses.

The 1st Marines were done as a unit that early into Peleliu. They had hit a brick wall of Nips at a place called the Point on White Beach, and now they could neither kill nor be killed any more than they already were.

We were ordered to get our gear together, told we were moving out and we'd draw ammo along the way.

As the remains of the 1st Marines flopped down on the beach, exhausted, our guys sidled up to them, quizzing them, as if their attempts to draw information from those grizzled marines would somehow imbue them with the power to face what we were about to. A transference of wisdom, if you will . . . yet the prophets had nothing more to give.

Me, I simply sat alone, watching the slow surf to my right lap lightly against the shore. I was usually one to cut up and shoot the breeze. Now, however, I had no desire to speak to those elderly young men of the 1st. They appeared too familiar. Slightly too real. To commune with them would tell me things that I really didn't want to know.

Here, our guys readied themselves, slowly, languidly, giving up our rotten piece of paradise to the boys who had come down from the mountain. We had already gone through the blast furnace, but the sight of the 1st Marines told us that there was something worse out there than hell. If only we had known. If only we had known that Peleliu was the place where even devils feared to tread.

I remember Corporal John Teskevich, Corporal Walter Stay, and Private Henry "Hank" Ryzner getting their gear together with their squad. Lieutenant Bauerschmidt was gathering up his things, too. He didn't have to say anything to get us moving. We were a good unit.

Private Joe Mercer didn't pal around with anybody, but he was waiting on the beach, too, ready to go.

PFC Lyman Rice was ultimately busy trying not to scratch the ringworm on his back. Little did Lyman know that in a few days ringworm would be the least of his problems.

Nippo Baxter carried more equipment than anyone else. Besides his Marine Corps issue, Nippo had a Japanese saber in his belt, a fur-lined Nip officer's pack that he strapped to the top of his gear, and on top of all this, his helmet fastened to his pack.

The pièce de résistance of his whole getup, however, was a Japanese-made phonograph, which he had hanging off the right side of his cartridge belt, complete with a full array of 78 rpms.

Nippo would play his phonograph all night long on Purple Beach, unless enough of us got together and told him to knock it off. The music (if you could call it that) was a grating noise of plucking and pinging sounds. Then, above the din, a Nip voice sang in tones that made it impossible to tell if the singer was a man, woman, or child. It wasn't lyrical, and it stung the Western ear; nevertheless, it was quaint—but only for a little while.

I'm not sure if anybody ever questioned where Nippo got all the best souvenirs; my theory was that he had to have been slinking off and scrounging around for that loot when nobody was looking. We had already seen Baxter in action on the airfield, a few days prior, but the trophies he had on Purple Beach were real beautiful things. They didn't come from the airstrips, that's for sure.

For all I knew, Nippo could have been slipping right into a Jap camp and lifting his swag from under their noses.

Now we are to head north, up the West Road, and into the hooks of the enemy.

Whether a marine lived or died, from there on out, none of us would ever be the same.

6

AND ALL THE MONKEYS AREN'T IN THE ZOO

The Battle of Ngesebus

THIS IS A BATTLEGROUND.

A conglomerate of filth and garbage, moving muscle, and the progress of steel. On a moonlike landscape, arid and blinding, thousands of us, the living and the dead, worm into an island that is only a few miles square from stem to stern. The smell is hideous. The noise of battle sings in all directions.

We pass a small aid station clogged with various casualties—immediate cases whose lives can be saved if they're rushed to a hospital ship fast enough.

Combat fatigue victims, who fall prey to themselves, look like mice trapped under a bell jar—clawing for a way out, around and around in circles, all within their own minds.

Dead marines, too. Dead. Just a couple of them outside the aid tent, covered with ponchos. The only sign that there had once been a life under the marine-issue poncho is the uncovered boondockers, roughly analogous to tombstones dotting Boot Hill. *Here lies PFC Chestwound, KIA, 09/25/1944. Beloved Husband and Father, Sgt. Avulsion to the Cranium, Killed in Action, Peleliu, 1944.*

Here, some sort of stretcher bearer is down on his knees,

scrubbing the red off a cot with a coarse wire brush. The cleaning agent he's using curls the blood up into a thick pink froth.

A group of Hellcats moan over the ridges (which now loom over us, so close we can almost reach out and touch them, if we dare), coughing bursts from their machine guns. Little rings of smoke drift behind the fighter planes, afterimages of the rounds they've just fired, as the pilots make quick time against the sun. Beneath them I hear the tinkling sound of spent cartridges, raining down hot, below their flight.

There, some orderly from the aid station, hands flecked with blood, shakily smokes a cigarette below the bags under his eyes as we pass by. He leans against the tent post, frowning, flicking his ashes into a bucket filled with soiled gauze, piss-soaked paper, and strips of stiff dungarees. I don't want to look at him. What would his gaze say if our eyes locked for only a second? *See ya soon, marine?*

Everywhere there is commotion, as jeeps and trucks in clouds of coral dust roll this way and that. The bite of diesel fumes and gasoline hangs noxious in the air. Marines, like us, march in single file, heads angling toward the sporadic pops of small-arms fire somewhere up the ridges. Muted thumps of explosives ring down, echoing through the caves and pockmarked surfaces of a cliffside that has been eroded, unnaturally, by the hammers of hell.

The ridges of Peleliu represent the healthless backbone of the island—a sickly spine that will never heal.

Yet the disharmony of our environment is not as chaotic as those first couple of days of the invasion. Although the battle still rages relentlessly, there are pockets of Peleliu (small though they may be) where marines can walk openly, if cautiously.

I know—the rifleman *knows*—however, that we are headed to places on tiny Peleliu, just a few yards from where the rear echelon guys feel safe, that nobody but the rifleman is expected to go. We're an elite fraternity of trained dumb asses. Damn the cost, we are expected to go, to get the job done, to spill the blood—be it ours or that of our enemy. For, the fact is, if we don't do it, then nobody will, and we'll all be stuck on this beautiful island for as long as we're unfortunate enough to live.

So they send us north, up a road lying on the extreme west of the island, to a place called the Lobster Claw. Gazing at a map, I don't think this western stretch of island looks anything like a lobster's claw. All the islands out here look the same, like Rorschach blots to a madman's eye—which is fitting, since anyone will believe what he wants out of all this lunacy. To one guy, the island might resemble the jaws of a monster. To another marine, Peleliu might appear like Saipan with a broken neck. To me, however, it all looks like a screwed-up version of the 1939 World's Fair. Here, the cotton candy is plumes of smoke. The exhibits are tanks and carcasses, howitzers and head lice . . . and a menagerie of young men slogging their way though Sniper Alley, up the West Road, muscling to the front of the line.

Sniper Alley is its own main event, although the Japanese along this stretch are not snipers at all. They are Japanese riflemen, pure and simple. Our yellow-hued brethren who, either by command or by their own moxie, have decided to harass us with fire from the mangrove along either side of the road.

That marines call them "snipers" gives them almost a bogeyman quality—a mythos that doesn't belong. That the Jap "sniper" is somehow more trained or more motivated than the marine is up for debate. Yet his effectiveness is not debatable at all. In fact, the little bastards must have nuts the size of cannonballs to be able to hold their breath out there in the heat, alone, just waiting to drill a hole through an American soul.

We're not thinking about snipers at all, though, by the time we get to where the road begins. We're hot. We're exhausted. The confusion and noise that surround us shake the nerves, like rattling a bean inside a tin can. We are the human beans.

"Goddammit, how long do we have to hump this friggin' island?" PFC P. A. Wilson mumbles.

"Hey, stow it, willya, Wilson?" Billy Leyden says, fed up. "We've got enough hot air without you addin' to it, alright?"

We've been marching since morning, and the scuttlebutt is that some of our guys from the company got to ride trucks across the island and up the road. Nobody says much about that. Somebody has to get the crap duty, so it might as well be us.

Before anyone can start bitching about the trucks, however, a Sherman tank chugs right up beside us, and Lieutenant Bauerschmidt suggests that at least some of us should climb up the tank and ride the rest of the way in.

It takes but a moment for those of us standing closest to the tank to toss our weapons up the side of the Sherman. Helping each other up, we perch against the turret, John Teskevich, Jesse Googe, and Sy Levy on one side, with Jim McEnery and me on the other. I can't speak for anybody else, but I am elated to be riding—because who knows how much farther we'd have to walk to reach our day's objective.

"Well, it ain't a Caddy, but it'll do." Levy beams.

"It's a goddamn limousine, is what it is, Sy." I smile back.

Kicking out of idle, the tank lurches forward as we hang tight to the beast; yet she's only crunched forward a few feet when . . .

We don't even *hear* the shot that hits Teskevich in the stomach. The whole world is a mash of noise and pressure. From where I sit I see John double over and grip his stomach, but it isn't until I hear the screaming that I snap that something is seriously wrong.

"Ahhh, I'm hit! Christ, I'm hit!" That's Googe yelling. *What about John?*

Quick, I'm off the tank; *every*body's off the tank, as if the Sherman is surrounded by plague.

"Stop this goddamn thing, now!" Jimmy bangs on the top of the tank. "Corpsman! Goddammit, where's Chulis?"

I run up to Levy. "What the hell's goin' on, Sy? You alright?" Levy is feeling around his leg, confused. Grabbing one of Levy's arms, I help him scoot on his rear, getting him behind the tank.

"Yeah, yeah. I'm fine," Levy says, out of breath.

"For chrissakes, corpsman!" Googe is on the coral, holding his right arm, which is a sad rag of useless meat at the moment. The blood is slippery down his arm and soaking into his dungaree jacket.

Teskevich, on the other hand, says nothing. Both Googe and Teskevich are being treated behind the tank when Chulis and Alfred "Doc" Jones decide they need to get John the hell out of here or he's not going to make it. In fact, John's *not* going to make it. No. His stomach is clotted with blood and some clabbered matter that must be John's breakfast from this morning. The square-set jaw and rugged looks that Teskevich once sported now appear gaunt and filmy. His body looks fragile. Yet his deathly frame isn't a product of the bullet that just killed him.

Things don't work that way.

The truth is, none of us realize that our lack of food and sleep, our gain of worry and fatigue—our general environment has been changing us into something else. In John's case the Nip bullet simply quickened the process.

Double-timing it, they evacuate Teskevich on a stretcher. Googe goes next, but the stretcher bearers are not in too much of a hurry with him. He'll be fine. Besides, it appears as though they gave Googe a shot of morphine; he isn't raising nine kinds of hell anymore. Teskevich, on the other hand . . .

You can see it in Jimmy's sorrow, that despite the best efforts of our corpsmen, Teskevich will die on Peleliu. He was dead when the Nip bullet hit him, though he clung to life a little longer, for all of us to see—more painful, to the living, than if he had died right away.

What happened was a one-in-a-million shot. The bullet had

passed through John's guts, out his back, and then through Googe's arm. Levy was holding his leg because the round had lodged in his legging, yet without piercing the skin, having lost velocity after spending itself through Teskevich and Googe.

"Sy, you're one lucky SOB, ya know that?" Chulis asks, patting Levy on the back.

"Alright," Jim says. He looks up toward the sun. "There's nothing more we can do here. Let's go."

John had been one of Jimmy's closest friend in the Corps. They had been on Guadalcanal together and Cape Gloucester, too.

"Let's go, guys."

Nobody says anything about John, just as nobody says a thing about the tank.

It's unanimous. We'll walk.

The road headed north might as well have been the road going south, because as soon as Teskevich was killed that's how everything went. South.

They've bulldozed the Japanese dead to the seaward side of this stretch. Pressed and torn among the mangrove on our left, the Nip corpses crack open like too-ripe fruit. They are sulfurous to the scent—brown uniforms painted with swarms of gut-wagon flies.

It's hard to imagine that when traveling from one small place to another on Peleliu—just a matter of feet or yards—there is something new to take in, to cope with, to experience, even to the point where the mind doesn't register it right away. The brain is forced to view it all impassively; otherwise the intellect will either go screwy or shut itself down completely.

Every few hundred feet or so an MP is posted along the road, moving men along, shouting out warnings.

"Hey, you marines, move your asses! Hot zone, next twenty yards! Hot zone!"

We take off on a dead run for the next twenty or thirty yards, because the so-called snipers are known to be picking off marines at different intervals. Me, Jim, and Levy. Run and pant. Walk, walk, and run. Fatigued. It goes without saying that nobody wants to end up like Teskevich; more to the point, the whole way up the sounds of combat have been fanning our way: bad breath, behind the decaying jaws of the little yellow imps from Tokyo. The jangle of marine gear bumps together as we speed it up. We sprint on sore feet, then walk some more; all the time we take sips from the tepid water in our canteens.

It's amazing how drinking hot water, even under such a humid climate, can cool the senses and quench the palate.

I don't think I'll get used to it, though. I don't get used to any of it.

What the hell am I even doing *here?*

All of us. Every man on this road is heading north for a purpose.

They told us it would be Ngesebus.

Ngesebus.

Sound it out. The word makes no sense.

Ngesebus is a baby island only six hundred yards across a causeway to the north of Peleliu's Lobster Claw. The island itself is only two miles from point to point, running SW by NE, yet it's a mere mile across its width, from west to east. Ngesebus looks exactly like a drop of bird shit on the windshield of a Pontiac. *Splat!*

Evidently, they had been holding K Company back for the invasion of Ngesebus. We'd even been told we would be pulling another amphibious assault, which came as a shock to us. For one thing, it was unheard of for a marine unit to make two identical beach landings in the same operation. Another thing, the Japanese garrison on the island (total forces unknown) was shelling the hell out of a regiment of the 81st Army Division, who had been raking across the upper portion of Peleliu for a few days and catching crap everywhere they went.

Ngesebus needed to be closed down—and closed down fast. The island was a sty in the eye of the whole operation, in that the northern portion of Peleliu couldn't be secured until Ngesebus was taken, too. With its miniature airstrip, Ngesebus was another vital key to unlocking Pandora's war.

So, once again, it was up to the marines to save the day.

Before we jumped off at Ngesebus, however, our job was to mop up and support the army on the Lobster Claw, as we secured the high elevation of Hill 80, protecting their eastern flank in the process.

Though the Lobster Claw was a frightening and miserable place, none of us knew what a rattrap Ngesebus would turn out to be. Then one night, we were inoculated to the facts in short order.

I had a front-row seat.

One of our last nights on Peleliu, before Ngesebus, was a particular stygian shade of black. An obsidian wall where light did not bend or break an atmosphere that was almost palpable. It didn't get much darker than that.

Quietly we set up a defensive position on one side of a dirt road. Across from the road, recessed about thirty feet, was a copse of tall scrub trees—probably the tallest we had seen on Peleliu.

Charlie Allmann and I were manning one foxhole. It was a beauty of a hole—simply beautiful. There was real dirt to dig in, not just sand, because of the rich earth near the phosphate factory. Everyone had great foxholes that night; the only problem was, the night was such an inky syrup that we didn't have any idea who was to the immediate right or left of us. We knew that Item Company was somewhere out there clockwise, and I knew that Hank Ryzner was in a foxhole, by himself, to my right (so close we could reach out and touch hands if we wanted), but beyond that I could see nothing. Only the same hard darkness everywhere.

Now I know why children are so afraid of the dark.

"Now listen, Charlie," I began, looking out of the corner of my eye where Allmann was sitting. "Levy's going to be in our squad now, but I want you to be careful because he draws fire, okay? Things are gonna happen—and when they *do,* the minute Sy gets in there the shit's gonna fly."

Silence.

"He's a good kid, but he's like a magnet for Nips, so we gotta watch out for him, understand?"

More silence from Charlie. Either he was sleeping or, knowing Charlie Allmann, my speech was going through one ear and out the other. Anyway, with losses to Levy's squad, there were no longer squads or fire teams. We simply divvied up whoever was left so we could at least function as makeshift combat units.

As always, I knew I couldn't count on Charlie; so I merely resigned myself to the night.

At that moment a voice came from behind us.

"Hey, boys, how's everything going over here?"

I looked up but could barely make out the face of Captain Haldane, peering out of the gloom. Evidently he had come up from the rear and was checking out our lines.

"Fine, Captain," I said. Then I thought about it for a moment and changed my mind.

I wasn't fine.

"Hey, Captain . . . do ya think we could get some flares up over those trees there? I'm thinkin' that . . . ya know . . . that would be a helluva great place for the Nips to come out an' sneak attack us or somethin'."

Haldane looked in the direction of the trees; his faint silhouette was shifty, hazy. "Yeah, I think that'd be a fine idea. Listen . . . you guys stay alert and take care, alright?"

"Sure thing, Captain," I said. Haldane moved again and was gone just as silently as he came.

Not long after, three flares shot up behind us and over the trees, light cascading down, turning the trees into dancing shadows, a shifting daguerreotype landscape. My mind whispered to me that behind the trees there must be ten thousand Nips out there, all bucktoothed grins and feeding off the night like a dog feeds off fear.

A machine gun popped off to our right.

Shit!

It never fails; the body goes rigid, with muscles you never knew you had going stiff. PFC Ray Cushing from I Company spotted some Nips, and in the half-glow of dwindling flares and arcing machine-gun bullets I saw them, too. *The Japanese!* These particular Nips were dressed in the black pajamas and split-toed sneakers of the "night fighters." In the distance, they were ill-defined man-shaped things, living shadows blending among themselves. Though before the light ebbed back into night, I clearly saw two of the Japs return again to the shelter of the woods, goblins having fun with the village idiots.

Respiration. Rapid.

Heavy.

Yet so damn tired.

Like the last flicker of a dying flare, sleep in a combat zone is the way station between stops of consciousness. It is one toe in the water, always testing the temperature, yet knowing that a plunge can drown you—but because the suction is so strong you cease to fight the feeling.

I knew the Japs were out there. I knew it. We all knew it—which is exactly the reason I asked Captain Haldane to light the woods up. Nips in the woods. Spooky little bastards. It didn't matter, though, because I was so goddamn tired. My adrenaline was seeping out of me with the dying light. Charlie was sleeping. I didn't know if Ryzner was asleep, but I was nodding off.

Then it happened.

I couldn't tell if it had been a minute or an hour, but some feeling—the childish part of my mind tugging on the coattails of my adult brain—woke me up just in time to see him.

A Nip running at a slash straight for us!

What . . . ?

Yet I wasn't fast enough to react. It was a dead feeling.

The Jap rammed into Ryzner's foxhole, only four feet away from me. I couldn't even move.

That's when the volume was turned down on the world. Silent sounds, everywhere, save for the thrum of my heart galloping in my ears . . .

Then gradually the volume came up. A few muted grunts and the swish of clothes on clothes, faint exhales. So close. *Not enough time, not enough time . . .*

More volume, but not loud. Instead of shouts I could hear the Jap's voice low in the dark, foreign lingo rattling around in the back of his throat. A prayer? A dirge? A supplication? A surrender?

At last I saw Hank's form move up in his foxhole, pushing the corpse of the Jap up and out of the hole.

There's not a clock in the world that could measure how slowly all of this happened, yet how swiftly the arrow of time flew. I was right *there* . . . yet where the hell was I? It all happened so fast that I didn't have time to react.

What followed was a lull that opened the silence.

"Hey . . . Ryzner?" I whispered, not really knowing what to say. "Are you alright?"

For a second there was only more emptiness.

"Yeah," he finally said, the arch of his back visibly heaving. I expected him to sound out of breath, but he didn't. Hank simply sat at the rim of his foxhole, his bent back drawing up and down. For all I knew Hank could have been gazing at the dead Nip with a big grin across his face. *How did he kill the Nip, anyway?* I thought. It was a soft slaughter: one so light that it never raised an alarm, not even a few feet down our line.

I ventured again, "What the hell you think he was tryin' to say, Hank? Trying to surrender or somethin'?"

Hank's garbled words were noncommittal—faraway and feeble.

Ryzner was a weird kid anyway. He was bowed at the shoulders, scrawny framed; his skin was yellowed by atabrine tablets, and his head was nearly shaved down to the skin. An odd duck. Nevertheless, one thing Henry wasn't was dead—and that was good enough.

As far as I recall, I never went to sleep again that night.

The next morning, just as soon as it was light enough to come out of our foxholes, I crawled over to Hank's Jap and checked around the body's waist looking for one of those "thousand-stitch belts" the Japs were so fond of sporting. The corpse didn't have one. In fact, his body appeared as if some marine vulture had already picked the Nip clean during the night. The fact that I didn't hear a marine creep up and scavenge the corpse was almost as eerie as groping over the Nip carcass in the first place. The dead man was a paradox: as stiff as a flatiron, yet cold and pliable. It was strange to think that he was killed just four feet away from me.

Later in the day, while we were lounging on the edge of our foxholes, talking and smoking, the press came to our company and began inquiring as to the whereabouts of Private Henry Ryzner, from Detroit. They asked about the story of how Hank single-handedly killed a Japanese night fighter.

Photos were taken. There was a lot of glad-handing. Ryzner was interviewed, and he was informed that his story would appear in his local newspaper. He was a hero for a day, and that was just as well for Hank.

We all thought the press hubbub was a load of crap, and I'm sure Hank felt the same. See, it's not that Hank didn't deserve the accolades, but there was a bigger story than Ryzner's that night, and it happened only about twenty-five feet from us.

When the flares went up and PFC Cushing let loose with his machine gun on the Nips in the tree line, the two Japs that I saw linger around the woods waited just a little while for the star shells to die down before they made their move. One Jap headed straight for Ryzner's foxhole, while the other one ran right into a rifleman and a contingent of mortarmen behind him. So while Hank was taking care of one Nip, another rifleman was fighting off the second.

Now, as I mentioned earlier, this wasn't that far from the old phosphate factory—one of the few flat pieces of land on all of Peleliu, therefore one of the few that could be built on. There were no cliffs and no rises—merely a level tract of soil, facing the western side of the sea. In other words, the Nips had a straight shot at our line.

Of course, I witnessed the struggle with Ryzner and his unwelcome guest, but it wasn't until morning that we found out about the second Nip and how he was dispatched . . . or rather, the tragedy that ensued.

It seems that while the rifleman was fending off the second Nip's attack, his foxhole buddy panicked, jumped out of the hole, and ran as fast as he could in the direction of the command post. As he hightailed it, one of the mortarmen, mistaking him for a Jap, came out of his foxhole and by accident hit the rifleman with his carbine, nearly knocking the marine out. However, accident or not, when one of the mortarmen heard the poor marine moaning out in the night, he slipped out of his foxhole and promptly shot the downed marine in the head with his .45, thinking he was a Nip.

At daybreak—about the same time I inspected Ryzner's Jap for souvenirs—PFC Gene Sledge, a quiet guy from the mortar section, made a grisly discovery. Not only did they have a dead Jap, but they also had a dead marine—PFC William Middlebrook, the rifleman who took off during the fight. It was Middlebrook who was shot by the eager mortarman with the sidearm.

Scuttlebutt travels fast, and we all heard about the killing, just as Captain Haldane was holding court over what to do about it.

It ended up being a big nothing, once they swept it under the rug—but we riflemen realized this was the second time an event like this had occurred among the mortarmen.

The mortarmen were good marines, by and large—the same as any other marines, from any other platoon. Nevertheless, while it's easy to overlook an isolated event, it becomes a real challenge not to cast an evil eye on what appeared to be a pattern. So when the press came up, Ryzner's kill was the perfect way to deflect any unwanted questions about what happened to PFC William S. Middlebrook Jr., from Houston, Texas. All they had to do was give the press a hero in exchange for a killing.

As for Henry Ryzner, true to the reporters' word, Ryzner's photo on Peleliu and his story appeared in the *Detroit Free Press,* about a week after it happened. The same day, in fact, that his mother got the news that her son had been killed on Ngesebus.

On the other side of the world (it might as well be a different planet), Bing Crosby croons over every Philco in America the song "Swinging on a Star," from the soon-to-be Best Picture *Going My Way.* Yet the best picture that any of us marines have is of our own pilots skip-bombing the hell out of the Japanese across the causeway on Ngesebus. Low flying, the F4U Corsairs skim so close to the ground, they appear as if they're going to bounce right into their exploding munitions. At any time we expect the planes to collide in midair, but they don't. These marine pilots are real pros, swishing and gliding through the air, sending up showers of flames and sparks in all directions. For many of us, it's a spectacle that will forever ruin even the best fireworks shows back in the States, as the world shatters and explodes across the water. In Queens, however, they never feel a thing. The price of milk is still fifty-six cents a gallon. A bottle of Coke is five cents. Admission to the Bronx Zoo will cost you nothing.

Coming down to the beach that morning it seemed we were all in good humor—or at least in a better mood than when we landed on Peleliu. It wasn't a long march—just a stroll of about sixty yards from our lines to the sand, where thirty army amtracs idled. The amtracs were lined up in a row, facing toward Ngesebus, waiting for us, as if to ask, *Going my way?*

It was a Thursday morning the day we walked aboard the tractors, heading for Ngesebus. Thursday morning, so different than our experience a week ago. We were a little wiser—maybe even a little dumber. What made us think Ngesebus would be an easy operation? Perhaps because Peleliu was such a shit-farm, nothing could possibly be worse. Maybe our temperament was lighter because the thought of a tiny island full of Japs gave us better odds than what the bookies on Peleliu were handing out.

Once inside the tractor, a couple of the big shots immediately moved up to the front of the vehicle. PFC Phil Magginello manned one .50 caliber machine gun on the left side of the amtrac, and McEnery stood at its twin on the right, both bracing themselves for the tractor to take off.

With a shift of gears, all the amtracs lurched at exactly the same time, right on cue, synchronized swimmers: a picture-perfect operation. There was plenty of firepower and support, to boot. Sitting atop the water we had a battleship, two cruisers, and a destroyer, leaning their guns landward and plastering the island with fusillade upon fusillade of scary heat—really breaking it up and claiming the island for the United States of America.

I sought out Levy and gave him a thumbs-up. He gave it right back and followed with a nod. *Yeah*—I looked over the side of the amtrac toward the smoldering island—*this will be a piece of cake.*

At least it appeared easy. Unlike in the first landing, we weren't catching any return fire. In the fifteen minutes it took to cross the six-hundred-yard causeway, it was the USMC who spent all the ammunition. No guff from the Japs.

On our way across, I spied a little island about fifteen feet off Ngesebus. Just a small thing—it was only another fifteen feet in diameter. I yelled up at Jimmy, above the din, "Hey, Jim, why don't ya hit that place with a few bursts! Looks dangerous!" I thought that little patch would be an easy place for some Nips to hide, so Jim let go with a few sprays from his machine gun just to be certain. For the most part, marines were pointing out obvious spots for Jim and Phil to hit as the beach loomed closer: a pillbox here, what appeared to be a hut there. It went without saying, the closer we got, there were masses of noise; our heads were in kettles and someone was beating the outside of them with ratchets. Yet there's one type of loud you get from the enemy guns, and another brand of bedlam you get from your own. Your own, you can stand it a little more, because you know it's the Nips who are sucking down flames. The Jap guns, on the other hand, even if they scream in a whisper, they lobotomize and turn the bowels to jelly.

Close.

The planes began pulling out, trailing vapor behind their tails like mirages on the open road.

Closer.

The amtracs are vibratory: a unified solid sound, a constant, as every one of the amtracs hummed the same. I peeked over the side of our amtrac and watched the other tractors glide on a glassy surface, a mirror image of what we must've looked like to the other marines. In fact, I couldn't tell us apart. We were one, like the thrumming of the amtrac engines.

Closer now.

There was nothing ominous about the shore. Only a beach, as thin as a thumb's nail, touching the meaty mangrove beyond it.

(*"There's not a Jap alive on the island, let's go!"*)

Suddenly our amtrac scraped and then shuddered against the turf. I wasn't expecting it so soon. The jolt pushed us back and then forward again as we tried to keep our balance. *Slap!* The ramp dropped at the water's edge. A fan of surf splashed up and broke my vision.

Here we go again!

Just like before, we pile out like gangbusters. I veer off to the right.

Somewhere, deep in the mind, behind the bangs and shouts, a dead marine screams, *"Just around the corner, hit on the beach, hit on the beach, Larry Mahan, hit on the beach, hit on the . . ."*

I don't have the time to dream about shit! Running up the beach I spy a pillbox, and I see someone scamper out the back. Alarms ring in my head. Shadows move within the rear of the box. Immediately I pop off eight rounds into the entranceway, as if to say, *If you're in there—stay the fuck in there!* I think they got the message, and I wouldn't be surprised if I nailed one of them, but this isn't the time to find out. I've got the muzzle of my BAR scanning everything before me. An extension of myself, this rifle is sacred to the point where my life dances on the business end of it. I'm scared as hell, but when I pull that trigger I'm invincible.

I keep running. The world is sped up like one of those old silent films—fragmented and jumpy—yet it's far from silent, as grenades explode and small-arms fire fills the air. I'm through the mangrove and across the airfield so quickly that once I'm on the other side, in a dumb-ass move I grab the barrel of my BAR with my right hand and burn the crap out of my palm. It's as if the chaos has control of me—and the strings that make me dance are being snipped, one by one.

My hand smarts—yet this pause gives me the first opportunity to scan the island, as marines pile in around me. We catch our breath and lean on a vacant bunker (the "bunker" really amounts to just a simple rise in the earth, little more than an anthill).

Simply stated, Ngesebus is the bastard child of Peleliu. The beach itself is perhaps a couple of yards in width, littered with rocks and bits of wood that have been washed up with the tide. Beyond that is some scrubwood, and just a jump farther is the airstrip—shot up and full of holes, filthy with debris. I'm not an expert in airfields; nevertheless, the airstrip on Ngesebus looks like it could scarcely accommodate a Piper Cub, let alone a Nip Zero.

What's more, just like Peleliu, Ngesebus has its own ridgeline beyond the airfield, only a lot smaller, akin to Johnny Roventini, the dwarf I used to work with back in my Philip Morris days.

"Call for Philip Moore-ea-es!"

Yet if there was a time for a cigarette, it wouldn't be right now. We're winded, and the whole place smells like live Japs.

"Hey, gimme a hand, willya, Mace?"

"Huh? Oh . . . oh yeah, sure." I help Roy Kelly get a foothold on the lip of the ridge, and then I sling my BAR over my shoulder and begin my own ascent. It's just a few hand- and toeholds up to a relatively flat surface. Then someone hollers, "There's one! Get that sonuvabitch!"

"Where?"

I see a lone Jap, about fifteen yards away, duck at the sound of rifle fire and then suddenly disappear. Just like that.

Bang! We're off! Scrabbling and running as fast as we can, giving chase, then quickly skidding to a halt at a hole in the coral—barely large enough for a human to slip through.

"This is where the Nip must've jumped! Don't let the fucker get away!" Ray Grawet growls.

Madcap follies ensue.

We get on our knees, gathering around the hole, about five of us—excited children, starting up a high-stakes game of craps.

Hurriedly I dig around my gear, finding my marine-issue pamphlet of Japanese phrases, while the other guys busily decide what to do next.

"*De te*," I begin, calling down the hole. *Christ, how do you say this?* "*De te ki te . . . ku da sai!*" Come out! "Ah, shit! Is that it? *Koufuckyou . . .* crap! *Koufuku sit e ku da sai!*" Surrender!

"Sterl, what the hell are you doin'?" Levy asks.

"*Watashi*—I mean . . . Oh, for chrissakes, I'm tellin' this goddamn Nip to come out an' surrender!"

I concentrate again. "*Wata*-shit-*shi* . . . Goddammit! . . . *Wa anata ni kigai wo kuwaeru tsumori wa arimasen*! There! That's it! 'We. Won't. Harm you!'"

"Hey, get a load of Mace, willya?"

Boom! I duck. Just as soon as I get the words out of my mouth a marine tosses a grenade down the burrow. One would expect to get sprayed by the grenade blast, but evidently the hole is so deep that none of us get hurt. Everybody laughs.

"Oh, Christ, that's rich! Throw another one!" Leyden smiles.

I laugh, too. It's hilarious as once more I break into my Nip lingo and start rattling it off.

Several more explosions go off as marines toss more grenades down the chute.

Bill hands me a grenade, too, and I flip it down the hole with one hand, my Japanese comic book of phrases in the other.

"It's okay!" Leyden calls down the hole. "Mace says we won't hurt you!"

Nobody had the thought that we were making so much noise, a whole company of Japs could've snuck up and blown all of us to high heaven, for not paying attention in class.

Eventually, though, everyone pipes down, wiping watering eyes, flushed in the face, as a few trailing giggles put the final touches on a chilling realization. Yes, we could've been killed—and for what? Suddenly everyone appears older . . . and embarrassed with age.

Presently a marine gets up, not looking at any of us, and says, "Well, either he's long gone or a goddamn goner, that's for sure."

That's all it takes. We pick ourselves up and move. The time for childish games was over before we grew up.

And so it goes. We creep up the ridge, slow ivy, olive serpents, twisting through the crags and gaps between the stones. The sizzling heat and sweat make the stock of my BAR slippery to the touch. Most of us have already turned down the back flaps of our helmet covers, so that the cloth hangs down over our necks, in an attempt to fend off the sun.

My part of the 3rd Platoon sets up on the left side of the ridge, which runs the length of the island—kneeling, lying prone, finding a perch to hold on to. Tiny pebbles of coral roll down the cliff, agitated by worn boondockers seeking purchase.

The other half of the platoon takes the right side of the ridge, and in the center of the ridge is where Corporal Van Trump and Lieutenant Bauerschmidt set up the communications area.

The "communications area" in this case consists of nothing more than "codes" that Bauerschmidt and Van Trump bandy between themselves from one side of the ridge to the other. They don't have radios, so the two of them are a little too loud for my taste. Every Nip on the island has certainly written down their name, rank, and serial number—and probably what they ate for breakfast that morning, too.

"Hey, Van," Bauerschmidt calls out to Van Trump. "Hey, Zero," is Van Trump's reply. As fast as Van Trump moves up on our side of the ridge is how quickly we move as well. It's a slow process—we're all jumpy and on edge, scanning for Japanese. We are the very front of the assault.

However, just as we're about to move up some more, Frank Minkewitz (who's standing on the beach guarding our rear) calls to us, "Hey! There's a Nip sitting on a rock over here!"

On a what?

"Then shoot the sonuvabitch, Frank!"

We're amazed that Frank doesn't do anything. He doesn't even raise his rifle to his shoulder. The Jap merely walks off, as easy as he pleases, leaving Frank on the beach by himself.

That was the start of Ngesebus: the first drops of rain that come before the gullywasher. The clues began coming in lightly, and it didn't take a regular Sherlock to decipher that there was going to be a storm. The Nips were right there—almost on top of us—only they were invisible, sharpening our nerves on a stiff leather strap.

Schwantz held up one arm and halted the column, gazing back at us nervously. I didn't know if he'd spotted something or if he was merely looking for Van Trump.

I was about to check on Levy when . . .

Ping!

What the, Christ!?

Something hit the right side of my helmet and careened off it, only moving my head half an inch in the process.

Corporal Alex "Hurricane" Hensen gawked at me with startled eyes. "Oh boy . . . I thought you were gonna go down!" he said.

"Did you hear that?" I asked, feeling around the top of my helmet.

"Yeah." Hensen still looked like he couldn't believe his lying eyes.

"Jesus, what *was* that?"

I didn't know what to think, or how close I came to being killed, but I sure as hell knew that we were close to the Japs—and they were close to *us*. Very close.

We got moving again, scrambling up the cliff in the direction of a loud banging noise coming from the little piece of flatland to our right, near the beach. Three Sherman tanks with a contingent of infantry were chugging up the turf, the tanks just blazing away, as groups of Nips ran up to the tanks, trying to climb aboard and drop grenades down the tanks' hatches. Naturally the riflemen were not going to stand for it. The turkey shoot began, with Japs getting shot and falling beneath the tanks' treads, leaving behind puddles of raw meat mixed with gritty dust. The ground was a sponge for gristle and blood.

Up . . . and move.

We were ten feet from the edge of the cliff, and Levy was on point. So close to the Nips. We had no idea how close. Behind Levy was Donald Schwantz, then Charlie Allmann, followed by Nippo Baxter. I was another ten feet behind Baxter, as a covering force to our rear.

I was in charge of covering the rear with my automatic weapon because the machine gunners were having a rough time climbing, with their tripods and extra ammo, their heavy weapons and miscellaneous gear. They were really humping it. The pangs on their faces were sharp and angular under the day's sun. If we were to get into a scrap with the Nips right then, there would be no place for the MGs to set up, with the ground tilting and the mangrove growing thicker up the slope.

"C'mon." I reached my arm out and gave Zombie a hand up.

Zombie. His name said it all. He was assuredly the tallest guy in the company, built thick across the chest, with muscles that could probably rip your head clean off, if he got you in a chokehold. The real kicker about Zombie was, he wouldn't win any beauty contests (not that many of us would), and every other word out of his mouth was unintelligible—a real zombie, nothing upstairs.

After I helped him up, something caught my eye, just lying off to the side. A Jap rifle! Not the ordinary variety of Nipponese craftsmanship I had seen before, either. No, this rifle had a yellowish tint, with a fine tiger-striped grain to the wood. It was a real showpiece. A high-sheen devil that made me think it would hit a bull's-eye every time.

I had to be fast. Quickly I stuck the rifle deep in some of the mangrove for safekeeping; the plan was to come back for the rifle after the island had been cleaned out—hoping the machine gunners were too absorbed in their labors to notice me messing around in the brush.

Just as I got back into position, two close shots rang out and I instinctually ducked, scanning where the shot came from.

Who's hit?

Levy rushed out of the thicket ahead, straight toward us. He looked flustered, brandishing his canteen. The dented metal of the canteen told the whole story. Sy had gone too far ahead of the squad, and as he went into the mangrove, a rifleman mistook him for the enemy and popped off two rounds in his direction.

Either the bullets hit the canteen or Levy smacked the ground so hard that his weight mashed the metal. Whatever the case, it was almost unreal that something like that could happen to Levy again. Levy was a walking rabbit's foot. Everybody knew it. We simply gawked at Sy for a moment, taking it all in. *How can anybody be so lucky?* There stood Sy, red-faced, embarrassed, his chest puffing up and down: a bellows stoking a fire. Nobody knew who fired the shots, or if they did, no one was telling.

Besides, who would've owned up to it? The dumb rifleman who nearly nailed Sy was probably just as thankful that he hadn't killed a kid like himself.

We were *close.* So close that Nippo moved up and took over point from Levy. All the time I really hoped I didn't have to look Allmann in the eyes, because *"Levy draws fire, okay?"*

Because . . . *Goddamn, we're close!*

Because . . .

The strangest thing unfolds before us.

In a world of brown, green, and gray, where even the blue sky has lost its luster, something attracts our attention like nothing else. There's a cave. In front of the cave hang the most vivid strips of red and yellow fabric that I've ever seen. The cloth is about as wide as a good scarf, hanging down from the upper edge of the cave's mouth and waving ever so slightly—ever so faintly, as soft air comes from within the subterranean cavity, just enough to curl the edge of the strips outward and up, like the tips of a pixie's shoes.

We give the cavern a wide berth, keeping our eyes peeled for even the slightest hint of something foul coming from the yawning entrance.

This has to be a trap.

I begin backing up, slowly, following Nippo through some foliage, watching the cave's mouth as I go. The machine gunners keep close to me, the ammo carriers trying to situate themselves so that if they have to grab their carbines, they can drop their load and start firing.

This red . . . so close . . . and this yellow, an abomination.

I part the scrub and find myself at the base of a small ridge. Nippo has already climbed up, firing his M-1. *Bang!* One! *Bang!* Two! I can hear some of the guys beyond the greenery, chattering.

"What's all this crap hangin' here for? This ain't right."

"Yeah, yeah, this is just *wrong.*"

Nippo holds up two fingers to indicate he has just picked off two Japs.

I eyeball the heights and figure that I should climb up, too.

By all appearances this is a Jap rattrap, just as I thought it would be, and if I don't get up there our guys might be ambushed.

Okay, this is what I'm here for. Go on, Brother. Start climbing.

It's a small climb. I get up, parallel with Baxter, and I surmise that on the other side of the small ridge is a drop below us—but I certainly don't have to stick my head over to figure that out.

"They're down *there.*" Nippo points. "There's somethin' . . . it looks like, I can't make it out too well . . . it looks like the entrance to a cave."

Angling my head in that direction, sure enough, from my vantage

point I can see the curvature of a cave entrance. Then I quick-look
and spy another ridge moving above and over me—so that if I climb
up there I might be able to come down over the top of the Japs, if
they're prowling around down there.

Leaving Nippo, I take one more fleeting glance below, where all
the machine gunners are crouched down, about six of them, as I
ease myself closer to the lip of the ridgeline.

The sweat is really cascading off of me. I can feel every loose
pebble and sharp crag, dry to the touch, running along the pads of
my fingers and becoming one with my grip. Against my chest and
stomach, it's the same thing, as the earth scrapes my ribs, even
protected as they are beneath my dungaree jacket. There's a difference in me now: Something the civilian version of myself would
never understand. Fear is a letter home that I forgot to send. Nobody reads it. Nobody wants to know. I don't feel anything. An
uncomplicated calmness descends on me, as the marine takes
over . . . and the kid from Queens with the dead sister melts away,
like the last rivulets of wax from a waning candle.

The candle dissolves into the crackle of a fuzzy and chopped
voice, coming in low and unexpected on the ridgeline. (Close to
the flame) I pause, as I'm about to come over the top of the rim,
trying to ascertain the direction of the voice, barely making out
the helmet of a marine, perched among the mangrove on a little
outcropping.

At first I don't recognize him. The marine is Charlie "Dusty"
Rhodes, an observer for the 81 mm mortars. *What the hell is he doing up here?* Rhodes, a kid who has a keen interest in baseball like
me, speaks into a field telephone, calling in coordinates, completely
oblivious that the enemy is right below him.

"Hey, Dusty," I whisper. "Nips! There's Nips, right down
there!" I point down, indicating to Rhodes their location.

Dusty merely looks at me as if I've got some nerve.

"Well, fuck you too, Charlie," I mumble under my breath. The thing is, Charlie Rhodes doesn't have a clue that he can get bumped off, right now, by the Japs below. I know, however—and that's part of what ticks me off.

What I'm about to do . . .

I get in position to look over the ridge, weapon at the ready . . . and what I'm about to do, I have no doubt that I'm going to lean over the edge and destroy whoever's down there.

It's an easy thing to do. Much easier than you'd think. To kill a man.

With my right hand white-knuckling the forestock of my BAR and my left hand gripping the trigger housing, I pull myself calmly over the ridge, without a thought of being killed.

What happens next occurs so quickly that I see every moment like the rising of the setting sun.

A Japanese soldier is only eight feet below me.

His moon-shaped face lifts and looks at me. (*I see the shape of his face so clearly.*) My reflection mirrors off the glossy surface of his pupils. His eyes never change. Only the moon. He knows, but he doesn't, what's about to happen to him. He sees. Only the big muzzle of my weapon. He swings his rifle around. (*There are two other Japs, lying on the ground, bringing their rifles around, too.*)

I aim at the moon. Shooting for the moon.

It's so easy. In a downward arc, I empty my weapon into his face, and into the bodies of the other two Nips on the ground, my rifle bucking in my hands.

Down! Behind the ridge, I turn around rapidly and wave three fingers triumphantly at the machine gunners.

Maybe it's so easy because I didn't actually witness how my rounds went through the Nips, but I can only imagine the first one.

I know, at such a close range, his head exploded, ripping instantly through bone, cartilage, brain, and muscle.

"Hey, you guys, pitch me up some grenades!" I yell to the machine gunners.

A few of them relay some grenades up to me, and I pull the pins on two of them, dropping one and then the other, pitching them over the side for good measure, muffled thumps followed by acrid air.

Jim McEnery comes up, a bazooka man in his wake so that they can shoot some heavier stuff over the side of my ridge. I think to myself, as I hop down, *What the hell is this? What're they gonna do, kill 'em twice?*

They have a better idea when they finally call up a flamethrower team to torch any Japs who still might be in the cave. Here's the gag: The Marines with the flamethrower can't get their gear to work, so they have to go back and send another crew up in order to spark the entrance. Eventually they light it up.

At the mouth of the cave the reds and yellows of the streamers are engulfed in a brighter shade of orange, mixed with the sooty by-product of liquid fire.

Jimmy looks on with satisfaction. It is good.

"Okay, guys, I guess that about covers it," Jim says. "We won't worry about those Nips anymore. Let's move up."

As we move along, we just about get to where Van Trump and the rest of the squad are situated when a shout comes from the rear, "Fire in the hole!" We duck automatically. The ground warbles and the air folds as a great boom collapses the cave behind us in the final act of sealing it up. Rubble falls in a great sheet, flinging out pebbles and a cloud of dust. Nobody goes in . . . and nobody comes out. In essence, the demolition marines have taken some C-4 explosives and laced them around the cave, effectively entombing any Nips that might be alive in there.

And that's it. Unfeeling and uncaring—why should anybody care? Any compunction to reflect on what I just did to three human beings is swallowed up by the chaos that's intrinsic to war as a whole. Callousness and indifference are not symptoms of the state of the soul, but instead, they are symbols that one's gratitude is intact—that my life is still in my own hands, and not bleeding out in the palms of yellow-tinted villains.

Stigmata for the lambs of Pearl Harbor and Peleliu.

Night came and the rain came in blankets of wet, some of us climbing the side of a ridge, seeking a different level, as the water seeks its own.

"Christ! What are we supposed to do, climb a tree?"

No dice. The weather was edging into misery, and the sky was falling down. We couldn't dig. Setting up some semblance of a line, the best we could do was slip and fall on tangles of vines and porous rock. The earth became more atrocious the thicker the rain fell.

Poncho clad, Allmann and I—with Jimmy following behind—finally made our way up the side of the ridge, wiggling up and nestling against the rock, and whatever mangrove happened to peek from its coral prison. There was very little light, and the closest sound was the constant drumming hum of the rain. I had my foot stamped down hard against a medium-sized trunk on the ridge—the only thing that kept me from tumbling, head over ass, to the coral below.

Through the hazy rain I barely made out a navy destroyer, moving at a snail's pace out on the water. *Jesus Christ, what a place!* Weapons under our ponchos, helmets pouring rain into our faces; I shook my head to clear my eyes of water, but that was a futile act as well. So I buried my face into the stinking rock, with little choice but to wait out the night under the downpour. *Where the hell was all this water when we landed on Peleliu?*

Suddenly four shots rang out.

"What the fuck? Who's that!?"

The shots were so close that I almost fell from the precious piece of mangrove holding me up.

It was only Jimmy, test-firing the tommy gun he had picked up from Sergeant Thomas Rigney when Rigney was killed on the beach that morning. *Only Jimmy, yeah, right!* I thought to myself. *Sonuvabitch, Jim, if the Nips find out where we are, we have nowhere to run in this shit—and here you are testing your goddamn piece in the middle of the friggin' night, no less!*

Names of dead marines began to come to mind, drips from a leaky roof, and into the place where home used to be. The leaks needed fixing, so I shook them off, just as a wet animal flaps his shaggy coat to shed the rain and the wild.

Today we lost Private Joe Mercer and Gunnery Sergeant Thomas Rigney. Lost is Anthony Putorti. Lost, Lyle Van Norman. Charles E. Williams, lost.

Not lost the way a marine misplaces his mess kit, or lost as if I can't find my flashlight in the dark. These things I would find again . . . even in the dark. Lost as in killed, destroyed, where you will never see them again, *never* . . . not even in the light.

When I look up, the sky is a dead slate of gray.

I try to find the moon, but it is lost to me.

Morning arrived, and as the rain left us, in came Lieutenant Bauerschmidt and suggested we'd better not get acquainted with the Japanese dead, looking for souvenirs or shaking their hands.

It seems that two guys from L Company killed a Nip, and as they were taking the gold from the corpse's mouth, some live Japs snuck up on the marines and slaughtered them both.

Hearing this wasn't the best way to start our morning, yet since none of us had any *real* sleep last night anyway, it didn't really matter. Scuttlebutt aplenty, the grapevine was like that all the time: It was always everything you didn't want to know, and nothing you did.

"Holland . . . Minkewitz . . . Mace." Van Trump called the closest BAR men over. "Come over here and test-fire your weapons, willya?"

"Yeah, sure, Van. What's goin' on?"

"Ah, I don't know . . . I just got a feelin' an' I wanna play it safe. So let's hear 'em."

Minkewitz pulled the trigger of his BAR and nothing happened. We looked around curiously at one another. Gene Holland moved forward and it was the same. Bupkes. I expected my weapon to start sparking fire, but I got zilch out of mine, too.

"Say, what gives?" Gene asked.

"You guys strip your weapons." Van raised his eyebrows, as if he were expecting that to happen. "It rained last night, so I dunno . . . just clean 'em before we move out."

It was the greatest idea I had heard from Van Trump the whole time I'd known him. Van Trump, the guy who, whenever he got the chance to rest, would sit down and immediately start polishing the revolver he swiped from the dead Hellcat pilot. Thanks to Van, if we ran into Japs we'd be ready, instead of pissing ourselves because our BARs wouldn't fire.

Under the circumstances, there was not a quicker trio of marines on the island than the three of us, sitting down with our toothbrushes and scrubbing over the vital parts of our weapons, the trigger assemblies, the chambers, the magazines, until everyone was satisfied that his weapon was clean—ready for business.

They all fired again. So we moved out.

That's the way it was done. A marine had to be quick and efficient, cleaning his weapon in the field. On very few occasions did we have the time to completely fieldstrip the entire weapon and give it a thorough bath. The simple toothbrush was probably the marine's closest friend, besides his weapon itself.

No sooner were we on the move, though, than they had us stop and wait for more orders. I gave Sy a thumbs-up, and he gave the same back. That was starting to be a comforting ritual between him and me.

Yet comfort is a bed of nails when the mortars start raining in.

You couldn't mistake the sound of mortars for anything else—screaming mortar rounds are distinct—as we hit the dirt, covering our helmets with our hands. I landed right next to Don Schwantz—so close, in fact, that we were Siamese twins. Dirt huggers. Grubworms.

The first mortar round exploded in the tree right above us. The explosions were black flowers, death lilies, their petals blooming out dark tendrils of swirling shrapnel, falling from the leaves and down atop us. The second mortar round was from the same garden, and it planted itself in an almost identical spot. That time, however, its brimstone seeds hit Donald in the back, six times. I watched blossoms sprout up in his dungaree jacket where the shrapnel ripped through and lodged in his flesh. No blood. Only the torn jacket. Schwantz didn't make a sound. Not because he was hit so bad, but due to the fact that he was just as shocked as the rest of us.

"Corpsman!" I yelled. Donald was writhing on the ground, holding his back . . . and there I was, literally touching Schwantz, and I didn't so much as scuff a knuckle. Lucky.

Doc Caswell and Chulis worked on Don as I got to my feet, peering up into the trees, looking around. *Everybody* looked around. Something was strange about those mortar rounds.

"Say, did anyone see where those mortars came from?"

"I don't know." I paused. "But *those* things? There's probably about forty yards left of this goddamn island, *tops*. So how're the Nips gonna get that kinda elevation to spot us in, huh?"

Van Trump came storming up. "Get your gear together. This is bullshit! Those were our own goddamn 81s that hit Don, sure as shit they were!"

Van was probably right again.

"Okay, fellas, let's get outta here," Jimmy said, getting his word in.

As we shoved off again, I'm sure, to a man, everybody thought about what just happened to Schwantz. *Somebody should get on the horn and see about those 81 mortars . . . find out what's goin' on.*

Van Trump pulled me aside. "Mace, you and Allmann—you take Allmann and move up about twenty yards, alright? The Japs might think we're tryin' to surround them and come on out."

For moment I thought I heard Van Trump say something about me and Charlie moving up, alone, twenty yards ahead of the rest of the squad. That couldn't be right, *could* it?

"You want us to move *where*, Van?"

"Just . . . oh, about twenty yards, I'd say. If the Nips think we're surroundin' 'em, it'll be hands up or lights out for the bastards."

I didn't say anything for a few seconds. It almost sounded like a joke without the punch line, yet I was waiting, like a dummy, for one anyway. Nevertheless, I didn't even attempt an argument.

"Sorry, Van," I said, "but there's not much room to surround *anyone*."

I merely trotted off, looking for Charlie so we could start the half-baked quest for Corporal Richard Van Trump and be done with it.

For Charlie and me, isolated somewhere on blistering Ngesebus, the sudden sound of twigs snapping all around us both inflames and quiets us. I have never been so close to death as I am in this moment.

The Japanese are very near to Charlie and me. Their smell is unmistakably rife with curdled sweat and ricey brine. Even alive the Nips have a clear odor to them.

We cannot see them. They cannot see us. We are two marines

recessed in a crevice of rock, shaped like a small bowl, surrounded by thick foliage. Still, we know they are here. We *hear* them, shuffling among the mangrove. Black marbles for eyes—searching, darting back and forth. They are as scared as we are, I'm sure, even though they have the upper hand.

Nips push aside branches and brambles, just as Charlie and I had done less than an hour ago, when we traveled up on Van Trump's orders and found this little place to wait.

Alone. Encapsulated in the deep vinery. Suffocating.

If the Nips find out that two marines are within arm's length of them, I doubt they will even bother taking us prisoner. They will butcher us just like we would butcher them.

I'm looking into Charlie's eyes, and I mouth the words, "Do. Not. Move . . . Keep. Quiet." Even the effort it takes to move my mouth in silence causes an automatic cringe response inside me that says I've done too much, said too much, I've given us away.

Where the Christ is everybody? Van Trump's gonna get us fucking killed out here!

We don't dare fire at the Nips (*don't even think about it*) because we don't know their strength. There could be two of them, maybe four . . . even one hundred and we wouldn't know it.

So we are forced to wait . . . waiting out the itch in the center of our brains, with no means to scratch it. Waiting . . . as the movement and footfalls ebb into nothingness, leaving only the sounds of bugs crawling on low leaves—and the occasional click in my throat. Even without the seemingly immediate presence of the Japs (*are they really gone, or just faking?*), there's something even more empty and dead about the absence of marines in the area. We are anxious for the sounds of friendly boondockers replacing the hobnail pad of enemy boots. Nobody calls for Charlie or me. No Corsairs zoom overhead. There's nothing tangible that lets us know that reality even exists in the here and now. There are only the thin minutes of decision and indecision, playing themselves out beyond the scope of infinity.

Ten minutes pass, and I can count each breath, each exhale. The air comes out as hot as the tropical sun.

Twenty minutes, and Charlie looks deeply pale, a disembodied spirit, whose only color is the plum-tinted splotches under his eyes. Pitiful being.

Thirty minutes, and I'm eyeballing the way Charlie and I came up; the eyes play silly games, seeing a kaleidoscopic image as the leaves overlap one another, seemingly a millionfold.

Forty minutes pass. I know then that we've been forgotten. It's almost impossible to believe, yet it's true—as if the thought of being disremembered is somehow foolish against the foolishness of war.

This can't *be right. There's no way this is friggin' right!*

"Charlie," I whisper breathlessly. "Charlie, we gotta get the hell outta here. This is *not* right." I pause. "C'mon . . . but *slowly*."

Slipping through the leaves, which sigh against our dungarees, we glide smoothly out. Every step we take seems choreographed, as if we know what we are doing. We don't know what we're doing, though, any more than we know what the face of dumb luck looks like. As it is, dumb luck is staring us right in the eyes. No Nips. This is as clear as the coast will ever get.

Eyes open, Mace; don't be stupid, now, I tell myself, over and over.

Down a little slope, Charlie and I creep along, fingers on our triggers with just enough pressure to keep them from going off, yet squeezing them firmly to the point that if needed, not a split second will go by and we'll rattle off with tympani and trumpets.

My heart triple-pumps, seeing the telltale signs of Jap footprints in places where the earth has yielded from last night's double rain. It doesn't take a keen eye or a Nippo Baxter to make out the unmistakable marks of the Japanese pigeon-toed gait upon the soft earth.

When I see the last Nip footfall, I tell Charlie to come on, and we make a quick dash into a small clearing, not even ten yards from where we started.

We skid to a halt. There's something before us both gruesome and unexpected.

Flat on the ground, there's a marine poncho, laid out and disheveled, smeared slick red with blood. Fresh red. *Fresh dead?* Fresh blood. Mixed into this madness are at least a dozen unspent .45 caliber rounds, bright in the day's clear brilliance, some of them submerged in itty pools of blood and whorled with fingerprints, outlined in scarlet.

"What in the . . . *world!*?" Charlie gawks.

Corpus delicti. Where the hell's the body?

"C'mon, Charlie." My mouth barely works. "C'mon, *Charlie,* let's beat it!"

We take off down a little weedy path, Olympic sprinters. Second gear. *Christ!* Third gear, all the way, assholes and elbows, all the way!

Even when we hit the jungle we don't break speed. We're scratched and cut by whipping vines, and even that feels like a million bucks simply because it's so good to be alive. Even if the Nips were to take shots at us now, I don't think they could hit within ten feet of us.

No gas mask to tangle me, no beautiful Jap rifle (*that sonuvabitch can rot on this stinking island, for all I care*); we're not even out of breath. The jungle scenery flies by and breaks open in a blur of green speed. Faster, faster . . .

Charlie and I burst out of the mangrove in record time and into clear daylight and sandy beach. There's the ocean—azure surf, and as blue as the sky is vast.

Spread before us on the beach, maybe one hundred yards away, scores of marines, chatting and grab-assing, line up as they prepare to enter amtracs, heading back to Peleliu—all of them oblivious to our presence.

"Hey, *hey!*" Charlie shouts. "Don't leave us!" We wave our arms so that we can be seen, and at the same time we try not to be mistaken for the enemy and be shot by several hundred anxious marines.

By the time we're going down the line, scouting out our platoon, marines are ogling us as if we are two nutcases. I don't care. I'm gunning for dumb-ass Van Trump and anybody else who didn't think it was worth their time to come get Charlie and me.

Where is that ignorant sonuvabitch?

When I finally spy Van Trump, though, my anger washes back down with the rest of the bile I was force-fed today. Van is propped up on a stretcher, being carried into a waiting amtrac. His eyes are bulging, his whole head swathed in bandages, blood fighting through the cloth, on its way out of Van's body.

Bloody poncho . . .

The realization suddenly hits me: As far as Van Trump goes, he was in no shape to tell *anybody* that he sent two marines up ahead— and had no way of ordering somebody to pull us *back.*

I see Jimmy on the beach and ask him what happened to Van Trump, besides the obvious.

Jimmy scratches his head and looks over toward Van Trump, with an air of annoyance and disbelief.

"It was those damn code words of the lieutenant's and Van's," McEnery begins. "Shit, that's stupid. All day long this 'Hey, Zero,' 'Hey, Van' crap—and then some Nip must have gotten wise to it, I guess. Called out, 'Hey, Van, where are you?' and I bet Van calls back, 'Over here!' Picks up his head and takes one in the jaw. Just like that."

"Christ, Jim! That's too ba—" I pause for a moment . . . *wait a second!* My anger begins to percolate again. I can feel it in my throat, acidic.

"Wait a sec, Jim! So Van gets hit, right? You guys just pull out and leave me and Allmann out there, by ourselves. Is that it? That's it, isn't it?"

For a moment McEnery looks like he has just gotten bawled out by a PFC (which he has); then his expression goes dumb. "We didn't know you were *out* there."

"Oh, for fuck's sake, Jimmy, you don't count goddamn heads or somethin'?"

Before McEnery can open his mouth I simply walk off and stand in my own line to board an amtrac. I can't get off this island quickly enough. Anger, yes—but more relieved that I'm not out in the mangrove getting my pockets rifled through by Tojo and Co.

This island is a nightmare. However, if I'd known what awaited me on my return to Peleliu, I would have wished I'd never woken up.

Man, that was rough duty.

Our amtrac glides back across the water toward the mother island.

Just forget about it.

It's difficult to forget. Below the permanent hum of the amtrac's motor, marines talk in hushed voices, trading scuttlebutt about who bought it out of our company, as if their names have no meaning anymore among the living—merely daily topics to reach for, like the change in the weather or who won last night's ball game. Idle minds and tongues of fire. Flippancy makes the fear fly home.

Corporal Arthur W. Cook.

Lost.

Private Henry J. Ryzner.

Lost.

Corporal Walter B. Stay.

Lost.

Lost. Lost. Lost. Lost . . .

They say Billy Leyden was wounded in the head by a Jap

grenade. I'm concerned, but they tell me he'll be okay. Evacuated, but good.

Lucky bastard, Bill. No more of this crap for you.

The surf splashes up the sides of the amtrac and sprays a thin mist of Pacific blue against my face.

At least I feel something—*anything*—other than myself.

There's one other thing about Ngesebus I should tell. It's not about the battle. It's not about the island. It's not even about the war. It's about the people *inside* the uniforms.

As they loaded us into amtracs, the victors of Ngesebus—filthy and disheveled, dungarees as stiff as canvas, weapons carried at cocky angles—they told us we would return to the bivouac area on Peleliu, and from there, we were bound for Pavuvu. We had done our duty and we had done it well.

Just a ways on the shore, a camera crew filmed us file past, capturing the moment for posterity. Marines gave various looks into the camera. Some marines smiled wanly, bashfully, as if it were expected of them to say cheese. Other marines pointed at the lens and cracked jokes. There were even some marines, unfazed by the limelight, who were just too hollow, or too tough, or too bitter, to care what the United States thought of them at the moment.

The camera merely rolled, emitting a swirling purr, in contrast to the stomp of hard boots on coral ground. The camera's mechanical eye seemed so out of place in hell. Why would anybody want to see the sour underbelly of the world, when there were far more lovely things on God's earth worth capturing?

As for me and Levy, when we passed by the camera, we were both too "New York" not to ham it up—to have a hoot—even in the ass crack of the apocalypse.

I grinned at Levy and he grinned back, the two of us telegraphing our intentions in perfect unison—a giddiness that is only found in kids (just kids), not yet jaded by the prospect of imminent death. In fact, in that moment, right there, there was no war . . . no war, no boondockers, no bombs, no bullets . . . no bullets, no sting of death, no Japan, no Roosevelt, no pain . . . no pain, no hunger, no anger, no blood, no tears . . . no tears, no sacrifice, no race or color, no Peleliu, and no Marine Corps.

There was only the beauty of being young and all the freedom that comes along with it.

Sy and I broke ranks. Nobody called us back. For just a few winks in the eye of forever, Sy says to me, "Truckin'!" So the two of us began truckin'—dancing—right in front of the camera, arms waving in the air, just like we had done back in the boroughs, showing off to the girls, laughing, sipping soda from candy-striped straws . . .

The smile on Sy's face was unbelievable. Never to be replicated. Captured on celluloid for as long as film may last; yet forever etched in my mind for as long as I may live. A charm of friendship. A wonder of youth, immortal.

Hurriedly, Sy and I trotted back to our ranks, a spring still in our step, giggling the whole time as the aftereffects of our folly still lingered, despite being back among the Corps. Nothing on this earth or beyond could claim that moment from Seymour and me.

7

THE REAL PACIFIC WAR

THE GREATEST TRUTH ABOUT LIES is that there's a little bit of truth in every one of them.

The truth is, there is no truth. Because the greatest lie in every truth is that the truth will set you free.

Ammunition will set you free. Grenades will set you free. Death will set you free.

It doesn't take a bleak outlook or a hardening of the heart to realize this. Fifteen days since invading Peleliu, attacking Ngesebus, and then back again, it is easy to see that we're not getting away with anything. Like the getaway driver in a bank heist; it's guilt by association. We're not going back to Pavuvu, either.

"So did you hear that crap about Pavuvu?"

"What crap is that?"

"Yeah, you really think we'd still be sittin' in the middle of this friggin' island if they were plannin' on sendin' us back?"

"The hell you say, Magginello!"

"The hell is right. You . . . me . . . *all* of us here. We ain't gettin' outta this fuckin' place unless all the Nips are dead, or all of *us*. Look around you and tell me I'm not right."

The truth is . . .

 . . . this marine isn't lying.

Now there's blood coming down Sergeant Spiece's cheek and he's crying. I'm squatting right in front of Spiece, rifle leaning against my chest, reaching out for him, trying to calm him down.

At least Spiece had the presence of mind to remove his helmet after the piece of shrapnel zipped through its inner liner and out the back somewhere.

His eyes are begging and his whole face is a knot of a frown, tears rich with anxiety.

"How bad is it, Mace? Mace, how bad?" The sergeant appears too shocked to believe this could be happening to him.

I lean over and look at the wound in his head. Even if I were able to see his brains pulsing beneath his skull (which I'm not), I would tell him what he wants to hear.

"Hey, hey . . . it's alright, okay?" I say. "It looks like a kid skipped a rock off the side of your head. C'mon, buddy . . . you'll be fine, alright?"

I don't know if what I tell him registers in his mind; nevertheless, I'm not lying to him. That's exactly how the wound appears: like a neighborhood brat beaned him in the head with a stone, putting a groove in Spiece's scalp, a poorly dug trench, jagged and slick with a thin layer of red.

Christ, some neighborhood, this place, I think, as I take my eyes off of Spiece and look up at my surroundings.

Mere moments before Spiece got hit, we had moved up and were standing at the bottom of a cliff getting ready to climb.

"Remember, guys," McEnery said. "This is strictly a defensive move. So keep your heads down during the day and we'll all be fine."

The cliff itself, just off the West Road, is at a 20-degree incline; the same dirty white coral rock and mash of crappy vegetation we've been bouncing all over since the invasion began. The same all-invasive heat, weighty and sharp. The same putrid dungarees, sagging off the body. The only difference now is that it's our job and not somebody else's.

Our job.

The day before, after we came off of Ngesebus, they moved us into the bivouac area, close to the old makeshift aid station we had passed on our way to Sniper Alley and the Lobster Claw. In fact, in order to get back to the bivouac area, we had to run the gauntlet of Sniper Alley one more time, just to grab our much-needed break.

We grabbed it in a big tent they had erected, much like the one we barracked in on Pavuvu. A place we could lie beneath, attempting to escape the barbed blades of the sun. It didn't matter, however. No matter where we went, in the shade or not, heat waves laid into us so it was like sticking your head into a preheated oven. Suicidal.

As it turned out, the Pavuvu-like tent was the closest we were going to get to Pavuvu.

Magginello was right. We're not going anywhere.

Phil was the same marine who, in our early fight for the island—when we still thought it was three innings and the ball game would be over—pointed out the various ridges of the mountains and laid out the whole plan of how we were going to take this place in just a few days. Now, however, the strategic genius of Magginello & Co. had given way to a bleaker air of surrender and acceptance.

Although I didn't subscribe to their fatalistic way of thinking, I could see where ideas like that came from and how some marines were justified in their thinking. To their credit, those Guadalcanal and Cape Gloucester vets were pretty sharp—though even the sharpest knife becomes dull after gnawing against the coral of a place like Peleliu, day in and day out. Dull in the mind. Dull in speech. Just plain weary in every cell of our bodies.

Even the familiar surroundings—the aid station, the busy roads, the marines marching and working—which merely a few days ago seemed teeming with life and clamor, now appeared flat and two-dimensional, as if they were only sketches on a piece of paper, half erased and ready for the garbage.

Under the tent, I raised my hand to rub my face, and as my hand slid down my slow growth of beard, the grime on my cheeks collected into small balls of dirt, mudslides rolling downhill. The same slime was on my neck, my chest, under my arms. Filthy. I could only imagine what our dungaree pants must've reeked like, too, after fifteen days. If we took a piss in a hurry, and anything splashed on the front of our dungarees, it stayed there. There was a constant sweat in the crotch—a pasty feeling down there.

There is nothing more certain than that if you want to make an animal out of a man, you merely have to treat him like one and the beast will follow suit—baring his canines all the way.

As for my teeth, I ran my tongue over the top of them, and where they normally felt sleek, now their surface was filmy. Where the bone met the gums I clearly detected deposits of bumpy mulch that had collected there after some long-forgotten meal I had attempted to eat.

The groan in my stomach told me I was hungry, yet the thought of Marine Corps food killed the sensation to eat just as soon as it had risen.

There were salt tablets, meant to rehydrate a marine. I rarely took any of those. Then there was one kind of food bar that looked like crushed raisins and ant corpses. It made me ill. There was another kind of bar that appeared to be made of smashed antacids. I didn't eat that either. The chocolate that came with our rations was a brick of shit. Old shit, too—because the chocolate was no longer the color of cocoa; instead, it was white, like a sun-bleached animal turd. As advertised, at least, the chocolate didn't melt in the heat. Of course, all it did do was sit there. It was debated by marines, if a guy tried his luck on one, what would come first, a chipped tooth or chipped chocolate.

On the other hand, lucky for us, being in the bivouac area, they eventually told us to line up for chow. There was a mess tent down the road, and we hadn't seen a tented chow line since . . . well, nobody wanted to say it . . .

. . . since Pavuvu.

Our spirits were immediately lifted. Hurriedly, marines took out their mess kits and prepared to line up. If mess kits were not available, as was the case for myself and a few others, we simply took the inner liner out of our helmets, swabbing the inside of the metal bowl with the elbows of our dungaree jackets. I was ready for my first real meal since Sy and I put one over on the navy boys on Purple Beach.

Plop!

"What the fuck is this?" I glared at the stuff the cook slopped into the bottom of my helmet. It seemed like something to eat (maybe), with bits of meat and beans floating in a greasy sauce . . . but I wasn't quite sure.

"It's chili," the cook said in an emotionless tone. His eyes were already looking toward the next person to serve, as the other cook in line handed me some white bread.

Chili? I thought. *What the hell is chili?*

"Ah, to hell with it!" In disgust I poured the chili on the ground, leaving me with only white bread and a greasy helmet.

If only I had known chili was good.

Being from Queens, I didn't have a clue. Therefore, I merely sat there, alone, picking the sand fleas out of the white bread and drinking the metallic-tasting water from my canteen.

If the bread didn't cure my hunger, well, at least I had cigarettes. The perfect Marine Corps food. Cigarettes. Camels. Chesterfields. Lucky Strikes. The nutritional value of cigarettes could carry a marine a long way. Have some. Bum one. Crinkled or broken. This foodstuff didn't spoil.

Goddamn, chili. They expect me to eat that crap?

Stupid. If chili had been on the Mace family menu in Queens, the sand fleas could've had all the white bread they wanted on Peleliu.

October 1, 1944.

We've taken over from the 7th Marines, preparing to climb a cliff they had occupied for the last few days. Facing east—the West Road and the ocean are to our backs, and in front of us, about fifty feet up, is our destination.

There is light conversation. Marines here and there adjust their gear for the climb up. I sling my BAR over my back and begin looking for Levy, since he has my smokes.

Suddenly we hear a rapid fluttering noise, very similar to the way a thrown baseball sounds when its flaps have come loose from its stitching. There's very little time to react. The brain registers what the sound is just a fraction before the muscles record the same.

Boom! There's an explosion—shrapnel and hunks of coral whip through the air as marines scatter . . .

All but one marine.

Only a few feet away, Sergeant Spiece falls flat on his ass, his eyes the size of pie plates. My own eyes vibrate in my head for a moment, like the last frames of a roll of film, flashing out their final scene on-screen. The scene in this case is Spiece taking off his helmet, and he gawks at it as if he's never seen a helmet before in his life.

"Hey!" My ears are ringing too loud for me to hear my own voice—and before I know it, I'm right there by Spiece, in the middle of the dust-congested air.

"Corpsman!" I shout.

I look at Spiece and then at the helmet in his hands. There's not a dent or ding in the helmet. Whatever hit him must've gone up and through the underside of his steel pot, cutting a groove in his head in the process.

I can't stop thinking of the fistfight Spiece and I nearly got into on Pavuvu. I can't even recall what it was about—just that Spiece isn't the same man now as he was with his fists up.

Jesus Christ, that was close!

They whisk Spiece away.

We've grown accustomed to crap like this happening to marines, so nobody even mentions Spiece or the other couple of guys who were hit by the same knee mortar. We simply begin to climb, hands grabbing for branches, mangrove, and any rock that looks strong enough to hold us up. It's not that tough a climb, but it's difficult not to think about where that Jap mortar came from. It surely came from the same direction we're climbing. Into the claws of another creature. Feeding the war effort with spoonfuls of blood.

A silent place.

When we reach the top there is only silence . . . and a little trail leading to some of the most ghastly scenery I have seen thus far.

On our left, to my astonishment, is what looks like a field of snow. Of course, it's not snow. Instead, what appears to be powder is really long streamers of toilet paper, about forty yards in length, stretching out and showing how far the 7th Marine riflemen could crawl from their protected areas to relieve themselves. There are hundreds of pieces of toilet paper—and at the edge of the paper are the corpses of Japanese in various stages of decomposition, some mixed in with the paper, all mixed in with the feces of marines. Excrement sticks to the coral surface; flies congregate for church in mass sheets of worship; the smell of shit and liquefying flesh floats as a palpable thing, suspended in the air, as if I can reach out and touch the melancholy—as if I can hold a conversation with the sadness that lives here. The horror blanks out all other thoughts and tells a story of how life used to be okay.

Silence, as each marine is left to digest this charnel house in his own way. Besides, we don't know if the Nips are two feet or twenty feet away from us; therefore, silence is the best policy. It's goddamn golden.

We spread out, north to south, every marine seeking any protection he can find: coral outcroppings, spines of rock along the trail, and any little divot against the face of the smaller ridge to our right. With our backs still oceanside, the other ridge—the one right in front of us, looking east—that's where the demons dwell. Beyond the eight-foot-high ledge, the Nips are surely sharpening their bayonets, angry at having to suffer under the same green stench of their decaying brethren, just as we are. Beyond the Nip camp is another ridge. Beyond that is another ridge . . . and another, and another . . . all of them infested with Japs to the very brim. If you can see it from an aerial view, the lay of the land is what's killing us. The whole surface of the mountains is merely a series of ridges that resembles the shallows of a waffle iron. Soft marines keep pouring into the crests and valleys, and when the Nips get ready, they merely press the handle down and Americans come out crispy and charred. Mostly dead and undone in the middle.

I pass Levy and Frank Ocepek and some kid named Matheny (who I really don't know from Adam), moving north on the winding trail until Allmann and I find a tight hollow against the east ridge.

Keeping our heads down, we slide against the wall at a crouch.

We're in defensive position, yes. I suppose to keep the Nips from spilling out onto the West Road and cutting open our vein of travel on this side of the island. Yet I'm not a general or a chess player, so what do I know? I *do* know, however, from my vantage, if the Nips decide to come over the ridge in force, we'll only be able to defend our ground for a few minutes and then we, too, will be dead among the crap paper, the bloated bodies, and the waste of whatever made the 7th Marines shit so much.

Nonetheless, up here, tactics are not the point of the lecture.

The minutes that creak by are rungs of the ladder I descend. For every moment that passes without a bullet in my head is another moment of triumph I hold over the power of death.

The minutes . . . The hours . . . The everlasting moment between the seconds . . .

We haven't been up here ten minutes when I hear the pop of something very akin to a firecracker, somewhere south of me. That's easy; I know that sound. The small-arms snap of a Japanese rifle. My body tenses for a second, waiting for someone to shout for a corpsman. I listen, nerves as tight as piano wire. Yet it's only when the call doesn't come that am I able to relax again. *Jap must have missed, I guess.*

Feeling around for my cigarettes, I don't find them. That's when it dawns on me that Levy has my smokes. *Dammit, I need one.* I gave them to Sy this morning, at the bivouac area, because I didn't have enough room in all my gear without crushing the pack, and since Levy doesn't smoke I could trust him to hold them, as opposed to some of those other smoke hounds in the squad.

"Crap!" I whisper. Allmann looks up at me, his expression asking what's the big deal. "I left my goddamn smokes with Levy, for chrissakes," I hiss. This is nerve-racking.

A few minutes pass and I can't stand it anymore—because there's no telling how long we'll be up here.

"Look, Charlie," I begin, antsy. "I'm gonna go down there and get my pack, alright? I'll be back in a flash."

Moving again at a crouch, I shuffle and zig along the trail, going down to where I saw Levy and Frankie stake their ground earlier.

When I see Frank, by himself, I skid to a halt and sidle up to him, dispersing a few loose coral pebbles in the process.

"Hey, Frank, where'd Levy run off to?" I quick-look to the right and left, trying to see where Sy moved his position. When I gaze back at Frank there's something in his downturned countenance that looks a little off. Out of focus.

"Frank?" Ocepek remains with his head down. I wince inside, where a tiny spike of nausea flips in my stomach and jumps around in there. *What the hell's goin' on here?*

"Frank?" I try again. I can hear the shaking in my voice. Desperate. "Where the fuck is Levy, *Frank?*"

A pause in my life. Just a pause.

"Nobody wanted to tell you . . ." His words barely audible under his helmet; he begins to raise his face to meet mine, and all the time this crazy flipping in my belly gets wilder and wilder. Then I know. I *know*. I know before I see the gray tone of sadness in Frank's eyes. Even before he finishes the words. "Nobody wanted to tell you, I'm just . . . Sorry, Mace. He's *gone*. He took one in the head as he peered over the edge, to have a look. He just . . . he just said was tired of this shit, and then he looked . . ."

Oh, Jesus, Levy . . .

"Where is he, Frank? Where'd they take him?" I hear myself say in a flat tone—as flat as the earth was once . . . a thousand years ago. I could fall off the edge of the map—a place marked *you are here*—but I'm not here. I'm not anywhere close to being here.

I hear Frank say something about them taking Sy's body back down the cliff, and all I can imagine is them carrying Levy's body over the spewing bellies of Japanese carcasses, rife with gas and hatching fly larvae; over the piles of human excrement, which speaks of how we come into this world and how we'll leave it, too; and then over the streams of toilet paper, so white and out of place, much like the beard Levy wore when he returned from the hospital ship an eternity ago.

I wasn't able to see Sy off, again, just as I wasn't able to say good-bye to him when he was hit the first time. *He should never have come back, that stupid fucking kid! He should be home!*

I simply sit—miles away from anyone living, and all those who wish they had never been born. Head in hands . . .

. . . I cry.

Jesus Christ, Sy, why'd you have to come . . . back!?

... --- -- . / -... . .-.. .. . ...- . / .. -. / .- -. --- . .-.. ...

-.-. .. .-. / -.-. .--. -. . .-. . ..-. / .-... .- ..- --. ..... - . .-.

-.-. .-. .-.. --- ... . .-. / -- -.-- / ..-. .-.. .- -- . / - --- / - ....

"GODDAMMIT! I'LL KILL ALL YOU JAP SONUVABITCHES! I'LL SHOOT ALL YOU FUCKING BASTARDS!"

There's the sound of a thousand voices spewing from my mouth as the thundering din of my boondockers claps the ground and splits the stones as I move up the line, my BAR pointed at the ridgeline where the Nips are hiding.

Only now, I've become bigger than myself. So fired with anger I could kill the whole Nip army with one spray of my weapon!

There's Jimmy, keeping up behind me, viewing me for what I really am—merely a young man, changed, but still just as small to the world as he was before Levy's death. All because Sy was "tired of this shit."

"Mace! Hey, Mace!" Jimmy hollers over my shoulder. "Goddammit, Mace"—Jim wheels me around by the arm—"Stop! Just stop, ya stupid shit!"

October 1, 1944.

I face Jimmy, but for a second I don't see Jimmy's face at all. Instead it is Levy's face, grinning at me like when he and I were truckin', giving a thumbs-up to one another on the amtrac coming in. Then it is my own reflection, where Jim's visage should be; my face wet with sorrow, ashamed, even though I shouldn't be. Finally there is only Jim. Jim McEnery. Despite all of his failings. Despite all of the failings we share together as marines, Jimmy had faced more death and decay than I have ever dreamed of.

At the sight of Jim's true face, beyond what the marines have made us, I deflate just as quickly as I had blown up.

"Mace . . . *Sterl*," Jim says, his hands on my shoulders. "Listen, Sterl . . . You've gotta get your shit together, ya got that? You can't do this. Not like *this*. You're the best BAR man I got, and you're just gonna get yourself killed, like this . . . and for what? Tell me that. For what, huh?"

I wish I could say something to Jim, but I can't. Jimmy's words have no lies in their truth. His expression is a rarity on Peleliu, unbridled in its honesty, even for two raggedy-ass marines, standing at the gates of one another's private nightmares.

I would hate to be killed by the Japanese, but I don't hate the Japanese man.

Yet I'd hate to think that after throwing all these grenades over the ridge I haven't killed the man I'm supposed to hate.

The thing is, I don't like the bastards very much, though.

(Throw!) (The sound of grenades exploding over the ridge at the Nips feels good, simply because I hope to be ripping them apart in the process. American iron flies in all directions, rending the life from Nip bodies.)

I'll continue to dislike the Jap because if it weren't for him, I wouldn't be here right now. All of us would be alive. I wouldn't be pissed because this generation's war is my war. *Rotten stinkin' luck!*

(Throw!) (Other marines join me in tossing grenades over the ridge. The only thing better than the explosions would be the screams of the Japanese. The fact that we don't hear anything other than our own blasts means nothing. Or it means everything. We can't even see what we want to annihilate. For all we know, the Nips are watching our efforts from a distance, laughing to themselves at the futility of it all.) (Throw!)

(Throw!) (Like I'm standing in the outfield throwing to home plate—the ball arcs in the crystal sky, tumbling over itself. Except unlike in Queens on a beautiful spring day, gathering my breath to pitch one over the ridge is like having my mouth wrapped around the tailpipe of a car. When I suck in a breath, someone starts the engine and my lungs fill up with heat.)

No, not hate. To hate the Japanese would mean to lose my self completely. My mom might not recognize me now. My dad, my sister, might wonder who this stranger is beneath my green veneer; nonetheless, if I gaze at myself in the mirror, I know I would still be able to make out the chalk outline of myself, akin to what you'd find at the scene of a crime. At least there's *that*. For one day, if I were to wake up dead, or view myself at a distance, killing with a smile, like some pulp villain, that would be too much to bear.

(Throw!)

Rather, I have become an automaton, a mechanical thing, a robot out of one of those Buster Crabbe serials.

Okay, Mace, if you've gotta kill somebody, you just do it. You do it, so you don't get killed and you can get the hell outta here. Get the hell outta here! (Throw!) *And you don't think about home too much, don't daydream like a sucker, don't volunteer for anything, yet for God's sake don't shirk your duty! Don't loaf. Keep your head down and your eyes open. Squeeze the trigger; don't pull it. Don't be stupid, and* (Throw!) *get the hell outta here!*

October 1, 1944. The day is setting like a stone in the horizon of my heart.

I don't think about home, yet I would kill every Jap on the island just to get back there.

Presently we exhaust ourselves throwing grenades. Grenades I *do* hate. I never carry them. You cannot trust the pin on them like you can trust your finger on a trigger. It's when you pull the pin and let go of the spool, and that thing starts sizzling in your hand as the fuse inside burns down—who knows if some munitions worker back in the States didn't come to work after pulling a bender, or fighting with his wife, and absentmindedly gave a whole batch of them a few seconds less in the fuse before they explode? I remember lighting a firecracker, when I was a kid, and the fuse burned down before I could get it out of my hand.

Lyman Rice pitched a grenade a few moments ago, and it careened off the mangrove, exploding back at us. The guys swore the Nips were throwing them back—but I know different.

Still, that pretty much ended our grenade throwing for the day. *Besides, this was supposed to be a "defensive move," remember? What's that saying? The best offense is a good defense? Or the best defense is a good offense?*

Whatever fire had burned over Levy's grave has turned into smoldering embers in the pit of my stomach. A weak flame: I hurt now about as much as one of Flash Gordon's robots. Dumb skin. Clipped circuits. Burned vacuum tubes.

Exhausted and alone in a crowd.

With the ridge and the Japs to my right, I settle back, chest heaving, watching the sky bleed out with the dying sun, as I phase into thoughts of the previous night, when our squad lay beneath a tent at the bivouac area, knowing nothing about the events of October 1.

That evening we lay on the ground beneath the tent, Levy on my right, all of us shooting the shit, smoking cigarettes and not paying much attention to the call for "smoking lamps out." The brass weren't going to come down on us smoking after dark, anyway. We were in a secure area, and we knew it: feeling good about being out of the crap, even though we had just found out we weren't going back to Pavuvu after all.

Nonetheless, young men will invent ways to take it all in stride, as long as the next knucklehead has it just as bad as you do.

What keeps us in the war, though, is the random shots coming from deep in the ridges and the occasional *budapbudapbudap* of a machine gun up there.

Intermittently Sy breaks into his best Sam Jaffe impersonation from the film with Cary Grant and Victor McLaglen, about the water bearer and such. By now we all know the lines and we've all seen the picture, so we indulge Levy and cut up a bit, despite ourselves.

We're tired, though—bone weary. Even though the ground feels like a plank of wrought iron, it doesn't take long for most of us to fag out, without so much as a word or a good night.

Maybe Levy could have gone on all evening, but I doubt it, though the kid is nearly inexhaustible. Soon, however, I'm falling asleep as well, when something in the corner of my mind catches the sound of Levy's voice downshift and drive into words not made of this earth—not fashioned by ink and paper, by men made of dust and clay.

In fact, Sy's utterances are a sacrilege in reverse, joined as we are to Lucifer's hip on Peleliu. Yet the words are as lyrical and divine as they were intended to be, the lines originally gifted to a little Jewish shepherd boy who would one day rule a kingdom much greater than this twisted devil's dominion we presently die on.

Seymour Levy speaks of green pastures and still waters, of fearlessness in the face of evil, even in the presence of his enemies . . .

Although I was there, in the moment . . . it was not my moment. It was Levy's moment in time.

Me, I was gently wrapped in the arms of sleep. Me, I say my bit to a long-dead sister, every morning: as a shield, as a guide. To me, however, God is a busy guy, and since he didn't start this crap on Peleliu, why should we think he needs to bail us out of it? Why muddy the waters, when nearly every marine, including the little dog we left on the beach, has already given God an earful of entreaties and supplications?

But Levy . . .

But Levy . . . his words ring true in the presence of his enemies—as his last words of prayer marry with my last bits of consciousness . . .

"Surely goodness and mercy shall follow me all the days of my life, and I will dwell in the house of the Lord forever."

So Levy said and so Levy did. It just turns out that the rest of his life was less than a day away. Less than a day, but no matter. That he dwells in the house of the Lord, at this very moment, I have no doubt.

Later that same night I awoke in the tent, with all thoughts of Levy's prayer out of mind. The night was deep and dark, only slightly illuminated by orange and red flashes blanching the sky-line. Explosions in the mountains, gone just as fast as they appeared. The flash and then the thunder, mocking nature, chain lightning.

I could be up there now, and don't you forget it.

It was just me awake. The whole squad, as far as I could tell, was fast asleep. Still a machine gun rattled off in the distance, *budapbudapbudap* . . .

Then to my right I heard a sighing sound. It was Levy, and with each burst from the gun Sy groaned in his sleep. Just a soft moan, which only occurred right after the machine gun tapped out its rhythm.

What the hell is he dreamin'? I wondered. Certainly not still waters and green pastures.

Lying on my back, listening for a while, eventually I fell back asleep. It was a dreamless evening for me, unlike Levy's sleep, where machine guns echoed out the final ticks of seventeen years in forty winks.

Now, one night later, up on the ridges, I think about those things as I drift off to sleep once more. However, this night, the evening of October 1, I *do* dream—and in my dream you can take out everything Levy recited in the Twenty-third Psalm, and roll it all down the hill with the toilet paper and the rotting Japs, leaving me with only one line out of God's sacred stanzas—taken out of context, sinister in its meaning, alone . . .

"In the presence of my enemies."

That's what I dream. The presence of my enemies.

Darkness engulfs Peleliu as if the whole island is wrapped in the tenebrous wings of a nightmare. It has a beat, a pulse, this night, a fever and a whisper. Of course, it is a nightmare, awake or asleep, it's a nightmare. My eyes scan the lip of the ridge to my right, over and over, marking every dip and rise, every stone and pebble, all the outcroppings of mangrove, the slots over the side where a Nip might appear and shoot me full of holes. For some reason something's missing. It's not the landscape. No. I've made sure of it. I've held the same small features of the ridge steady, in my mind, as if my eyes are shutters and the earth is a still-life image captured on glossy 8×10 paper. I simply want to believe nothing has changed out there—for if Japs are about to come over the ridge, I want to be able to get the drop on them before they get the drop on me. Survival by inches, yards, and feet. Yet something is definitely missing. Vaguely, I'm aware that other marines are around me. Yes. This place smells like rotten meat. I have no idea where Allmann is—but that's nothing new. Then I realize what's missing. This whole time on the island there's always been the sounds of combat emanating from somewhere. But not now. Always, no matter how near or far, the racket of war keeps you in the here and now. It's almost a comfort to hear the din of combat, because it lets us know either that we're not alone on the island or that we're not quite dead yet. But not now. No single rifle shots, no mortar thumps, no machine guns nor flares, no cursing of men, no cries for corpsmen, no shuffling of gear, no drone of fighter planes, no radio crackle or cannonades whooshing from navy ships. Life in a void. Yet suddenly there's a small lump on the ridgeline, only a few feet above me. It wasn't there a second ago. So I check again the mental photograph in my head against what's before my eyes. *Jesus Christ, what the shit is that?* The lump inches up and becomes wider in its silhouette . . . and then up a small amount more, and then more it rises . . . until I can now make out the turtle-shaped outline of a Japanese helmet, the crease of its brim flaring out, and then the darkened face, beneath the helmet—and I don't need a light to make out the features looming over the ridge; for in my photograph the face is a mocking moon, with the same slit-eyes, flattened nose, and tanned, emotionless features, the same . . . *I've got to shoot this bastard* . . . but then an arm comes up, bent at the elbow, in a high arch, splayed fingers gripping my side of the ridge, and then another arm comes up and does the same, *he's pulling himself over the goddamn ridge*, his arms appearing much like the forelegs of a spider, with another six legs sure to follow; and his back is bowed at the top just like an insect, too . . . a half-arachnid, half-man creature (*but this is only my imagination, right? Fighting me back? This is a man and I've got to kill him*). *Kill him, goddammit! Kill him!* My breath hitches in my chest and I believe I can feel my finger on the trigger . . .

I close my eyes.

I open my eyes.

In the exact spot where the Jap was coming over the ridge, in my dream, there is now a big empty space of night, looking identical to the photograph I had taken in my mind right before I fell asleep.

That was some friggin' dream ya had there, Mace, I tell myself. Despite the heat, you could probably chill a beer in the cold drips coming off my body.

Here and there, the familiar noise of sporadic combat echoes across the island: small arms popping, machine guns burping, and the occasional grenade littering the night with its garbage. There's my BAR lying across my lap right where I left it. The trouble is, I'm not in a very good spot. My position is too cramped. If the Nip from my dream comes over the ridge, I don't think I can whip my rifle around fast enough to pop him off before he gets to me.

I get up and slide down a ways, down the rough path, remembering that there's a marine who carries a pistol as a sidearm. Because I know that if I'm stuck up there where I can't use my BAR, a pistol will do the trick in close quarters.

I find the marine quickly—he's only down the path a few yards.

"Say, you still got that pistol you been carryin' around on ya?"

"Yeah, I still got it. What's—"

"Lemme borrow it, willya? I'm in a pretty tight spot up there, an' I don't think I've got room to use my rifle if one of those Nips comes over the ridge, ya know?"

He gives it to me. It's only a small peashooter, probably a .32 caliber Colt or S&W his parents sent to him as extra protection. Nothing like the .45 caliber revolver Bauerschmidt totes around with him, or the .38 service revolver Van Trump pilfered off the dead pilot. Still, beggars can't be choosers. I've caught a break with at least something I can shoot the Jap with; otherwise I'd being zinging pebbles at him. Or good luck with this crappy knife the Marine Corps issued me.

So there I sat, pistol in hand, BAR draped over my legs while my eyes sting from staring at the same spot for hours. Sleep had been the only thing I'd been fighting since I came back with the peashooter.

Then just at daybreak something happened.

First light brought with it a sudden noise—not human, yet familiar, and nearly as quick as blinking an eye. A chicken! Appearing right in the spot where the Nip should have been. *A goddamn chicken!?* The bird was flustered, perched on the ridge. Closer to the point, it's not as if the chicken could have climbed up there! No way. Feathers all in a ruffle, wings batting the morning air—that bird was thrown up there by a Jap, sure as hell it was!

The bird scared the crap out of me—just not enough for me to pull the trigger on it.

I had seen and known plenty of shitbirds on Peleliu, but a chicken? The only birds I had known on the island were the indigenous birds, with their eerie exhale/inhale call in the mornings. Otherwise, Peleliu was a wasteland, devoid of anything larger than a blowfly; meaning that my feathered friend up there was domesticated, and more than likely a trap set to entice a marine to give his position away by taking a potshot at the bird.

Watching the chicken for a while, waiting for the Nips to complete the caper that never came—eventually they pulled us off the line and we were back on the West Road, having said good-bye to the chicken, the turds, the corpses, the shit paper, and the place where a seventeen-year-old Jewish kid from Brooklyn lost his life because he was tired of this shit.

We all were. Sick and tired of this and that. Once more, *this*—the moth-worn scuttlebutt about going back to Pavuvu. "You guys put a cork in it, willya? We're not goin' back to Pavuvu." Once more, *that*—"They don't care about us."

Mostly we made small talk, as we headed south, keeping the conversations light. Nobody said anything about what happened back there. It would've broken our hearts to even try.

I damn sure wasn't going to tell anybody about my dream and the chicken. I could hear it now, exactly what the boys would say if I told them.

"A chicken? Oh, for chrissakes! Ya know what that dream means? It means you're gonna lay some goddamn eggs, Mace!"

Yeah, I'm sure that's what it meant.

The real Pacific war.

8

THE FIVE BITCHES

We start off in a skirmish line, a zigzagging group of marines, taking furtive steps through the morning mist toward a place that looks more ominous and foreboding than any other place we've been on Peleliu. There is nothing more real than this.

We're in a draw composed of nothing but heat-baked coral, littered with mangrove, bits of wood, discarded marine gear, spent ammunition, and the scent of putrefaction and cooked blood, a silent testimonial that bodies once lay here, long carried off, leaving only their memories to linger. At the end of the draw, before us is a sixty-foot sheer cliff, running a thousand yards up the island. Its upper edges are cannibal's teeth, eating away at the sky, breaking off pieces of the firmament as if it's the end of the world. In many ways it is.

On the opposite side of the cliff is more uneven ground, yet more punctured and blistered up close than it looks from afar.

I was mistaken; right on top of it, it doesn't resemble the surface of the moon at all. With the naked eye, you can see occasional craters on the moon's glowing face. Down here, on the other hand, the ground is dull—millions of pores on a dead man's skin: showing the effects of the constant bombing and shelling since D-day.

This cadaverous earth. Man, what an earth!

In the middle of it all sit two Nip pillboxes that had taken direct hits from incoming navy mail. The pillboxes are merely small pimples in the overall picture, yet I can only imagine the fits they would have given us if the navy had not taken them out first.

From where I stand the panoramic view below is of the newly erected supply depot, the refurbished airstrip, and the blue Pacific Ocean. Beyond that? New York? Queens? *God, I hope so.*

Tanks move up with us, and it feels swell having them here—assuredly just as good as the tankers feel about having marine infantry at their side.

The tanks make an awfully big racket, and they churn up coral powder as if they're slapping a thousand blackboard erasers together in front of our faces. Well, it isn't like we're sneaking up on the Nips anyway. As with the marines before us, slamming their noses against the ridges time and again, stealth isn't the issue when brute force is the order of the day.

It's insane to think this way when it comes to tactics—and I don't know tactics from Shinola. All I know is what's right in front of me, and that's the way it's been since we landed on this island paradise.

Soon, the fundamental theory of blunt action pays off, when a group of marines spots a pillbox about thirty feet up. They claim it's bursting at the seams with Japs. Instead of taking potshots at it, though, a tank is called up: one with a gun like a long nozzle, very akin to what I'd seen back home, when the fire department was called in to quell a riot.

Slowly the tank's turret turns around to where its nozzle is facing squarely into the eyes of the pillbox, and with an air-sucking *whoosh*, a long stream of liquid fire belches out of the tank, trailing plumes of black soot and waves of heat that twinkle in the dry air.

At first I'm encouraged by this, especially if there's somebody in there, but after a few moments, *Enough's enough already, for chrissakes!* The Nips come *boiling* out. Literally, *boiling* out of the pillbox, all from one exit, rife with mayhem—the whole lot attempting to get out at once. I wince at the burning clothes, licked with flames, the sizzling hair and charcoaled faces, and the sporadic cracks of ammunition detonating in cartridge belts from the compressed heat inside.

The first Japs only make it out about eight feet from the exit, and the rest pile up behind them, doubling up and tripping on themselves, falling onto one another, creating a layer cake of crusted victims, and still this tongue of flame from the tank roasts whoever can't make it out—gooey and tarlike they slip on their own liquefied fat, hot gelatin within their Imperial Japanese–issue uniforms.

A magical voice rings out, "Hey, Mace, cover that mess over there and see if there's any movement, willya?"

The voice quickly snaps me out of my trance.

I trot off.

Sonuvabitch, why me? I swear it's always Mace who does it.

Dutifully, however, I do it, despite the natural protests in my mind. Picking my way gingerly up the small slope, rifle at the ready, I notice that this is a fool's errand anyway. These Japs are dead beyond dead. They might as well have never been born. Around fifteen to twenty of them, stacked and black. Nearly inhuman looking, as the heat has just began to cool somewhat, allowing the melted skin of one Nip to solidify with that of his comrade below him. Just like melted wax, a glue that binds them into one entity. The only things that identify them as being human once are their talonlike hands, their lips peeled back against their gums exposing white teeth, and their hollow eye sockets (the eyes, composed of mostly liquid, are one of the first things to evaporate when you crank the oven on full blast).

I look away, but that doesn't help much. I can still smell

them—enough to make a vulture gag; though more perversely, I can still hear them. The massed bodies crackle and hiss just like frankfurters on a grill. *Exactly* like roasting frankfurters.

I swear to Christ I'll never eat another goddamn hot dog!

Oh, and there's movement within the corpses, alright—yet nothing to shoot at. It's only escaped gas making the frankfurters shift a little as—

Pop!

One of the corpses makes a loud noise, and it startles me so much that my foot slips off the loose coral gravel and down I fall a few feet—head over end—to another sandy perch below. Just like slipping on a banana peel in one of those vaudeville acts back home. No harm done. Merely stupid looking.

Red-faced and ashamed, I quick-spy around to see if anyone witnessed my acrobatic flip; but no, it doesn't appear anyone saw it. Someone would have ribbed me already if they had. A nice bunch of fellows—yet if some other marine had taken a crazy crash like that, I would have been the first to give him the business. They'd never let me live *that* one down.

"Okay, fellas, that's enough of this stuff. Let's get movin'."

We don't stay there long. We know where we're going.

The Five Sisters.

On the approach, the Five Sisters were nothing more than chewed-up humps on the ground, covered all over with half-charred trees, appearing like roach legs poking out of the earth. The first rise in the earth was a shattered pyramid, dead to the pharaohs, blown to bits by the constant drop of napalm and 500-pounders.

The Hellcats and Corsairs zoomed up from their runways, making their runs only fourteen hundred yards away. They were so close to the Sisters that the bombers didn't even have time to retract their wheels. Now *that* was close combat. With a roar the napalm dropped, and it was a wonder the splash from the deadly incendiary bombs didn't melt the wheels off their landing gear.

Napalm we had more faith in, over the 500-pounders. Napalm looked like it really penetrated into the nooks and crevices of the terrain, while the big bombs just skipped off the surface and exploded on top of the coral. Napalm, made of jellied gasoline, was designed to stick to the skin while it burned, bathing the Five Sisters with a spray of fire. It was also created to suck the oxygen from the air and suffocate its victims. In theory, any Nips within the area should have been shriveled, burned husks of men. Either that or they should have asphyxiated in their holes. Hopefully both. There was no desire to face what the planes or the tanks could take out for us.

That's what made Corporal Raymond Grawet's death so bitter. He didn't have to die just to prove there were Japs still in a cave.

At a slow move up to the Five Sisters, a Sherman tank spots some Nips hiding in a cave. Maybe there's only a few of them. Maybe a few hundred. So, at point-blank range, the Sherman blasts a round right down the spout of the cave, sending up a lot of smoke and flames.

Right by the tank, shirt open, bare-chested—Ray leans over a little, his M-1 rifle at the ready, trying to get a better look into the cave.

Corporal Grawet takes a Nip bullet right in the chest, before he can take two steps. Killed before he hits the ground.

Quickly they rush Ray out of the way, and the demolition marines implode the cave, sealing up Raymond's killer, along with any other little bastards who might be sucking air inside.

They take Ray's body back down the draw, moving right past me, at a trot. As they flash by, I remember the tattoo of a bulldog on Ray's left deltoid. *What's the rush?* Any life that was left in Grawet's body had seeped out through a little round hole in his chest at the mouth of the cave.

No matter. Before we even reach the Five Sisters, there's more of this kind of slaughter. I am merely waiting, like Corporal Raymond Grawet, to enter my own cave.

They will bury Ray's body here, a side of beef, so far from his life and home.

We move up and see five dead marines, nothing but sacks of bones lying up the path to the Five Sisters—all of them skeletons in saggy, discolored dungarees. One is on a stretcher, and the other four are obviously the stretcher bearers, caught coming down from the Sisters and wiped out where they now lay. Nobody even moved them. Then again, we might be the first marines to come up this way since the 1st Marines pulled out.

"Oh my God, would ya look at the poor bastards?"

"Yeah."

"What the hell is this!"

I was breaking all the rules by dwelling on such things—I couldn't help it. I could only imagine, here's this poor wounded marine, lying up there for a couple of hours, watching his funeral play out in his mind . . . and then here comes salvation. Stretcher bearers! Now the wounded marine is delighted. Instead of imagining his mother getting a telegram, he's making plans for what he's going to do when he gets home and then . . .

It's all over. All of them dead. Just like that.

I looked away and up as sun flares made rings of light in my vision; the sweat was bitter in my mouth. All that time I had dead marines to think about while trying to keep my eyes peeled for Nips. It was too hot. It was too crazy to the senses. I glanced over my shoulder a final time at the dead Marines, with their bald faces in perpetual skeletal grins, with remnants of skin clinging to their bones, marking the time in which they'd lain exposed to the elements. If there'd been even a slight breeze, those flecks of skin would have drifted in the air.

Lyman Rice and Lieutenant Bauerschmidt, on the other hand, had climbed up the side of one of the Sisters, about twenty-five feet up, and there they perched as one of our tank escorts pulled up to the edge of the draw and parked himself. If the tank went any farther, he would put himself in real jeopardy. In the case of a hand grenade attack, he would have to back out of there in a hurry.

What're Rice and the lieutenant doin' up there, anyway?

Frank Minkewitz stands at the base of the Sister looking up at them, and he's talking to them about something, but from where I stand I can't hear their conversation. I'm right by the tank, and everybody else is spread out around the base of the hill, all of us simply waiting for the orders to move up, or move out, to move somewhere, to do something . . . to do anything! It's difficult to decide what's worse, to sidle up by the tank and choke on its fumes in the shade, or to simply sit out in the open, baking under the sun.

"Hey, you, marine!"

I look up to see who's calling me. One of the tankers is leaning out of the hatch in the turret.

"Yeah?" I say back.

"Here, I got somethin' for you here." He holds out a big can, probably a gallon of something.

"What is it?"

"It's apple butter."

"Oh, no kiddin', yeah?" I ask. I don't realize how hungry I am until this moment. "Thanks!"

So I take out my marine-issue spoon, clean it off with my tongue, and begin to dig in.

It's not dining at the Ritz-Carlton, but this thick, greasy stuff sure hits the spot, it's so different from the common fare.

The thing is, the war doesn't give me time to wonder where the tankers got this delicacy before I spy one of the oddest things I've seen so far:

Only about sixty yards away, four Marines come out of an opening in the ridge. One makes a strange little right turn, and the rest follow suit.

What in God's name's goin' on?

Except they're not marines. They are Japs in marine uniforms. Americans don't walk like that. Americans don't crawl out of the ridge like that. I start to bring my rifle to my shoulder. *Sonuvabitch, those are Nips!* I can't get my weapon up before the last one disappears into the slice of ridge he had just come from.

Almost instantly the intensity of the combat began catching fire somewhere in the middle of the Five Sisters. But those Japs? The ones in marine uniforms? I immediately felt they'd brought something sinister with them. Don't get me wrong, I wasn't superstitious, but on Peleliu I came to know these moments for what they were. The Japs' appearance alone called forth a sense of doom. I could have dropped them all, only I hesitated slightly before I figured out they were not marines at all (and somehow, in the back of my mind I found it chilling that the Nips were wearing dead Americans' uniforms). Yet I didn't kill them. I knew then that something bad was going to happen.

From that moment forward, everything seemed like a mad rush, although none of us were rushing anywhere. We merely pulled back a little. Slowly. Methodically. It's just that time was on a racecourse around a bend that we didn't know existed, let alone could see with any real clarity.

"Bauerschmidt's dead," Jimmy says. "I guess that leaves me in charge."

"What happened?"

"Got it in the stomach. Said somethin' about the shot coming from behind him. From one of us maybe. Don't know what the hell he's talkin' about, though."

"When?"

I had only moved twenty yards behind the tank; I was amazed how I could be right on top of a killing and not even know that it happened.

"What about Rice?" I ask.

"Lyman? I dunno nothin' 'bout Rice."

Minkewitz lopes by, and I recall him talking to Bauerschmidt and Rice about something. Suddenly it hits me that Rice is dead, too. It appears that whatever Minkewitz was talking about with the lieutenant and Rice, it involved either Frank staying put or Frank refusing to go up there with them. I'm guessing the latter. Nevertheless, I still can't figure out what they were doing up there in the first place.

Forget Minkewitz. My problem is that I can't stop wondering if the Nips who got Bauerschmidt and Rice had on marine uniforms. *No, it can't be.*

Whatever happened, it was confirmed that Rice was killed a short while after the lieutenant.

On this horrible landscape, tits up and covered with insect feelers, it even smells like heat: This is where we stop for the day. We have pulled back forty yards from the Five Sisters, yet the whole monstrosity looms over us.

Charlie Allmann and I take the extreme left flank of the line, only about fifteen feet from the base of the cliff. There, the work begins as marines scrounge around for riffraff, wood, junk, anything that will make a marine feel secure against a hand grenade attack. Anything before the sunlight bends into darkness. A sleepy red glow is already filtering through the last haze of a scorched earth, though it's ridiculous to think that some scraps from the ground are going to protect us out in the open like this.

Charlie and I put together some bits of wood, arranging them in a U-shape around us—about five feet across at the inside of the U and only about a foot high at the most. Some pieces of wood are as long as two feet, while others are mere splinters at about two inches in length. I might be able to blow on the weakest portion of our little campground and the wood would tumble straight down, it's that skimpy.

Yet there's always this false sense of security that keeps us moving.

It's akin to the same phony protection we feel by merely moving back a few yards from the most dangerous spot on the island. The reality of it, however, is that fifteen, twenty, or even forty yards doesn't make a lick of difference as the bullet flies. Still, it's the choice we make, to believe against rational thought, because rationality tells us that we've got no chance in hell. It's the analytical mind that gets blown out the back of your head for believing you can think this thing through, without your instincts in the driver's seat.

Any marine who believes he can think around the next corner is only deluding himself. However, to sense what's coming next— from your gut—without bursting into hysterics? That's the free ticket to staying alive just a few minutes longer.

So we built our "protection" for the night. I came across a sheet of corrugated metal, thinking it would supply some good cover— maybe bent over us, or perhaps wrapped to our side. However, not long after I sat down on it and unlaced my leggings, the whole piece of flimsy metal warbled and warped so loud it made a din like a platoon of marines cleaning their mess kits.

I'd just gotten my boondockers off, too! I was really amazed at how fish-belly white my feet were. Palmolive-soap white. Not a smidge of dirt on them, not even between the toes. Since I hadn't taken my boondockers off since Purple Beach, experience told me that my feet would be as mashed up as poor Dennis Hoffman's dogs. Thank God they weren't.

What was equally amazing was my leggings—no longer pliable, nor a smooth marine beige; I sat them down and they stood straight at attention. More to my surprise, at the back of the leggings, molded into the fabric, was the perfect curvature of my muscled calves, detailing every line and fiber, as if they were made of Bakelite. I chuckled and wondered what the leggings would sound like if I knocked them together. A gong?

The corrugated metal was loud enough as it was, so I didn't try

Sterling G. Mace, the only son of Harry and Harriet: aged three, c. 1927. *(Courtesy of the author)*

Football in Queens! Aged sixteen, c. 1940. I really think I was able to hack the physical exertions of combat in the Pacific because I was so athletic growing up. I certainly loved football . . . but baseball? Baseball was king. *(Courtesy of the author)*

Here I am *(top row, second from the right)*, on the Richmond Hill Dodgers. This local team won the 1938 Jr. championship. That's my good pal, Tommy Colonna *(bottom row, third from the right)*. Note the mismatched uniforms. *(Courtesy of the author)*

The John Adams H.S. varsity baseball team. Right in front of me, sitting, was our Japanese batboy, Tommy O. When I think about the Japanese I've killed it makes me glad that Tommy O was born an American. *(Courtesy of the author)*

Two shitbirds from Yemassee! New recruits hamming it up for the camera, Tommy Colonna and I joined the marines together. Tommy liked basic training. I didn't. While I got Peleliu and Okinawa, Tommy got to play baseball during the war. *(Courtesy of Tommy Colonna)*

Wearing my pith helmet at Hadnot Point, New River, Camp Lejeune. This is after I threw my arm out, playing baseball in Casual Company. The opposing pitcher that day was Dan Bankhead, who wound up with the Brooklyn Dodgers. *(Courtesy of the author)*

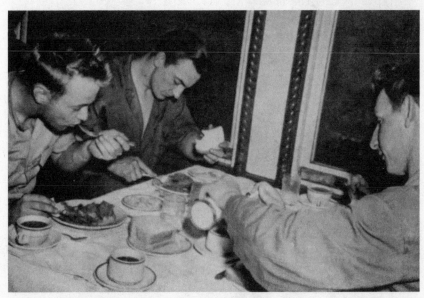

On my way to California *(far left)*. This photo was snapped in the train's dining car, by a Marine Corps photographer. *(Courtesy of Leatherneck Magazine)*

Wearing my "Mortuary Blues." I didn't own these blues. They were cut straight down the back, and you'd slip them on, just like the suits you bury people in. *(Courtesy of the author. Photo restored by Alan Bot)*

PFC. Seymour Levy, service number 540792, the only child of Jacob and Nettie Levy of Brooklyn, New York. A real tough Marine, through and through: a rifleman. *(Courtesy of the author)*

PFC. William Leyden. *(Courtesy of Marie and Brian Leyden)*

I've carried this memento in my wallet every day, since crossing the equator on my way to the war. The ceremonial crossing was pretty racy, to say the least, filled with "bowing before King Neptune" and a special "haircut." But that's a story for another time . . . *(Courtesy of the author and Skip Mace)*

Pavuvu May–August 1944—work parties and more work parties! Behind the workers you can see our tents, the rows of coconut trees, the company streets, and even a speaker affixed to a tree. *(Courtesy of U.S.M.C.)*

Heading into Peleliu! Marines in our amtracs try to get a look at where they're headed . . . and what's coming to them. *(Courtesy of National Archives)*

Get off the beach! Fast! Forget what you've seen in the movies, you don't stay on the beach, and you don't crawl on your bellies. These marines have the idea, while a few more are sighting in. *(Courtesy of National Archives)*

The Marine Corps rifleman: Going into the mangrove, off the beach on Peleliu September 15, 1944. This man is unique in his class and phylum: not susceptible to rot or decay, even in death. "Without my rifle I am useless." *(Courtesy of U.S.M.C./ www.ww2gyrene.com/Mark Flowers)*

PFC. Lawrence Daniel Mahan Jr., service number: 536009, L/3/5. He lived the real Pacific war, with a bullet to the chest as soon as he exited his amtrac. Larry was a very good friend of mine. I hope everyone remembers guys like Larry and what he gave, never asking anything in return. *(Courtesy of Dorothy McCarthy and Family)*

Marine riflemen preparing to move through the jungle after our trip across the airfield. The expression of wariness on their faces is telling of our journey on Peleliu. *(Courtesy of U.S.M.C./ www.ww2gyrene.com/Mark Flowers)*

A marine with a BAR, just like the one I carried, somewhere in the many ridges of Peleliu. Note the swamps in the background. *(Courtesy of National Archives)*

Cpl. Richard Van Trump. I don't imagine he'll ever lose the scars he acquired in the hellhole of Ngesebus. *(Courtesy of Mr. and Mrs. Richard Van Trump)*

PFC. Donald Schwantz.
(Courtesy of Paula Schwantz)

Marines of 3/5 on our way back across the causeway from Ngesebus. The looks on our faces and our body language doesn't tell half the story of the way we felt inside. *(Courtesy of U.S.M.C.)*

Peleliu, October 1, 1944, 3/5 Marines moving back into the lines. I'll never forget that day. *(Courtesy of National Archives)*

Lt. William B. Bauerschmidt, a Silver Star recipient on New Gloucester, was a fine leader who also posed as just one of the guys. *(Courtesy of Mr. and Mrs. Richard Rosendale)*

The watch I took off of one of the Japanese night fighters I killed. I sent it to my mother, and she had a new band put on it. When I told her where I got it, she really didn't feel like wearing it again. *(Courtesy of the author and Skip Mace)*

A view of Peleliu's 1st Marine Division cemetery, which happens to have a marine kneeling in front of a grave you might know. It turns out, however, that the kneeling marine was an actor. You can find dozens of photos with the same marine kneeling in front of crosses. Still, it's the thought that counts. *(Courtesy of Mr. and Mrs. Richard Rosendale)*

A close up of me after Peleliu, from the now famous photo of K/3/5. I'm alive and ready to get the hell off the island. *(Courtesy of the author)*

The photo that tells the rest of the story: The remains of the 3rd platoon, after Peleliu. *(Top row, left to right:)* Steve Collings, Marsdon, unknown, Frank Minkewitz, Toby Paulson, "Hurricane" Hensen, "Zombie," and Jack Baugh. *(Middle row, left to right:)* Roy Kelly, PA Wilson, Jimmy Moore, "Preacher" Wills, and Bishop. *(Bottom row, left to right:)* RD "Blowtorch" Wilson, unknown, Orley Uhls, Gene Holland, Jim McEnery, George Chulis, and Sterling Mace. *(Courtesy of the author)*

The burning of an Okinawan village, in northern Okinawa. Twenty years later the whole world would see similar burnings in another Asian war. *(Courtesy of National Archives)*

The two little Okinawan girls.
(Courtesy of the author)

Moving into southern Okinawa and preparing to attack. Marines are on break, taking in our new surroundings. (Courtesy of National Archives)

Okinawa, May 1, 1945, it seems we riflemen were always attacking across open ground like this, against the Shuri line. The whole ground was zeroed in by the Japanese on the high ground. We really took a beating once we cleared the rise. (Courtesy of National

Marines look on and prepare to attack, on Okinawa, hoping their time isn't next. Radiomen, like the one pictured, would convey information regarding our progress, calling in smoke or spotting for artillery. *(Courtesy of National Archives)*

If you make it across the open ground, like these marines on Okinawa, you take cover pretty quickly and await the next command. Sometimes it seemed like it was all for nothing. *(Courtesy of National Archives)*

Okinawa, May 2, 1945, we were carrying out Sgt. Heeb. Behind us you can see the draw and the embankment we fought up against for days. The marine *(second from the right, at the rear of the poncho)* has been identified as Cpl. Sterling Mace from South Ozone Park, Queens, New York. *(Courtesy of Infantry Journal Press, 1949)*

PFC. Robert "Wimpy" Whitby.
(Courtesy of Mrs. Robert L. Whitby)

On patrol, sniffing out the Japanese, on Okinawa. *(Courtesy of U.S.M.C.)*

Fighting like World War I with the mud and artillery on Okinawa. When the weather changed, it was always wet and miserable. These marines are exactly the way we looked: terrible! *(Courtesy of National Archives)*

A marine takes ten on a Japanese dud on Okinawa. Notice the wear on his boondockers. Notice the size of that shell! One in every three or four shells was a dud. It was one like this that nearly took my life. *(Courtesy of National Archives)*

Back home for good, at George McNevin's wedding. George had been wounded on Peleliu and sent back home. That's me on the left, George in the center, and his brother Arthur on the right. My pal George passed away in 2003. *(Courtesy of the author)*

Sterling Mace, USMC, 1943. *(Courtesy of the author)*

Whatever happened to PFC. Freddy "Junior" Hudson? *(Courtesy of Marlynn Allen)*

to find out. Any slight movement and the sheet rang out like Nippo's phonograph machine.

Oh, to hell with this! I merely tossed it aside. It made one last shimmying sound before it came to rest with the flotsam from which it had originated.

I couldn't imagine that Charlie was too pleased with my efforts, either, but that was alright. Matchsticks would do Allmann just fine. In fact, if Charlie had showed any kind of life whatsoever, I might have had to call a stretcher bearer to come take him away.

"Hey, I think this guy might be dead—he's movin'!"

Gilbert Amdur heard only two things right before he was killed: the sound of his own voice and something heavy thudding against the ground beside him.

"Who's out there? Gimme the password," Amdur whispers into the darkness, greeted only by the sound of nothing in the night. Gilbert waits. He's a nice soft-spoken kid you wouldn't expect to be in the MG section. Gil's not soft, though. He expects to hear the words "Bull Run," which would be the correct response from a marine. Somebody approaches Gil, a shadow slipping up behind his position. Whoever it is, he's as noiseless as he is wordless.

Either out of annoyance or fear, Amdur challenges for the password again. "Goddammit, who's out th—"

Thud.

The Jap grenade explodes right next to Machine Gunner Gil Amdur, killing him before he can register what happened.

The sound of the blast jostles me.

"Corpsman!" The cry pierces the night.

If I'd been looking straight at the explosion I would have lost my night vision. As it is, I merely catch the halo of a flash in the corner of my eye, coming from about forty yards behind Charlie and me where the machine guns are set up. *Fssssss!* There's a red

glow in the night and a sharp thunderclap, and for me it's immediate pins and needles. I'm sharp and alert to the sound of the grenade killing PFC Gilbert Amdur, just as I'm acutely aware that the
action behind us is worse than to the front of us. Like the cowboy
getting shot in the back by the villain, this is not fair play.

"Stretcher bearers, c'mon, you guys!" I swing my rifle around
in the direction of the commotion. The call for stretcher bearers is
a little more moribund than a simple call for a corpsman alone.

I stop myself from saying something to Charlie when I spy two
shadowy figures coming in my direction. Two heads bob up and
down as they steadily trot toward me. I've developed cat eyes now.
Seeing things clearer in the dark is something my eyes have adjusted
to, after spending so much time on this island. A form of necessary
evolution, where previously my eyes would have screamed at me for
trying to pick out something black-on-black, against shade. Now,
however, I can see just about every detail of these figures, with the
exception of . . . *Are these ours or theirs?*

My BAR is leveled straight at these two figures, coming in
closer and closer by the second. The pressure I'm putting on the
trigger is just a tad under letting the whole magazine fly.

"Charlie," I say, "look at that. Do I shoot these or do ya think
those are stretcher bearers?"

I'm seeking words of encouragement from Charlie; in typical
Allmann fashion, they don't come. Charlie raises up to take a look,
but he doesn't say shit. My mind tells me that the two figures can't
be stretcher bearers because they're heading in the wrong direction.
Japs in marine uniforms?

"Christ, Charlie, are those friggin' marines or—?"

The two outlines cut off to the right, toward elements of the
rest of the 3rd Platoon, where Jim McEnery is. This is followed by
peals of small-arms and automatic weapon fire as the company
CP lights up for a few seconds. The noise trails off with a few sporadic shots.

"Dammit, Charlie! Turn around, the bastards are comin' up behind us!"

Thump, thump, thump, thump, thump, thump, thump . . .

I begin to wonder what this new thumping sound is before I quickly realize it's the sound of my heart lightly thrumming in my ears. Lightly, because I'm otherwise calm, when under the circumstances I shouldn't be. I'm operating in a gear I've just now realized that I have within me. I've killed before, but now that the shark has smelled the blood in the water he has no compunctions about doing it again. It's as if every Nip that I wipe from the face of the earth leads me one step closer to making it home again . . . and since I have no qualms about going home again, why should I care about how I arrive there?

"Charlie? Charlie, listen, we must've missed these bastards comin' up here. There's a ballroom fulla those suckers out there, an' they're gonna try an' get through us, sure as shit."

Time passes. Every so often a star shell floats up at the airfield below us, giving us just enough light to see our surroundings. White coral cliffs show up like drawings on a blackboard. Each rock, each pebble on the ground, gets its own shifting shadow, moving clockwise and fading as the star shell fizzes and pops, petering out beyond my view. Every so often I see the figure of a marine or two, hugging the coral, but no Nips. Only darkness or the sickly sameness of artificial illumination from below.

Still, the Japs are coming. There's not just one or two Nips out there, no. These yellow devils run in packs. They're caught behind us, and they're trying to get back to the Five Sisters where the rest of their army congregates. One more thing: They've been watching us this whole time. They watched us when we came down, when we set up, and when we organized ourselves for the night—and they sure as hell won't attack when the night is lit up by star shells. Instead, they'll wait until the lights fade to make their move. That's instinct. That's smart.

Okay, Mace, breathe easy. Wait for it. They'll come right after the next flare.

Suddenly I remember I have a full magazine of tracers in a cartridge pouch, and the last thing I'd want to do is use those rounds at night. So I take it out of my cartridge belt, slowly, and place it on a piece of wood in front of me. Deliberately, I inhale and then exhale.

I'm ready.

Five Japs run straight for me, black pajamas, split-toed sneakers; they all have grenades in their hands.

I can see them!

They are only eight feet away from me when I really put the brakes on 'em. I pull the trigger. Each of my twenty rounds makes a dull flash into the rushing Nips. Chests, stomachs, and faces light up. Some bend back unnaturally as they skid and fall, while others collapse to the side or simply fold inward at the belly. All of them crumple together, touching one another, in a soft cloud of coral dust and the afterglow of my muzzle flash.

Quick! I change magazines and I'm ready again. Scanning, scanning . . . There's the clamor of distant battles on other parts of the island, yet it's all quiet to my immediate front—only the unmoving heap of dead Nips before me. It's then that I realize that Allmann and I are so far on the left flank, this very spot we occupy is where the Nips decided they'd go when it got dark enough to make their move. Charlie and I are probably the closest marines to the Five Sisters—the chink in the armor the Japs were looking for.

"Do you need help over there?" Jimmy yells from somewhere in the area of the CP.

I don't say anything in response to this. *Jesus Christ, you dumb fuck, what the hell you wanna do, give us away?*

Gene Holland is closer to us on the line, however—just a few yards away.

"Mace," he whispers. "Are there Nips out there?"

"Yeah. I can see 'em."

Waiting. Waiting for something. Waiting for another star shell to go up. Waiting for the Japanese to make another run for it. I have no idea if there'll be any more Nips coming, but I'm not taking any chances. I'll stay awake all night if I have to, with my finger right on this trigger. Allmann is right beside me, under a poncho. I think he might be sleeping. If anything else happens I'll make sure I wake him . . .

. . . Up!

Boom! An explosion rocks me awake.

Oh my God, I fell asleep! You can go to sleep without even knowing it, for chrissakes. Just like that.

Another cry for a corpsman goes up. *Thump, thump, thump, thump, thump, thump, thump* . . .

"Someone's hit, who is it?"

Disoriented, I scan down the line where I heard the sound of the blast, and then quickly back out in front of me, my eyes sweeping for Japs again. I can barely shake the wool from my brain, my senses are so weak. To make matters worse, I don't recall this big pile of rocks eight feet in front of my line of sight. *How'd that get there?* I squint at the rocks and then glance back at where some corpsmen are working on a couple of marines up the line a few yards. The acrid odor of a spent grenade still lingers in the air, nearly singeing my nose hairs. The smell brings me back to the real world. *Those aren't friggin' rocks.* Those are the Nips I piled up with my BAR. *How long ago was that?*

I have no concept of time, but I *do* know we only have one wristwatch between us—and we probably paid the price for it.

The word comes over that it's Frankie Ocepek and PFC Bishop who've been wounded by a Nip grenade. Evidently they had fallen asleep. Everyone, like stupid asses, had fallen asleep, including me. Immediately I know it was the wristwatch to blame.

See, the gag is, since this wristwatch only has an hour hand, whoever is on guard will take the watch, wait until his buddy is asleep, and then push the big hand up one hour and advise his buddy that it's time to switch guard. Of course, everyone knows about the infamous "guard watch," so the punch line is, your buddy would do the same thing to you. Nobody gets any sleep.

Oh yes, it's really funny until somebody gets hurt because we're a bunch of clowns with rifles.

Holland asks again, "Are they still here?"

"Yeah, okay!" I yell back. "They're all around us! We gotta stay *awake*, dammit!"

I'm awake and more excited than I've ever been, as if I'm receiving a steady stream of juice from a low-voltage regulator. More wired than on Christmas morning with my Junior Racer Flexible Flyer. More charged than when I got my first kiss at the ballpark. More than when you're getting away with something that you know you shouldn't.

See, the Nips are coming again, and maybe two or three of them got through when they bombed the hell out of Frank and that kid Bishop—when the Japs took the chance to hit the left flank of our line (or didn't get the memo not to). Nevertheless, I've got this niggling feeling again, just like when I knew that hell was coming down before Bauerschmidt and Rice bought it.

Yet it's also a feeling of helplessness. Waiting. The truth is I can't wait to pull the trigger again. My oxygen and my blood, my heart and my breath, are all wrapped up in the power I have in my hands. Who the hell can approach me with this thing I've got blazing away?

All of a sudden, four more Nips run straight for me, almost the way the first five did. I tense up, but then I lay the steady down. Just a simple squeeze of the trigger and these four take the full magazine like the first group; stumbling and skidding, they rupture, spilling out on the coral, deflating as they fall.

I swallow hard and slowly crane my neck to see what I've done. Amazing. Their corpses appear too flat to have been human once. They must have only pretended to be alive just a few seconds ago. All an illusion.

Fast. I change magazines. The ammo slaps in with a click as I immediately begin to sight in again.

The Nips must be either stupid or desperate. Not only do they keep coming on the same route—*don't they see their buddies fall or my friggin' muzzle flash?*—but in order to detonate their grenades, they have to first prime them by hitting them against something hard, e.g., a helmet, the ground . . . their heads? The Nips are not wearing helmets, so they might as well be chunking rocks. Even at that, they're not even throwing them at me. They simply hang on and die.

I just can't figure it out, yet I don't have time to wonder as four more of them come zipping toward me once again, a sickly déjà vu.

Go!

This time, though, when I squeeze the trigger, the whole night lights up in blinding bursts of red and white, pumping the magazine of tracers through my BAR—just the opposite of what I wanted to do. I had put the pack of tracers there for the sole purpose of not touching them, but in a dumb-ass move that's exactly what I grabbed! Oh, but it fires up the Nips, alright: They fall under the stage lights of their lives in dramatic fashion, one atop the other, their pajamas smoldering from getting torched by the phosphorous tips of the tracer rounds. They must be boiling inside. All but one Nip. Despite the stars in front of my eyes, I see him veer off to the right and into a little bush only about eight feet away from me.

Holy shit!

I'm really shaken up now, not only because there's a live Nip a few steps away from me, but also because it was quite a shock to see those tracers shoot out like that.

He's hiding in that bush, my mind whispers.

They had told us to keep a full magazine of tracers ready, in case we ran across a drum of gasoline we had to torch up or something (I might not have been paying attention during *that* lecture). Anyway, these Nips got the rounds instead.

Quietly, I move into position facing the Jap in the bush, positioning my left knee on the ground, with the BAR propped on my right knee: My aim is squarely fixed on where I think the Nip should be.

Just.

Right.

There.

I don't want to move much, let alone breathe . . . but then there's Charlie Allmann. I forgot all about him during this fracas with the Japs. Leaning over ever so slightly, I can barely make out Allmann's face in the darkness. He's still under the poncho, so I take my hand and get it close to Charlie's face, pointing at the bush, and in a voice lower than a whisper I tell Allmann, "He's right there, Charlie. He's right . . . *there,* so keep quiet."

Yet I don't shoot right away. It's fire discipline. What if he's a little off from where I'm aiming and he gets away because I pop off too soon? *All I need . . . all I need, you sonuvabitch, is a noise. C'mon, make a sound and tell me where you're hidin'. Let's hear ya, big boy. C'mon, c'mon, don't let me down, ya slant-eyed fucker.* I've got all the time in the world. Time to kill. The funny thing is, I know I'll get him. I don't think for a moment he's going to nail me. If he's looking for a place to smack his grenade, then he'll give himself away for sure. Probably the worst thing that can happen is that he'll jump out and scare the crap out of me. So all I need is that one sound . . . and he gives it to me . . .

It's only a small scuffing noise, yet just enough for me to know that my aim was dead on the whole time. I squeeze the trigger even before the scuffing noise has faded into the night. All twenty rounds in 2.5 seconds (I don't even recall slapping another magazine in after I'd spent my tracers). No matter, this Jap is now a figment of his own imagination, as if he never existed. Mist and nothing more.

I hear a small voice at my elbow, from underneath the poncho. Charlie Allmann.

"Did you get him?" Charlie asks meekly.

What a stupid question.

My breath is coming back to me. *Oh, Christ!* Maybe I'm more shook up than I realize.

"I'll show you in the morning, Charlie."

I'll show you in the morning . . .

Good night, Charlie. Good night, Peleliu.

Daybreak comes, and the Nip bodies are lying out here for everybody to see. They look like dancers who have collapsed after a long night of revelry. *Yeah, dancers, sure. I had them doing the Big Apple, alright. That must be spilled wine all over their tuxedoes.*

Every marine is too busy with his own worries to worry about mine. No one says, "Hey, good job, Mace." Nobody marvels, "Wow, that's a whole lot o' Nips you killed there!" Maybe nobody notices, because that's not the way things happen in real life. We'd all seen the films *Wake Island* and *The Flying Tigers* before we entered combat, and any illusions of how we imagined battle to be were dispelled as soon as a marine took the first bullet. There's none of this shouting loud orders in combat, or dodging bullets, or waving the boys on. All of that is pure fiction—and there's a reason that the marines who win the big medals are mostly dead when they get them. You've got to do something either incredibly brave or incredibly stupid to get one. Just doing your job doesn't count.

The marines pay me fifty-seven dollars a month, so that's three dollars a day, plus all the chow I don't eat, for the nineteen days I've been on Peleliu. So for every Jap I kill, I estimate that each of their lives is worth less than one cent in American money. That's eight cents for a loaf of bread back in Queens. That's American wartime economics at its greatest.

I'm more curious, however, about the Jap I killed in the bushes, as I slowly make my way over there.

I only have to part the scrub a little to see the Nip propped up in the thicket.

First I only see his right cheek; his head is bowed as if in prayer. His torso is doubled over in the middle, a mangled mess of blood, meat, and dry tripe, where he took all twenty rounds straight to the breadbasket. He clutches a grenade in each hand, a grim testimony to plans gone wrong. This Jap doesn't wear the black pajamas like his buddies. He's got on the typical Japanese khaki, browned over where his blood has stained through. It's not until I move around him, to the other side of his body, that I notice the left side of his face—the side his heart's on—is a sky blue, where the unoxygenated blood became trapped in there, exactly at the moment my bullets pinched him in half. He died instantly. Not that I care either way, though. He's only a study. I can see how taking a full magazine of .30-06 will kill a man, just like that, but what of his brethren? Come to think of it, I haven't seen a Jap in captivity, wounded or otherwise, since I've been on this island. There's a fundamental difference between the way an American dies and a Nip cops it. It's as if the marine, while shot up and bleeding from every orifice, will cling to life with everything he has—hoping against hope—yet the Japanese would rather lie down and die, quietly, than give in to the natural will to live. This is the enemy we live and die with on this sorry island. He has a different concept of heaven and earth, and he'd rather take the former and rot on the latter.

That's fine by me, too. Who am I to argue with the sun and how it rises or sets?

That's all I need to see. No need to rifle around in his pockets for souvenirs. Besides, if this Jap has photos of family or children in his pockets, the sight of living things might make me feel something. I don't want to feel anything. It's better that way.

As I walk away, though, something glints in the morning sun and catches my eye. Something shiny, a glimmer, coming from one of the other Nips I shot during the night.

This Jap's elbow is crooked so that his arm sticks nearly straight in the air, and on his wrist is the shimmering object that attracted my attention. It's merely a wristwatch—yet a very curious one, at that. The only problem is that he's still got the live grenade in his grip. In fact, all the Nips I killed last night didn't drop their grenades as they fell. Curious. They simply clung on to them, as they phased into the next life.

Squatting down to get a good look at the watch, examining it from all angles, I start to plan. *How am I gonna get that friggin' watch off of this guy without setting off his grenade?* Even without the grenade in his hand, I certainly don't want to touch him. They've all got flies rubbing their legs together on their dead flesh—and who knows what other creatures are hatching their larvae inside them.

Even so, a wristwatch, a fellow can always use.

After a few minutes, I manage to attach a little twine to the watch, then scoot back on my heels a ways, until I run out of line. *Careful . . . careful, now . . .* Tugging lightly on the string, I try to make the Jap let go of the bomb. Yet he's not having any of it. This Jap likes the watch too much or he's going to blow us both up either way.

After about a minute or so of this pulling and tugging, however, I've had enough and I merely get up, reach over, and snatch the watch off his wrist and slap it on my mine. *Stubborn bastard!*

No wonder he liked it, though. The watch is probably cheap as hell; nevertheless, it has a lid with a clever little design at the locking mechanism, with a nice clean face and American numbers that really pop out. Written right across the top is SEIKO. It's a military watch, though, for right on the cheap leather band is the star of the Japanese navy or army. I couldn't ask for a better souvenir without sifting through his garments or looking for a thousand-stitch belt. Besides, we are leaving already, and at least for now, I've done my duty.

"C'mon, Mace, we're pulling back a little."

"Sure," I say absently. "One sec."

Before I trot off to catch up with the rest of the guys, I take one final look at the scene of last night's massacre.

I did all that. It's normal. I don't have to look at the corpses for long to know that normally the last thing on somebody's mind after killing a dozen men would be getting some breakfast.

I'm hungry as hell, though.

Where's the breakfast?

9

A CONSTELLATION OF GHOSTS

"... And there's a solid left *hand to the body by Louis, and Conn takes it, rolls off the ropes out into the center! But Louis did not follow up the punch! A bit more action in this round than in the previous two! Conn strong with a left hand into the body! ...*"

We're outside a tent in the bivouac area, and they've got a spam-can (one half of a military two-way wireless radio) in the tent, and we're all lying around listening to a broadcast of the Joe Louis and Billy Conn fight in New York.

The heat is still unbearable, which makes the fight a fever dream rolling in on an alien shore. I don't care anymore. I don't care about anything anymore.

"*... Conn is very wary in there! He's gotten wary all of a sudden! ...*"

This is the point where every day it's two or three marines getting killed, and I just don't want to hear about it. Then when you think it's all over, it's one more marine dying.

PFC Alden Moore, KIA.

PFC George Parrett, KIA.

PFC Clarence Morgan, KIA.

"... *There's Louis getting away from a left jab shot at his chin by Conn! Conn, his guns down by his side. Time's running out in this round* ..."

The day before, the Louis and Conn fight we were coming down from the Five Sisters, making the thousand-yard trip out of Death Valley and back toward the bivouac area near the airfield.

We were slugs in marine uniforms: Listless, bone-weary, heads lolling on our shoulders—I'm sure that some of us were walking in our sleep. You could take a look in your buddy's eyes and there was no life in them. The tiny capillaries in the eyes became magnified. They bulged out as if they were stuffed with every nightmare we had seen on this island to date. So if the eyes are the windows to the soul, then there was no soul in there either. We sacks of bone, blood, and muscle, we're merely going through the motions of living ... and it will happen ... something will inevitably stop that activity, too. It was only a matter of time; and time was running out ...

Just over the last rise in the coral I heard an explosion and saw the smoke, only about thirty yards away parallel to me and three other marines. Then came a clamor and a call for a corpsman, yet our company kept moving. Nobody stopped, just those in the immediate area.

"... *There's Louis taking a left jab on the chin, and LOUIS IS DOWN FROM A RIGHT CROSS TO THE CHIN! CONN FLOORED LOUIS, WHO GOT UP WITHOUT ANY COUNT! LOUIS GOT UP QUICKLY! Here's Conn driving a right to the chin! Again, Louis has been on the floor! Time is running out in the round, about twenty-five seconds remaining!* ..."

Some guys began stripping the body of whatever marine was

killed over there: Gear, ammo, socks, his souvenirs, whatever they could use.

I hailed a Marine who had just come from that area. "Say, who got it back there?"

"Oh, yeah, some Polish kid and Baxter."

"Nippo?"

"Yeah, Nippo. Mortar round came right in and *splat!* Killed Nippo and wounded the other guy. A real mess."

I didn't look back. I simply kept walking.

Besides, I don't think there's anything left to say.

"*. . . Conn, coming in on Louis, and Louis driving a right to the chin and Conn scoring with a left high on the head! Here's Conn taking a left hook to the chin and driving a right to the jaw of Joe Louis! And the fireworks, so much talked about, are here! . . .*"

October 6, 1944.

We're at the bivouac area listening to a fight happening so far away. The fight is a real treat, despite the feelings and thoughts of home it gives you. I can't help but think of how we used to sit in parked cars in front of Ben Goldman's candy shop on 124th Street and listen to boxing on car radios. They are pleasant thoughts, but not ones I want to have here where I can be killed.

"*. . . Louis scores with a left hook on the chin, a right over the head by Conn, who's very wild! And now they go into a clinch, one of the few clinches in the fight so far. Time almost up in this round, Conn short with a right hand . . . the bell . . .*" Zztt!

Some marine walks up and snaps off the spam-can. First there's a shocked silence, then the whole audience yells about it.

"Hey, what the hell's goin' on here?"

"Yeah, buddy—what's your fuckin' problem?"

"Turn it back on, dipshit, we're gonna miss the friggin' fight!"

"Hey, keep your shirts on, ya dopes," the marine says to us. "There is no fight, okay? This whole thing—"

"The hell you say!"

"—the whole fight is a *sham*," he continues. "Coupla guys in L Company are just foolin' around with a spam-can of their own. One of 'em's callin' the fight an' the other one's hissin' into the can like it was crowd noise. Saw 'em on the way up here."

We laugh and shake our heads in disbelief. Not even a good time is what it seems on Peleliu.

"Well, I'll be a sonuvabitch!"

"Hey, yeah, whatcha think of that, Mace, sounded good, huh?" Gene Holland grins at me.

It's the first good laugh I've had in days. "Yeah, right, only wish I had thought of it first, not a coupla limpdicks from L Company. Had *me* fooled."

McEnery walks up with a big smile on his face. "An' ya know, I shoulda known better. Goddamn Conn and Louis both joined the friggin' service! Ain't a chance in hell they'd be fightin' each other."

"No foolin', Jim?" Gene looks up.

"Yeah, no shit. That's gotta be the best chisel ever, fellas."

It was, too. I don't know what tomorrow will bring, but for now this is just what we needed: Fun-loving American ingenuity at its slyest.

Our artillery has been pounding into the Japanese-held cliffs for hours now: the Five Sisters and the Five Brothers, heading up the mouth of the Horseshoe, shooting the heavy stuff right down their throats. The earth warbles beneath our feet. With each shell that lands in the battered cliffs, large black spirals of smoke touch the sky, accented by fiery orange balls of flame in the center. Jagged chunks of coral and dust rain down in the air, only to be lifted up again by the next explosion, and the next, and the next. The debris from the explosions never seems to touch the earth. The finer particles just hover there, where they can't seem to make up their mind whether to float like clouds or settle into the valley.

The hope is that when we go up the cliffs again, we'll go up walking on Nip corpses.

We move up the Horseshoe, the infantry at a snail's pace, staying well behind the barrage and the tanks ahead of us. If there was ever a time to be a combat fatigue victim, this would be the perfect time to do it. It's nerve-scathing, to be sure. I can almost see the air move in great heated shocks toward us, giant ripples in a pond, a palpable rush of wind. It must be a souvenir hunters' paradise up the cliffs, because all I can imagine is our bombardment rattling the gold teeth right out of the Japs' jaws.

Allmann says something to me, but I can only see his mouth move; I can't hear a thing he's saying.

"Whaaaaat?" I ask. I can't hear myself either.

The eyes water at the constant hum of the largest tuning fork in the world being set off by my ear. I grit my teeth and it hurts to do so. It's better to let the mouth hang slack rather than create a conduit for the noise to rack the body. I even let my BAR rest as gently in my hands as possible, despite the desire to hang on to it for dear life.

By the time the artillery stops, however, the tanks start firing into caves—or anything that *looks* like a cave (you can never be too sure), and although the tanks are not nearly as noisy as the heavy stuff, they still grate on the senses.

Our job is to cover the tanks in case the Nips try any funny business. If they come out and make for the tanks, we shoot them. If they head higher up the cliffs, we shoot them. If the Nips get cute and try charging us, we laugh—and then shoot them.

Thank God there's not a Jap in sight. The demo marines and flamethrower operators are rushing up in short spurts, doing their jobs, sealing or searing up the caves, and then they move back again. All the while we have our weapons trained on the porous cliffs for any movement. It's actually amazing to watch all the marines work in perfect conjunction. It's a symmetry that would make me proud, I'm sure, if I weren't too occupied with my own job. First the artillery and mortars tenderize the area, then the tanks concentrate on smaller pockets, as the demo teams and flamethrowers seal up what's left, and all the time they are getting covered by us, the riflemen. It works. If there's a single marine casualty, I don't see one. Conversely, I don't see a single dead Nip either. Yet that's the thing about this whole operation. I know we've killed loads of Japanese. In fact, the whole island reeks of the dead more than ever. Their bodies are everywhere, still piled up in putrefying heaps. Where they come up with these figures of 75 killed this day, and 111 killed this day, I don't know. None of us have seen a bespectacled marine going around with a little notepad and a stub of a pencil tallying up the Nip dead. Even if such marines exist, when all the Nips look the same, how does he know he hasn't counted the same one twice, or even a dozen times, as the Japs change from blue to black under the hardness of the sun? Moreover, when we seal up a cave, how do you know how many Japs were in there—if any? I've never seen marines unsealing a cave to find out.

The truth is, I don't think they know much about this island. Not when we landed. Not right now. Not what the future will hold. It's been the longest three days in the history of mankind—and if they don't know about the five skeletal remains of marines going up the Five Sisters, how the hell are they going to know when to get us off this island?

On the move again. Somebody with stars on his shoulders must have hit the map room, because we're doing something we've never done before. This time we make a short move up the West Road and then a sweeping turn, the whole regiment, toward the east side of the island.

Add this marching to the list of miseries on already miserable bodies. I remember how the 1st Marines looked to us when they staggered onto Purple Beach. Like a rattle of rats. Now we look like them, but rolled in flour, dusted over by the coral on the road.

"Say, Gene," I say, "ya know where we're headed?"

Holland drops the canteen from his lips and wipes his mouth with a grimy shirtsleeve. Screwing the top back on, he squints up at the sun and then looks back at me. "No, I don't have a fucking clue where we're goin'. Do you?"

"Yeah . . . I do. We're gonna hit those ridges from the north. We're goin' south. Sure as shit we are." I adjust the strap of my BAR on my shoulder, trying to find a spot that's not raw.

"Yeah? So where'd ya hear that dope?" Gene is a smart marine, a good guy and a quick study—not much goes over his head—but Gene's also been trying to work an angle to get out of here without letting his buddies down.

"No dope," I say. "We've been bustin' our balls up against the same crap every day. Same results. Fuckin' Corsairs droppin' that napalm shit all over the Nips. What've we got? Artillery, navy . . . tanks? Nah, we're coming up their asses this time an' see if they don't feel it."

Gene chuckles. "Oh yeah? Ya think they'll feel it?"

I've never been a know-it-all, nor one to spread half-baked scuttlebutt. Nevertheless, call it simple, or even unoriginal—whoever or whatever I am—I always figured that if I just do my job in combat the rest will take care of itself. So far I've been right. At this moment, despite that I don't want to reexamine the concept of hope, I have almost a sixth sense that things are going to be over soon. I don't want to dwell on it. Anyway, if it takes ramming our way up the backside of the rising sun so that we can watch it set? Then that's what 3/5 will do to make it happen.

"Oh yeah? Ya think they'll feel it?"

For a moment I think about it and then get back with Holland.

"Hell, if they don't feel it, Gene, *we* sure as hell will."

Nobody's home. The back door is wide open, and that's what's really scary.

Up there on the ass side of the cliffs I finally realize the ultimate paradox of combat: When you're surrounded by the enemy, you feel alone as can be. Yet when there's nobody home, it suggests that all their guns are pointed straight at your heart.

Cautiously we move from cave to cave, our weapons scanning the mouth of each hole in the rocks as if it's filled with a thousand Nips. Occasionally a marine pops off a few rounds into a cave entrance, jittery, unbelieving that we're actually alone up here. It's nerve-racking just to know what *could* happen, but the dead Nips in the area let us know exactly what did.

We're in a graveyard of what the battle used to be. We dug the graves, but we don't know who to fill them with.

"Where do ya think the Nips are, Jim?" I ask McEnery. McEnery has the same look of cautious confusion written on his face as the rest of us (what remains of the squad, that is).

"Dunno," Jim says. "Not here. But still . . ."

He doesn't have to finish. I know what he's thinking. Either things are as they seem and there are no live Japs up here, or they're all over the place and this is a trap. That's the rub: We don't rely on our intellects or gut feelings. Neither do we hang our helmets on the five senses. We live only in the "but still . . ." realm of thought. It's not a realm civilians would understand. Not unless they've been here—and they haven't. I'm not even going to explain it.

That's when I realize that this really is over. We're not going to lose any more marines. We're going to make it.

———

All except for Lieutenant Hillbilly Jones and PFC Chas McClary.

We're close to the West Road, and it seems that some rear echelon shitheads from company headquarters got a case of "jungleitis" and decided it was safe enough to go souvenir hunting close to Sniper Alley. (Jungleitis only affects those marines who've been sitting on their asses behind the lines too long. With their ears to the grapevine, when they hear it's safe to come out of their holes, they get the itch to venture out into a combat zone, so that they can regale their sweethearts and folks back home with daring stories of how they slew a Nip to get his sword, or a Jap flag, or photos of the dead man's family. Or maybe it's that they don't want to feel as worthless as they actually are, when it comes to proving what salty marines they are. Whatever the case, jungleitis is a common affliction toward the end stages of any battle.)

Soon there comes a cry for help.

"Say, what do ya think those jokers are up to?" Allmann points out a couple of marines running back from the West Road in a cloud of dust toward the bivouac area. These marines are unarmed, and they appear comical the way they're really moving, taking constant looks back over their shoulders the whole way.

"C'mon, Charlie, show some respect, willya?" I rib Allmann. "That's the Marine Raider Battalion, fresh off patrol. They just, ya know, do everything really fast, those guys."

A few of us have found a place in the shade where we can sit for a while, smoking, eating, simply waiting for more orders to come down the pipe—hopefully something that brings us close to the rear, because coming out of those empty cliffs was just too creepy; we've earned a break. Nonetheless, sitting on our butts like this, it almost feels as if we're "Marine Raiders," too. It's a nice respite, despite the heat and the shouts of our mortar fire slapping into the cliffs.

You're not outta the woods yet, Goldilocks.

About fifty yards away, the 1st Platoon is set up by some tanks, and they appear to be simply idling there as well.

Quickly, a jeep drives past us and then careens off to the right, headed in the direction of 1st Platoon.

"Say, that was a major in that jeep, wasn't it?"

"Yep. Headquarters, looks like."

It's Major Clyde Brooks, USMC, in the jeep; what he's doing here nobody will say, but we know the score better than anybody. HQ doesn't go anywhere near the front lines, but it seems that some of the major's little chicks got their feathers ruffled and Brooks is here wanting us to find the fox who did it.

That's the stupidity of how Hillbilly Jones and McClary get killed. All because of a couple of stupid shits with jungleitis, wanting to prove the improvable, as gung ho marines.

"Come on, you guys, get your shit together." Sergeant McEnery walks up to us, his tommy gun slung over his shoulder. "Lieutenant Jones asked for a little support over there. Sniper's got this place crawlin'."

Holland looks like he's about to pass out over this order. "Oh, Christ, Jim! Because of those assholes from headquarters? Let 'em get killed, serves 'em right!"

"Gene . . ." McEnery doesn't know what to say. You can tell Jimmy doesn't believe in this mission either. "Gene, just get your weapon and come on." Jim walks off.

Holland looks at me as if I can do something about it. "Ya know we're not goin' to see a single fuckin' Nip up there. You know that, right?"

So 3rd Squad sets up about thirty yards from 1st Platoon and the tanks. We pretend to look for "snipers." Pretend because Gene is right. Just like the day when Teskevich was killed on the tank, there's no way of telling where the Japs are hidden along the road and in the cliffs. The Nips only shoot in the daytime, when the sun is too bright, and you can see neither their muzzle flashes nor the smoke spewing from their rifles.

"Hey, what is that guy doin'?"

Amazingly a marine climbs atop one of the tanks, potentially exposing himself to a Nip riflemen.

"I dunno," I say. "Must be a mortar spotter, but the marine's gonna get himself killed if he don't watch out."

No sooner do the words come out of my mouth than the marine falls from the tank.

Dammit! It is a sick sight to watch. I look for even the smallest puff of smoke anywhere in the vicinity, but nothing.

Then, to our surprise, the fallen marine gets back up and starts climbing up the side of the tank again, waving off the corpsmen who had collected by the tank's treads.

"Hey, maybe he just fell off on his own the first time." I'm too far away to really tell.

"Either that or this is one loony marine."

The marine is only atop the tank's turret for about two seconds, tops, when he topples again and hits the ground in a small fan of coral dust. He doesn't get back up. And here I am rooting for this guy, as if he had a chance in hell, after giving himself the best seat in the house.

All for nothing. If a single Nip is killed up here it's only because one of the mortarmen or one of our tanks got lucky. Otherwise, the only dead Japs in this area are the skeletal remains of the ones they bulldozed to the side of the road two weeks ago.

The real irony, on the other hand, is that if our illustrious Marine Raiders wanted souvenirs, they would've had to rummage through the skeletons of the dead Nips who had already been picked over by marines who had come this way dozens of times before them. The little turds from headquarters would have come away with nothing at all. Nothing for nothing. Now there are two more dead riflemen, who reached up for a hook in the sky and tumbled back to earth for a big nothing.

There is nothing more for us to do here. We simply leave.

Walking to the bivouac area, we hear that Lieutenant Jones was the marine who was killed on the tank, and some kid from the 1st Platoon, McClary, bought it in the same area, either right before or after Jones. Somewhere along the way they bring Hillbilly Jones's body down to the aid station, shortly before we walk up. We had already lost our lieutenant. Now it's the 1st Platoon's turn.

At the aid station I see Corporal Ted "Tex" Barrow, from Kemp, Texas, standing over a dead marine reposing on a stretcher at the side of the aid station. The dead man is covered with a poncho.

"Say, Tex, is this Hillbilly here?" I ask him.

"I don't know." Tex shrugs. "I guess so."

I reach down and lift up the poncho at the head of the stretcher, exposing only the face of the dead marine underneath. It's Jones, alright. I stand right behind his body, looking down at his face. His face is perfectly set in an attitude of calm and ease. There's not a blemish on him, yet his skin gives off a clammy sheen, as if the last beads of sweat his body produced had not finished drying in death. The only thing I'm really drawn to, though, is that his nose appears slightly skewed—broken at one time, perhaps playing football or boxing in high school.

"Yeah, that's him," I say, to no one in particular.

I don't know why I felt compelled to lift the tarp. I just did. It could have been me lying on the stretcher, gazing down on myself, dead, and I would have felt just the same. Nothing.

Now, you can do a lot with the wooden coffins they use to transport dead marines in, besides burying them in the 1st Division cemetery on Peleliu. In the case of the outpost off the West Road, they've turned several of these coffins upside down and then, with a circular saw, cut three holes in the underside of each box, packing dirt around the sides of them so the smell won't leak out, and voilà! A place for marines to take a crap. That's not where the amenities end, either.

After we come around a little bend on the West Road, on the Lobster Claw of the island, we see part of the 3rd Platoon already situated in a small patch of jungle on our left, where the army had cleaned out a place for themselves weeks before. The marines there are even making pancakes, sitting around drinking clean water and waving. Then, fifteen or twenty yards past them, we come up to another cleared-out area with a high hill to our right, and in a wide open space farther to the right of the bend, and up a little rise, is a fortress (or, not to give the wrong impression, at least it seems like a fortress to me).

This fortress is at least seven and a half feet tall, with wooden posts holding up a sandbagged top, and below that is a square-cut hole in the ground, about seven feet square and six feet deep. So if we jump into the fort, it looks like we can hold off the whole Japanese army with a bunker like this. It has an entrance, which you don't have to go through to use, and a machine-gun emplacement, which covers the whole area perfectly. To the sides are ready-made foxholes, and then down a little slope there looks to be a spot where the mangrove has been bulldozed out, nice and clean. They could have parked four of five trucks in this large, sheared-out area abutting the jungle. That's where they set up the three-holed crapper made out of coffins.

"Holy shit!" Corpsman Chulis says. "Did we wake up on another island or somethin'?"

"Wow! Wouldja look at this? Didn't I tell ya no more fightin'?"

We settle in. Jimmy and I go into the fort, where for the first time the coolness of the earth and the overhead sandbags impart the closest thing to real shade we've felt since we've been on the island. Everywhere else we've gone we've merely experienced subtle increments of hot and hotter.

McEnery takes off his helmet and props his tommy gun in the corner, and immediately he lays claim to one of the cots in the bottom of the bunker by stretching his stinking body out on it.

He closes his eyes and lets out a long sigh. "Oh, this is so good."

Taking off my helmet, too, I lean up against the inside of the bunker and rub my fingers through my hair, shaking out the crap: bits and pieces of foreign matter that's been lurking near my scalp for days now. The skin on my head feels slick with a thin layer of some sort of gunky matter.

I look at Jim. "Yeah, but ya know, Jim, if we've got a bungalow like *this* . . . ? Imagine what kinda CP Haldane and Stanley and them got."

"Ya know, Mace"—McEnery lolls his head toward me and opens one eye—"imagine if you talk too friggin' much."

A real funny guy, that McEnery.

As I'm about to leave, Jim calls out to me. "Oh yeah, and if you see that Greek, Chulis, tell him to come on down, willya?"

"Sure thing, Jim," I say. "I'll tell him you've got a football game goin' on down here and he gets to play center. That should do it."

By early afternoon Jimmy and Corpsman Chulis are piss drunk from a bottle of sake they were adventurous enough to drink. We passed up so many of these corked bottles of sake on the island, because the brass told us not to drink them. The scuttlebutt was that the Nips had poisoned their liquor, claiming that we Americans were nothing but a lot of bloodthirsty drunks, imbibing anything fermented, be it grain, rice, potato, or catnip, if you could get enough sauce out of it. That, of course, is a lie (for everyone except Jimmy and the Greek).

Nevertheless, poison or not, the last thing we need is to go on a bender with the Nips breathing down our napes.

We're safe here, though. It's real good. It's even real funny when McEnery and Chulis begin dancing together.

Arms locked, legs flying, up and down the two drunks bend and gyrate. Whatever half-in-the-bag dance they're performing is a wild mixture of the Greek Kalamatianós, the Russian Cossack dance, and the plain ol' American Turkey Trot. Around and around they spin, sake sloshing out of the bottle they pass between themselves, while Chulis punctuates the dance with roisterous attempts at carrying a melody between slobbery lips.

"Jesus, Sterl, look at 'em go!" Holland beams at me.

"Yeah, ya know what I think, Gene?" I've got a smile of my own. You just can't help it, even here. Everyone is grinning, except for maybe Allmann—who wouldn't know a smile from a bucktoothed Chink.

"I think we've been on this island for too goddamn long, Holland!"

It's a real riot until the shit hits the fan.

"Hey, Nips! Nips!" One of Pappy Moore's marines comes running up the slope toward us, trying to pull his dungaree pants up, looking as if he's about to trip on the pants if he doesn't get them over his hips quick enough. He's sprinting from the direction of the shitboxes.

Instinctively I reach out for my weapon, as if my BAR's right beside me—but it's not. It's in the bunker with all my other gear. *Dammit!*

Another marine runs up to the guy who sounded the alarm and holds him by the shoulders. "Wait, wait, wait . . . hold on, hold up, buddy . . . what's goin' on? Nips where?"

The first marine bends over double, with his hands on his knees, trying to catch his breath. "Down there," he says. "I was . . . I was, ya know, takin' a crap, when alluva sudden I hear this moanin' . . . and *Christ!* I look around an' there's a live Nip right behind me—in the mangrove—just layin' there moanin' an' groanin'. Scared the shit outta me!"

At this a couple of marines chuckle and wink at each other.

The second marine asks, "He still there?"

"Hell, I hope not!" the first marine replies, rebuckling his belt. His cheeks are clearly flushed with excitement as well as a little hint of embarrassment.

Soon two armed marines cautiously head down the slope. We don't have to wait long until they return with one of the most pitiful sights I've seen on Peleliu.

They've got a Nip with them, one marine carrying him by the back of his black pajama collar while the other marine totes him by the waist of his britches—or, closer to the fact, the two marines carry what amounts to a human matchstick, swathed in tattered raiments.

"Hey, put him over here. Over here," a marine says, and they drop the Nip in the dirt right by our fort. Everyone crowds around just to steal a peek at him.

The Jap is more than a mere curiosity to me, however. To me, he's the first live Japanese I've seen that isn't trying to kill me . . . and I'm not trying to kill him. In fact, he's a human being, despite my mind telling me otherwise. I see him and immediately realize he's on his way out of this world.

As a matter of fact, he's the most emaciated, sickly-looking thing I've seen in my life. From his close-cropped hair, pushed down on his forehead, to his obsidian marble eyes, he lies there, in an awkward heap, bent in ways that would make a contortionist tremble. I can only imagine what's going through his mind, how we marines must appear horrid, hovering over him as we are. For God's sake, his muscles appear to be mere tendons; his bones have a fragile birdlike quality beneath his paper-thin skin. It's a wonder he can even move, though he manages to bring his fingers to his lips, miming that he wants a cigarette. His face is asking and anguished. His eyes never appear to blink, and his mouth hangs slack, showing off a perfect row of yellowed Asian teeth.

"Oh my God, what do ya think happened to this guy?" a marine asks.

"I don't know," I say. "Looks like he wants a smoke, though."

A marine gives him a cigarette and lights it for him. The Jap takes two puffs off it, drops it aside, and then goes through the motion of asking for another one. So we give him another one . . . and then the same thing: Two puffs and he drops the smoke. It's a curious thing to do; we don't care. We squat around him, and everyone genuinely feels sorry for him. We even want him to pull through.

The only thing that we can gather is that this Nip had been hiding out in the mangroves since D-day, just waiting to take his shot, but for whatever reason, his chance never came. So as the days went by and the area got cleaned out and situated, the Jap just lay out there, scared or ashamed to go back to his unit, content to die at the edge of the mangrove, until we came along and rescued him. Fat chance of a rescue, though.

After we've ogled the Jap awhile, the highest-ranking officer remaining, Lieutenant Charles "Duke" Ellington from the mortars, comes over to see what's going on—to figure out what to do with the Nip. Ellington brings with him an interpreter, but from the looks of things the interpreter doesn't get two words out of this sorry creature.

"Well . . ." Ellington sighs. "Let's at least get the poor devil off the ground and get him on a stretcher or something." Evidently Duke hears that McEnery has a cot, so he goes over to the entrance of the fort and calls down for Jim to bring up a stretcher.

Duke waits for a few minutes, and when nothing happens he goes back to the bunker and asks again.

This time, though, he gets a curt answer from McEnery. "No."

Whatever is going through Ellington's mind at the moment, he doesn't show it. Basically, Ellington was just told to go to hell by a sergeant. Yet, in a situation like this, there's not even any face to save. What is Duke going to do, run Jimmy up on charges and take him to the brig? Over a Jap who's probably going to die anyway? Besides, the fact is, with Bauerschmidt killed, Rigney killed, and Spiece wounded, Jimmy is the highest-ranking marine the 3rd Platoon can find. Just a sergeant, and most of our fire team leaders are gone, too.

Duke's no dummy, and as the leader of the mortar platoon, he realizes he's out of his element among riflemen—it's simply not worth it. Still, Jim was insubordinate. Yet they take the Nip away, as is, no questions asked.

"Boy, that McEnery's got some nuts talking to Duke like that." Jack Baugh shakes his head.

"Yeah, and if Duke knew he was drunk, he would've run Jim up on a drumhead, nuts and all."

Later we find out that the Jap died on his way to the company CP. He must have been ready.

We really hated to hear that.

Back on the line. October 12, 1944. D-day +27.

When you're a kid, they make you read in the history books about all these famous battles that ended in big cavalry charges, great bloodbaths, and climactic clashes that changed the course of wars and indelibly changed the lives of the men who fought them. Names like Waterloo, Thermopylae, the Little Big Horn, and York-town ring down through the ages as final conflicts, which ended with such big bangs that little men with pen and paper have spent their whole lives edifying the sacrifice, the glory, the human trag-edy, and the necessity of the thousands of men who fought for their lives in those battles. Their guts spilled out on foreign soils, gagging on their blood, dying in their own excrement, the men who fought those battles never knew that their lives would one day be reduced to mere words in a schoolchild's eyes—and in turn, those children themselves would one day fight in battles with equally strange names, like Tarawa, Guadalcanal, and Ngesebus.

Peleliu does not end with a bang. Instead it dies with a whimper. There are no great defining moments, no last *Banzai* charge from the Japanese, and no bloody stories to tell. History is doomed to fail itself.

In fact, we're on the line on October 12, 1944, when Peleliu has been deemed "secure" by the brass. In effect, they say it's over. Yet we're still here.

The truth is, if there is any last bang to the battle of Peleliu, it is for our company CO, Captain Andrew Haldane, and the poor suckers like us who have climbed one last hill on Peleliu only to face death in a very different way. It's as if they had to invent a new way to kill us when the Japanese were not enough to finish the job.

This dung heap, Hill 140, is the last dumb analogy to how Peleliu ended for us in the middle weeks of October 1944. We climb, climb, climb . . . fight, fight, fight, only to reach the summit of the biggest gag since "Three days and this will all be over."

Atop Hill 140, not only are there no Japanese, but we were also told to relieve some marines on the hill . . . and when we get here, there is only emptiness and waste, no marines.

A lone airplane, a U.S. Kingfisher—the type of small pontoon plane a battleship catapults off the back of its fantail—circles above us in near-silence. It's a funny-looking little aircraft, with skinny legs angling down into big pontoons for feet, but it's also majestic. It's beautiful not because it's a great bird of war, but beautiful because there are no Japanese trying to knock the little gnat from the sky. Such a slow target as that would surely be a luscious target, even for a lone Nip rifleman.

"Say, would ya get a load of that guy? What's on this jerk's mind?" A marine nods up toward the plane. "Must be a big ship nearby or something, ya reckon?"

"Probably," I say. Then I see the pilot's arm come over the edge of the cockpit. "Look at that! He's waving at us!"

There's something curious about the pilot's arm, though. "What's that he's got in his hand?"

"What?" Marines look up and shield their eyes from the sun.

"Shit! That's a gun!"

"*What?*"

Before we can scramble, we hear the dull thud of a slug thumping the ground nearby, and then the pop of a small-caliber handgun.

"Christ, the dumb sonuvabitch is shootin' at us!"

Thump! Thump! A few more slugs smack the ground, way too close to where they might actually hit somebody.

"What'sa matter with this dumb fuck?!"

"Hey, hey, we're marines, ya stupid ass!"

A few of the guys look like they are about to bring their rifles to their shoulders and shoot back at the Kingfisher, but they don't, despite it taking all their effort to hold themselves back. We are simply so accustomed to retaliating when fired upon. At the same time, however, we also don't want to kill anymore, especially an American. Besides, if we fire on the Kingfisher, who knows, he might call in a whole barrage of artillery from the ships, dead on our coordinates.

Other marines jump up and wave their helmets, and we all shout as loud as we can for the pilot to peel off, we are not Japs!

One more slug hits the ground before the pilot finally gets the message and slowly veers off, heading back over the water. I don't feel sorry for the pilot, but I'm sure the guy felt like a real heel when he realized he mistook us for Nips.

"Goddammit!" Jimmy throws his helmet down in disgust. "As if we didn't have enough!"

Jimmy speaks for all of us—even Charlie Allmann, who doesn't have anything to say. I don't think Charlie has fired his weapon the whole time we've been here. Charlie Allmann, from Colby, Wisconsin, just sits on the coral, his face in his hands, preferring the darkness to whatever runs wild in the real world.

For the marine in combat, however, ignorance is the closest shot toward the victim known as bliss.

When we come down from the hill, the evening of the twelfth, we hear that our company commanding officer, Captain Andrew "Ack Ack" Haldane, was killed earlier in the day. *Bang!* He took one right through the head like Levy.

I don't think very many marines know what really led up to Haldane getting killed. We hear all sorts of scuttlebutt, but since every marine claims he was right there when Haldane bought it, the picture is a little unclear.

The word is Haldane was on an unfamiliar ridge with a few of the sergeants, trying to register in a machine gun over difficult terrain, when he poked his head up—only for a second to get his bearings—and a Nip rifleman just drilled one through his cranium.

It sounds about right.

Since D-day we had already lost a lot of brass. Lieutenant John "Moose" Barrett, from 1st Platoon, bought it early in the fight, our own Lieutenant Bauerschmidt, up on the Five Sisters, Lieutenant Hillbilly Jones, and Captain Smith, the L Company CO, got it—and now K Company's CO is killed as well. I might sound callous, but in light of all that, how am I supposed to care? It's sad, sure, when any marine is killed; nevertheless, once it's done, there's nothing more that anybody can do about it. Even if I had known Haldane well, my tears wouldn't bring him back to life, as if we were living in some sort of fairy-tale world. I met the captain once, and he was the sort of guy who seemed to genuinely care for even the lowliest marine. A marine can appreciate and respect that. On the other hand, it takes marines who are always hanging back by the company CP to really moan about a guy they've had a love affair with every day. I didn't have that sort of luxury, so my eyes are dry.

"Well." Gene eases himself down beside me. "Shame about Haldane, ain't it?"

"Sure is," I say. "A swell marine."

Gene thinks for a moment and then says, "Hey, don't that make Stumpy our new CO?"

"Christ, you're right." I let that digest. It's sort of funny. "Well, at least the thing about Stumpy Stanley—he don't have a chance at gettin' it if he never gets outta the goddamn CP, huh?"

Gene whistles. "Ain't that a fact."

It *is* a fact. A much more acceptable fact would be not losing any more marines, rather than just knowing whose voice was going to be the next one to lead us from the comfort of a foxhole and a spam-can. At least Haldane wasn't that sort of marine. He's just a dead one, is all.

Semper Fi.

On October 15, 1944, after thirty days of combat, K Company, 3rd Battalion, 5th Marines, was finally taken off the line, holding the distinction of being the last 1st Marine Division unit to see combat on Peleliu.

Since October 12 we had played witness to massive bombardments of the cliffs in the Umurbrogol Mountains, napalm runs by our navy and marine planes, and the destruction of countless Japanese weapons, supplies, and corpses, in the attempts to lay waste to the last Nips still holding out on Peleliu.

"Hell, this is what they should've done in the first fucking place!" Bomb it out. Destroy it. Kill the earth.

Hollow-eyed, we watched the shelling belt into the terrain, in sheets of fire so hot you couldn't imagine anything could live through such a conflagration. Numb and uncaring, our nerves no longer winced as witnesses to the pain.

In a dreamlike trance, if they had asked to us to march into the belly of the cauldron to our front, we would've had no qualms about doing it.

What's one more flame to marines who are already creatures of ash and soot inside?

Instead, they pulled us off the line. We headed to a newly constructed bivouac they told us was dubbed White Beach.

So they marched us just a short stroll from the area with the fortress, around the bend and onto the West Road, then another hundred yards down and to the right, between the West Road and the Pacific Ocean, and there was White Beach. It was as lovely to us as the name sounded.

The whole area was about the size of two tennis courts, with a smattering of palm trees—a few of them standing and a few of them fallen and twisted from taking some shells at one time or another—the entire scene surrounded by clean beach sand. Pretty as a picture.

As we came down to White Beach, however, there was nothing pretty about us.

Our faces were grimy and caked with sweat, dirt, and flecks of coral, as well as being heat-blasted from explosions and the rays of the sun. Light to heavy beards itched on our faces, clotted with filth and sand fleas. We were sunburned and raw on our shoulders, in the crooks of our elbows and knees, and on our feet. Our boondockers were shredded in the leather and shaved off at the soles, to the point where they were almost disintegrating. Some of us no longer even had dungaree jackets, but for those who did, their jackets were begging for the fire. Most of our dungaree pants were torn at the knees and split at the bottoms; our leggings were either missing or plastered to our legs like casts. All of our dungarees were tinted white with perspiration and coral dust. Not only were they stiff to the touch, but they also inflamed the skin beneath them, rubbing the legs sore, inciting ingrown hairs on the tops of our thighs, where the material rubbed the flesh—scraping like sandpaper anywhere that was tender and apt to fester. Scabs fell off and then grew back again, never quite healing because of the constant cycle. Our hands ached and were cracked at the knuckles. Overly long fingernails were chipped and packed full with black matter. We had smoked too much and eaten too little. We were at least twenty pounds too light. I could feel my ribs, even beneath the herringbone of my dungaree jacket. The only things clean and in good order about us were our weapons. Those we kept immaculate. Our weapons were our livelihood. Not our bodies, not our clothes, not even our minds—only our weapons.

It was odd, but when we arrived at White Beach, it appeared that some of K Company had been there for a few days already. There were familiar marines walking around White Beach with clean dungarees, shaved faces, and fresh smiles.

I didn't know what to think.

"You see this crap, Mace?" Frank Minkewitz asked.

"No," I replied. "I don't see nothin'."

It didn't matter. What mattered was that they told us to draw hammocks and set them up between the palms so that we would have a place to sleep. When that was done they lined us up and issued us clean dungarees, boondockers, and a ditty bag, which contained simple toiletries. However, I had a little extra in my ditty bag. Someone had placed a corncob pipe in there—identical to the one that made Olive Oyl go nutty over a diminutive sailor.

"Say, what the fuck is this?" I pulled out the pipe.

"Eh . . . well, I'd say that it looks like a pipe, Mace."

"Oh yeah, ya think it does, do ya, Holland? That's why they put mugs like you inna rifle squad. A regular goddamn Edison. I *know* it's a friggin' pipe, but what's the fuckin' thing doin' here?"

"I dunno." Gene smiled. "Maybe they took one look at ya and figured you was a pipe smoker."

"Ha. Ha. Screw you, Holland. You just make sure your hammock isn't anywhere near mine tonight."

We laughed. We bathed in the ocean. We donned our new dungarees and boondockers. We shaved and ate. We put our immaculate weapons away where we didn't need them.

It's amazing what a little good treatment would do to the frontline marine. It was as if somebody reverse engineered a weapon, so instead of pulling the trigger and killing us, it brought us back to life.

For the rest of our time on White Beach, I carried the pipe in my mouth. I never smoked it—hell, I had never lit a pipe in my life— but it was goofy and I liked it. Whoever decided to put the pipe in my ditty bag had no way of knowing, but just that simple thing, that one little thing, was enough to bring a skinny twenty-year-old marine back from everything that hurt so much about war.

The last days of Peleliu, for me, ended with a grave marker, a stolen jeep, a photograph . . . and a fistful of stars.

After a while, just hanging around White Beach, we began to grow a little bored.

I've heard it said that the experience of the combat infantryman is one of boredom, followed by brief moments of intense slaughter. Then the cycle repeats itself until you're KIA. That might be the experience of other battles, but Peleliu always kept us jumping—until the very end.

They had told us a couple of days after arriving at White Beach that we were now waiting for a ship to take us back to Pavuvu. This was fantastic news. They never should have told us that, though, because the more we sat around doing nothing, the more we got antsy. The more young men get antsy, after escaping something as hard as death, the more they are likely to ramp up and stretch their legs.

"Say, Gene, whattaya say we get out of here and go do somethin'?"

"Do something? Like what?"

"I dunno . . . Like go see Levy at the cemetery. Anything to get the hell outta here. Maybe go scrounge up a meal of somethin'."

So Gene and I begin walking. Eventually we're able to hitch a ride on a few trucks, until we make it all the way south, between Orange Beach 2 and the airfield, where they set up the 1st Division cemetery.

We're greeted with rows upon rows of white crosses, all laid out neat, in perfect straight lines. The outer edges of the cemetery are still a bustle of work, however, as fresh holes are dug, Marines are being placed into new graves, and all the while boys from Graves Registration are using rakes to smooth the spaces between the graves, keeping a tidy look around the area.

It's a lot to take in. Gene and I walk the paths between the graves, gazing at the various names etched upon the crosses, neither one of us saying a word, both of us adrift in the heat of the day: the same sun these marines died under, the same sky, the same ground they fought for, and now they own this coral rock in ways they never thought they'd own anything in their lives . . . much less their deaths. This ground is rich with the blood of proud American sons.

I stand over Sy's grave, trying to keep the thoughts at bay. I know he's down there, wrapped up in a bag or something, sightless, unmoving, unfeeling. Brooklyn. He's from Brooklyn, the same place my folks are from. I look around the island, beyond the barrier of crosses, and I'm disgusted with the place because it's nothing like New York. It's nothing like anything we've ever known. We'll leave here knowing that we left a whole lot of marines behind who couldn't have cared less about coming to Peleliu.

At least they didn't die for nothing. People do that—"die for nothing"—back in the States all the time, but they'll care about these boys of Peleliu forever.

All I can do, rather than dwell on it all, is look down at Levy's grave and say, "Well, this is it."

It's the same words I waited my whole life to say, right before the ramp of our amtrac dropped the day we arrived here.

This is it, Sy.

So why am I not satisfied?

"Hey, buddy," I call to one of the Graves Registration marines.

"Who, me?" He stops what he's doing and leans on his rake.

"Yeah, come over here. Look, this guy . . . this guy is Jewish. What's he got a cross for? Shouldn't he have a Star of David over here?"

At first the GR marine doesn't say anything. He simply gazes around the graveyard, as if he heard a ghost calling his name.

He looks back at me. "Well, umm . . . we don't have a star like that. I don't know, *buddy*. I mean, what do ya want me to do about it? I just work here, okay?"

"Yeah, okay." My eyes meet Holland's. "Let's get the fuck outta here, Gene."

Forget it about it, Sterl. Sy's only goin' to be here temporarily, anyway.

Gene and I leave for Purple Beach, not looking back across the cemetery. I did what I came for, and once I had seen Levy off, that's all the satisfaction I needed.

On the way to Purple Beach, we have to cross the airfield. This time, the airfield is chock-full of American planes, spread out, so that if the Nips came by on a strafing run they couldn't hit our planes in a straight line. Moreover, the planes are all parked on a newly repaired airstrip, which shows no sign that we'd ever had the hell shelled out of us when we made our run across it a month ago.

"Hey, how's it goin', guys?" a young pilot greets us.

Gene and I stroll over to a lanky blond-haired pilot who's sitting by the runway eating his lunch. This pilot looks like he can't be more than twenty-three at the most.

Gene says, "Okay, I guess. Looks like we'll be leavin' this place soon."

"Yeah," I say to Gene and the pilot. "Place looks a lot different from when we took this damn thing."

The pilot drops his spoon in his can of food and looks at us slack-jawed. "You mean . . . is that *right*? You people have been here since *D-day*?" he asks.

"Yep," I reply. "Say, tell me, you made any runs at Babelthuap?"

Babelthuap is the largest of the Palau Islands, a place we've heard is brimming with Nips—a place none of us marines want to go. With all the brass jerking us around, with talk about going back to Pavuvu, and so far none of it has materialized, it wouldn't surprise us if Babelthuap is the next item on the menu.

"*Have* I?" The pilot laughs. "You kiddin'? Place is almost finished. Lemme tell ya somethin' funny. The Nips, they've got this tower over there, right? Glass windows. A radio tower or somethin'. Anyway, boy, we come flyin' over and shoot the hell outta them glass windows. *Then,* and get *this*—we come back, right? And the sonsabitches have put the glass right back in the windows! So we just flyyyy back over and *tatatatatat*—blow 'em out again!"

We all laugh. "Yeah, that's great!"

I think the pilot notices us staring down at his food. I don't even realize I'm hungry until I'm caught eyeballing his food, embarrassed.

The young pilot puts a smile on his face again so that we won't feel bad as he holds out a gallon can of something.

"Hey, fellas—you guys want the rest of this? I'm, umm . . . I'm really not hungry. It's not much, but it sure is tasty. Chicken and gravy."

We thank the pilot and part ways. Now we have something to eat on our way to Purple Beach. Sure, they're feeding us on White Beach—already we're starting to regain some weight—yet the food on White Beach is a part of the same problem, the monotony that made us want to get out of there in the first place.

Purple Beach this time around doesn't look anything like it did when we were there the first time. Now Purple Beach looks like a navy paradise: Ships moored up everywhere, LSTs snug to the beach, a veritable swarm of swabbies, all ranks, milling about, laboring on their ships, huddled in circles playing cards, smoking, probably yucking it up over some photos of geisha girls they've traded for.

I'm not sure the navy guys take much notice of us, but we sure feel out of place.

Eventually, after we hang around awhile, some sailors take us aboard ship, where we end up with a lunch of Spam and dehydrated vegetables.

We thank the U.S. Navy and begin our trek back to White Beach, meeting up with Hurricane Hensen along the way. Hensen gives us some cock-and-bull story that he got lost and he's been looking for K Company this whole time. Look, the feeling is, you don't have to lie to us. Just tell us you've been loafing around for a few days and we'll believe you; otherwise you can dispense with the bullshit. It's not like Gene and I are exactly toeing the company line either.

Presently, Hensen pipes up. "Say, take a look at those army boys."

Off the side of the road is an army bivouac area, a smallish campsite, about half the size of ours on White Beach. There are just a few tents erected, so it's probably for a special unit, especially isolated like they are, out here on this desolate stretch.

Splitting up, we sort of skirt around the camp, cautiously—each of us eyeballing whatever it is we hope to find here. There isn't much, but there's a jeep. The vehicle is parked out by itself, near a tent with its flaps closed. Suddenly I've got an idea. My grin grows as wide as the infamous Cheshire variety. I'm back in Queens and there's no such thing as a war in the Pacific. I've never known combat. I've never killed a man. I'm only a kid.

Keys in the ignition? Check.

Nobody around? Check.

Property of the United States Army? Precisely.

And I'm gone!

Boy, it feels good driving a car for the first time in . . . Jesus, I don't know *when*. If someone had stepped out of that tent, while I was in the jeep, I'd have had my speech ready: "Oh, I was just gettin' that homesick feeling—how it feels to ride in a car again, ya know?" Thankfully nobody saw me, and here I am skidding around to where Holland and Hensen are standing, their jaws nearly touching the ground at the sight of me in this beautiful piece of machinery.

"Hey, fellas," I say, pulling up in a cloud of dust. "Did somebody call for a cab?"

And we're gone!

It's a joyride up the West Road—a place that had caused us so much trouble in the past—through Sniper Alley, the whole megillah. Yet this time the only shots we take are from the eyes of angry GIs and marines as we pepper them with coral powder, zipping by as we are.

"Hey, watch it, assholes!" somebody yells at us.

Who cares? We're whooping it up and laughing the whole way, stealing quick glances over our shoulders, seeing who's receiving the butt-end of our joke. It's a freedom. It's freedom that, by God, we've earned! It feels as if we have eagle's wings—and nobody clips the wings of those sovereign birds. They just fly, without a care in the world.

By the time we pull into White Beach I've already got it in my head that we need to dissociate ourselves from the jeep—but fast!

"Wow, look at this!" a marine says as some of the boys begin crowding around the jeep.

I don't want anyone to ask too many questions, so quickly I say, "Hey, yeah, why don't you guys go take her for a ride?"

Just as soon as two marines hop in the jeep, I grab Holland and Hensen by the elbows and navigate them into the crowd. "C'mon, let's take a walk inside here. Mingle . . . mingle with the boys, huh?" So we mail into camp like we know from nothing. My accomplices know exactly where I'm coming from. If somebody gets caught with the swiped jeep, it's not going to be one of us.

Still, when the other marines take off in the jeep, Holland pulls me aside. "Look, Sterl, I didn't wanna tell you then . . . but when we were at that army camp, I dunno, it must have been about . . . say, a minute, at the most . . . when you pulled up in the jeep . . . Hensen and I saw this army lieutenant get outta the jeep and go inside the tent. Yeah, he couldn't have been in there *a minute* before you took the thing."

"No foolin'?" I ask.

"Uh-huh, no foolin'."

I've got a knot in my stomach as big as a baseball, having come so close to being caught. If I had known then what Gene just told me now, I would have never taken the jeep. It would have been a hell of a thing to spend my last few days on Peleliu in the stockade (or whatever passed for one here), considering that Peleliu was a prison in its own right. Nevertheless, what's done is done, and we had a great time doing it.

I thought of Private Mercer, and how he'd spent his days on Pavuvu secluded in a tent and how lonely he had been in life. That wasn't me. I wouldn't spend my days on Pavuvu like a hermit, not after all this.

Was it worth it?

Let me think.

You bet your ass it was.

Click.

The shutter opens, then closes, capturing one moment in time on a strip of celluloid.

Taking a photograph is a wholly mechanical act, chemical in nature, yet not totally dissimilar to how the human brain traps within its memory stark moments of fear, love, pain, happiness, and beauty, if the instant is powerful enough to etch its way in forever.

Back in the early 1920s, hundred of thousands of flashbulbs went off, some of them simultaneously, as cameras around the United States captured still images of thousands of American male infants within the camera's eye. Proud parents arranged for these photographic sessions, wanting their new baby boy's photo to sit upon the mantel, or by the bedside, as a display of love and warmth and of memories that will forever shine, as long as the living eye is around to behold them.

Nobody knew, nor did it ever cross their minds, that in twenty years' time the photos would remain, but the infants emblazoned on the paper would have vanished completely from the earth beneath the undertow of a war that took memories as much as it took lives.

Memories and lives are the same. For after the lives have passed, so go the memories, if there is no longer anyone around to remember whose photo they're looking at.

We did what we did on places like Peleliu so that at least the memory of freedom would live, if not the real artifact in time.

So when they took us down to Purple Beach, before we loaded up on the *Sea Runner* for our trip back to Pavuvu, a simple photo was taken.

First Sergeant David Bailey in our company had the idea to take a photograph of us for posterity. He took the now semifamous photograph of what remained of K Company. Out of 235 men who landed on D-day, September 15, 1944, only 85 of us remained by the end of October. A rotten casualty rate.

That's not the photograph that tells the whole story, though.

There was at least one other photograph taken that day.

Bailey lined up the remainder of the 3rd Platoon and snapped a quick photo.

Click.

Out of thirty-nine riflemen in the 3rd Platoon, across three squads, only nine of us remained unscathed: R. D. Wilson, Orley Uhls, Gene Holland, Jim McEnery, Sterling Mace, P. A. Wilson, Roy Kelly, Frank Minkewitz, and Jack Baugh.

Also in the photograph was the remainder of the machine-gun squad assigned to our platoon and George Chulis, our corpsman. That's it.

Most of us smile. Make of that what you will. Perhaps we're pleased to be getting off the island. Maybe our smiles are what civilized men are supposed to do when a camera is pointed their direction. Smile.

Or maybe we're laughing at a mysterious joke; one whose punch line will be forever shrouded within a piece of celluloid and time—our eyes gazing back across the span of years separating *our* moment from yours—a clear instant in our lives between those who know and those who know not.

That the truth is, the survivors of Peleliu had it easy . . . while those who died there did not.

I've never seen anything this beautiful in all my life. Above me the tapestry of night is perforated by millions of points of light, winking, twinkling, like diamonds scattered across the firmament by God's great hand. Not the God we met on Peleliu's scorched shore, but the God who made the calm Pacific Ocean, the effervescent scent of a lightly salted breeze, and the constellations, so very near, yet so very far, as if I can just reach out and touch them, coming away with a fistful of stars.

I lie on my back, aboard the *Sea Runner,* as the sky appears to rotate, very slowly . . . very, very slowly, the billion luminous pinpricks reflecting in my eyes—and in my ears there is the sound of waves gently lapping the sides of the ship, as she cuts through the water on our voyage back to Pavuvu, and the soothing sounds of David Rose's "Holiday for Strings," lilting out of the ship's speakers, wafting toward my open mind—a record the ship's disc jockey plays to ease the savage soul.

Only now, allowing myself to be hypnotized by the show of sky, am I able to reflect—not upon the dead, or those who fell by the wayside, but upon my own well-being. I made it. I really made it. I'm alive and I didn't break. If it's selfishness, then so be it. If I can't stand to hear the guys talk about what happened on Peleliu, or who got killed, or how bad it was there, then I merely have to crack open the night for solace, for forgetfulness, for nothing at all.

It's as if I've waited twenty years for this very moment.

I've never been more ready my entire life.

This is it, Sy.

This is it.

10

TRUE CONFESSIONS

*Combat plays a more significant factor in
developing an anxiety state than in the other
types of psychoneuroses. It is not satisfactory,
although obvious, to assert that a soldier
develops a combat anxiety from fear of
battle. Nearly any battle-hardened soldier
speaks freely of being "scared like hell" prior
to and in combat. Fear is a natural component
of battle . . . The possibility of concussion with anxiety added
must be considered. Perhaps there have been
cases of brain concussion with anxiety symptoms
diagnosed only as anxiety states, because
a majority of anxiety cases give a
history of blast exposure.*

"Psychoneuroses, Combat-Anxiety Type"
Capt. Robert B. McElroy, USMC
American Journal of Psychiatry, January 1945

Okinawa Shima, Ryukyu Chain, April 1st, 1945,
Codename: l-day (love day).

The amtrac driver shifted gears on the tractor while taking a quick peek between the two shields in the front of the boat.

"Lucky bastards!" the driver said between smacking lips. His jaws looked like something mechanical, maybe a nutcracker, chewing a stick of gum, much faster than a human should be able to chew.

"What's that?" I called up, barely able to hear anything over the thumping engines of the tractor. The last gear the driver hit really made the tractor skim faster across the ocean.

"I said, you're lucky!" The driver leaned closer to me. "The landing's unopposed!"

"The hell you say!" I said, unbelieving.

I looked over the side of the amtrac, and out there was the largest armada of ships I had ever seen. They stretched out as far as the eyes could see, to all sides and beyond. Closer to the point, there was the occasional geyser of water that splashed up between some of the amtracs coming in. *Someone* was shooting at us.

"Suit yourself!" the amtrac driver said. "You'll be walking ashore!"

We did, too. We walked ashore, as if it were only a training exercise, leaving our makeshift ladders in the amtracs.

"Wow. Wouldja look at this?" PFC Eubanks said, grinning. This time K Company was in a much later wave, and there were already tanks and bulldozers, scores of troops, and hundreds of tents being erected by the time we got ashore. Fighter planes zoomed above us by the dozen, making a lot of noise, yet their guns were silent—nothing to shoot at. We could see marines in skirmish lines, sixty yards ahead of us . . . and then another group of marines, another sixty yards in front of them.

Marching single file, we looked back at the bustle of activity on the beach, in awe. Even as hectic as any landing was, marines were relatively languid in moving the huge artillery pieces out of the LSTs, along with crate after crate of munitions, rations, water, fuel, jeeps, and medical supplies that heretofore had no use.

The truth is, unlike before Peleliu (when they flat-out lied to us), as we prepared for Okinawa, the brass basically informed us that we were heading into a meat grinder. All things considered, I don't know what I preferred, the truth or the lie. Having already been on Peleliu and Ngesebus, I was pretty much scared shitless about the Okinawa landing. Everybody was. Not only was Okinawa Japanese home soil, where we expected the worst; moreover, the navy constructed ladders that we were to use to scale a big seawall right off the beach.

"As soon as you hit the beach, you can expect knee mortars, and heavy Nip artillery, and when you get up the ladders, expect intense machine-gun fire, sweeping the seawall across the landing zone. So, do not stop. Keep moving, as you were trained, and you should be just fine," they briefed us.

Just fine, huh? Just fine? We looked around at one another, dumbfounded. *What the hell did I miss, what with all this talk about mortars, artillery, and machine-gun fire?*

The ladders themselves were a joke, too. They were simply made of two 2×4s, the thin sides out, with smaller planks nailed to them as rungs—exactly the kind of ladder Bruno Hauptmann used to snatch the Lindbergh baby. I don't suppose the craftsmanship of the ladders mattered, though, when all I could imagine was marines' brains smeared atop the six-foot seawall while scores of empty helmets littered the sand, rolling down the beach.

When we landed, however, instead of a seawall, there was only rubble, where the navy had really pounded the beach, reducing any surface higher than a marine's knees to powder.

Off to the side, a camera crew was setting up their gear, and in their midst was the actor William Lundigan, another California type turned marine.

"Say," Eubanks gawked. "I seen that guy in that *Dodge City* picture . . . and what was that other one? *The Fighting 69th*, too!"

"Hey, Hollywood!" Some marines whistled and shouted, giving

the young actor their approval. Lundigan simply nodded back good-naturedly, then resumed his job with the camera team.

"You *know*," I told Eubanks, "that Lundigan fella is really from Syracuse, New York."

Bob Whitby smiled at me. "This is great, ain't it, Mace? Looks like a real piece of cake."

"Yeah, looks like . . . maybe something like that. Hey, you just keep your head screwed on, alright, Wimp?"

I couldn't help being apprehensive. Too many things just didn't add up. The anticipation of combat is nearly as intense as the genuine article.

I'm sure that if the Nips had let us have it right then, the marines unloading the boats and stacking the boxes would have grabbed their carbines, but none of the brass would have actually called them up to use them. Each man to his own job—so you can be damn sure it would be the riflemen at the vanguard of the attack.

The press, or marine film crews like Lundigan's bunch, would start rolling film and snapping photos, but more often than not, the pictures they'd send back to the States would be of the carbine-wielding ammo carriers at the back of the train. Like any smart guys, the photographers wouldn't run right into the teeth of the action if they didn't have to. In fact, the only shutterbug I knew who did ended up KIA on Peleliu—him and his camera both.

Every so often they'd hand out some copies of *Stars and Stripes,* and we'd read the caption at the bottom of a photo with a marine in it: MARINE IN ACTION ON IWO JIMA. Then you'd look closer at the picture and there'd be a crate of tropical chocolate beside him— further proving that like most captions in life, this one only contained a fragment of the full paragraph.

Things never add up. War was like that.

They called the whole Okinawa invasion Operation Iceberg, for reasons that I couldn't comprehend. Though the climate was cool to the skin, and the countryside reminded me of northern Connecticut, there wasn't anything icy about it, except for maybe the chill that ran up my spine.

Just a little ways up the beach, in a shrubby area, we happened upon a whole platoon of Japanese who had taken a direct hit from a navy 14-inch shell. It had landed right on top of them; those poor souls were mutilated beyond recognition, not even appearing human anymore. The Nip platoon was now two thousand pounds of carnage—stacked, spread out—hacked meat, chicken parts, pork carcasses, sides of beef, looped intestines, and a few odd organs, all mixed in together, raw to the smell; you didn't want to open your mouth for fear that you might taste the stench. The only things that told you they were once people were a few scattered bits of tan clothing, a couple of shattered helmets, and their rifles—which weren't really rifles anymore, they were pipes; the wooden stocks had been sheared clean off by the impact of the explosion.

I had never seen mutilation like this, not even on Peleliu. I had never seen an unexploded shell, either—but there it was. It scared the hell out of me.

Right in front of the chewed-up Nip platoon, burrowed two feet into the dirt and sticking out another three feet, was another navy 14-incher. What made it so menacing was that we didn't know if it was a dud or if it was going to go off if somebody bumped into it. If the round had turned sixteen Japs into some sort of potato salad, what would it do to just a few of us? We'd be mist. They might find enough of us to stuff in an envelope to send back home. Imagine, the only letter I wrote home from a combat zone has me stuffed in it. *Sonuvabitch.*

"Say, Wimp?" I called.

"Yeah, what's goin' on?"

"C'mere and take a look at this, willya?"

Bob walked over. "Yeah, sure, what ya got?"

He stopped in his tracks and merely stood there, his eyes

confused, squinting, trying to make out the pieces—trying to make sense out of what his brain didn't want to register.

"Wimp?"

"What? Huh?" He looked at me, an amnesiac. He didn't know who *he* was anymore, either.

As I walked off, I simply cocked my thumb back over my shoulder, leaving Whitby where he stood. "Piece of cake, Bob," I said.

They called it L-day, or Love Day, the day we landed on Okinawa. It was also Easter Sunday, as well as April Fool's Day. It was the sort of landing any marine could only dream of. Yet there we were. It was real. We only heard a few scattered shots here and there. Nobody knew where they came from. I ran into PFC Harry Bender, who witnessed two little dead girls not far from the beach. Harry said he had lost his breakfast, right there, at the sight of them—and he wasn't ashamed to admit it. Later on, the scuttlebutt came down that some major was killed, but again, we didn't know how it happened, or even who he was.

All I knew was that the whole 1st Marine Division was moving eastward across the waist of Okinawa, with the 7th Army Division on our right flank and the 6th Marine Division shoring up our left. According to the original battle plan, the 1st Marine Division was supposed to be at spot X, but we had surpassed that by making it all the way to spot Y, on some general's map. At least that's what we heard, anyway. The rumor was that we had moved so far, so fast, that we were in danger of becoming unsupported and alone at the forefront of the American lines, possibly running into a large number of Japanese troops bearing down from the east coast.

Soon after hearing this news, K Company was called to a halt. My fire team and I picked out an abandoned farmhouse to set up camp, the four of us settling down in a patch of land behind the farm—or whatever passed for a backyard, in that neck of the woods.

"Think we'll run into any Nips tonight?" Weisdack asked.

"Don't worry about it. We'll be okay, and if we do, just keep Eubanks loaded, alright?"

Bob said, "I'll take first watch if you guys don't mind."

"It's okay, Wimp," I said. "I'll take first watch. You guys get some shut-eye."

"Well," Eubanks said, "I don't know about you fellas, but I don't think I can sleep, even if I was in my own bed."

The marines in my fire team were a good group of guys. I say "my" fire team simply because I inherited them by default—much the same way I made corporal on Pavuvu, when we got back from Peleliu. I certainly didn't ask for the promotion. Someone must have thought I had done pretty well to earn it. Since it was only me and Charlie Allmann left of our original team, I got the stripe, and Charlie got a new fire team. By the time the replacements arrived to bolster our depleted ranks, my BAR was taken away from me, and I was given an M-1 rifle and a new BAR man in PFC Eubanks.

Now, if I was just a kid at twenty-one, then nineteen-year-old Eubanks was just a baby—and a country bumpkin, at that. He was tall and lanky, the sort of guy who if you put him in a new suit, the suit would never fit, no matter how much tailoring you did. A product of the Appalachians, Eubanks seemed to me like he would have been more at ease in a pair of bibbed overalls with a piece of straw hanging out of his mouth—or maybe stumbling down a yellow brick road, with Dorothy and Toto in tow.

A marine could say anything he wanted to about Eubanks, but he could never say anything negative about his dedication to the marines, or his readiness for action.

Then there was our BAR assistant, PFC George Weisdack, from Donora, Pennsylvania. George was a little older than me, though not by much, short, good-looking, with dark hair, and a real pencil-thin mustache—a touch of the Hollywood look, by Weisdack's own design.

Poor George, exactly like Lyman Rice, had all those nickels and quarters on his back, red-ringed and sprinkled with white powder: totally infested with ringworm. It must have hurt like a sonuvabitch; nevertheless, Weisdack didn't say much about it—though I knew it was just a matter of time before he wouldn't be able to lump it anymore.

Rounding out the bunch was PFC Robert "Wimpy" Whitby, from Solon, Ohio. Our scout. A real good man. A real good *family* man. I had no idea how he even ended up in the marines. They would say that the marines didn't draft married men with two young daughters, but with Bob they certainly did. There's no way a man like Bob Whitby was going to volunteer for the service, the marines no less, with several mouths to feed, a mortgage, and everything that went with the white-picket-fence life. Furthermore, Whitby was about thirty-two years old, only a private first class, and no more than 5'7". He was a little chunky, with dark, sort of curly hair, already graying at the temples. Not your prototypical poster model for the Marine Corps. Yet, who knows, by 1945 maybe Bob was.

All of them were untested in combat. They relied on veterans to give them the skinny on what combat was like—but short of giving them a line of bullshit, it was a difficult thing to describe. The straight dope was about as crooked as a crooked mile; whatever you told them had the potential to either scare the crap out of them or give them a false sense of reality. It was a lose-lose situation, no matter what you said, because you never knew what shade of green a new marine was.

Before Peleliu, my squad leader, Sergeant Thomas Palmisano, bunked with Jim McEnery. Jim told me on Peleliu that Palmisano was constantly asking him what combat was like—what to expect, what to do, how to do it. I don't know what Jimmy told him—something ambiguous, I'm sure. Nevertheless, the reason we never saw Palmisano on Peleliu was that as soon as we landed, he took another amtrac right back out to the ships, and there he stayed, having crapped out on the operation. Maybe he had cold feet, or maybe he simply realized, right there on the beach, that the Marine Corps wasn't for him. Whatever the case, when Peleliu was over and we reached Pavuvu again, they lined us all up to witness Palmisano's court-martial.

They gave Sergeant Thomas Palmisano five years in the naval penitentiary on Mare Island for cowardice. And there we were, on Peleliu, almost near the end of the operation, thinking that Palmisano was either killed or wounded in the landing.

Maybe he would have been better off with the latter two options.

Then there was Lieutenant Robert Mackenzie, "Mac" for short—Bill Bauerschmidt's replacement as leader of the 3rd Platoon. Mac wanted to know what combat was like, too.

After Peleliu, we had only been back on Pavuvu maybe a week when, much to our surprise, Mac called a few of the riflemen to his tent in Officers' Country.

"Huh, I wonder what he wants with us?" Orley Uhls asked.

"Beats me," I replied. "Maybe he's got a medal to pin on ya, Uhls."

"Sure." Orley laughed. "In a pig's eye!"

All joking aside, we couldn't figure out what Mac's angle was, why he'd call the enlisted men to his tent. If it was for debriefing, wouldn't he be better off talking to what was left of the sergeants or the other officers?

Mac was new, so maybe he was simply inquisitive.

When I went inside his tent, he asked me to have a seat and relax. Before me was a real healthy-looking man, robust, a true marine-type officer in appearance and demeanor, only not too overbearing or blusterous. What he was missing, however, was that "salt" that gave the combat man his natural air.

"PFC Mace," he began, after I had seated myself. "So, I understand you spent a considerable amount of time on Peleliu, in combat, is that correct?"

I informed him that was correct.

"Made the landing, did you?" He looked up at me, from whatever papers he had in front of him. "What was that like?"

I proceeded to tell him how we had come in first, and how the machine guns and mortars had come in right behind us. How there was a lot of shelling, and Nip knee mortars peppering the beachhead—machine-gun fire, etc. I also told him about Shifty Shofner and how Lieutenant Moose Barrett was killed soon after landing.

"So . . . the mortars and machine guns"—he appeared to jot something down on his papers—"the mortars came in right *behind* the first wave?"

"Sure," I agreed. I almost said something about that being standard operational procedure, but since I was talking to an officer, I figured he already knew that. Plus, I didn't want to come across as a wiseass, so I just left it at that. First the infantry goes in. Then the mortars and heavy weapons have to follow close behind for immediate support. The setup was both practical and logical.

"Okay, fine." He paused. "Did you see any Nips? Kill any Japs?"

Boy, this guy sure doesn't have any idea, does he?

"Yes, that's right, Lieutenant; you didn't have to go far to see Nips. We came across some in a cave. Between me and Nippo—"

"Nippo?"

"Umm . . . PFC Thomas Baxter, sir. He's dead."

"Oh. Okay, carry on." Lieutenant Mackenzie looked a little green around the gills when I mentioned a dead marine.

"So," I continued, "we got a few of them. But you get down real quick, like, because you never know when a Nip might have you sighted in at the same time."

I paused, thinking that was all he wanted to know. Then I

added, "Also got a lot of them by the Five Sisters. Like I said, you don't have to go far."

Later that night, I was playing 500 Rummy with George Weisdack, and during a lull in the game, he said to me, "So . . . I heard the new lieutenant wanted to see some of you guys today?"

"You heard that, huh? Yeah, new lieutenant's got somethin' cookin'. Wanted to know all about combat, this and that."

"So what did ya tell him?"

"Oh, you know, this and that."

"No, I mean, what *is* combat like?" George gazed at me intently. This was Weisdack's perfect chance to broach the subject, without appearing too desperate in the attempt—without sounding too green himself (although George was as green as a new crabapple).

"Look, George." I laid my cards down and peered straight into his eyes. "It's hard for me to tell you what it's like because each campaign is different. All ya gotta do is stay alert. Don't anticipate something taking place; just be ready when it does. And don't goof off, alright? Stay alert. Be a smart marine. Everything after that will come to *you*. You don't have to come to *it*. You'll be alright, if ya don't think about it too much. You'll be alright, okay?"

Now, as we set up our little camp behind the abandoned farmhouse on Okinawa, I looked over at Weisdack and knew he'd be evacuated soon. His ringworm was about as bad as any case I'd seen. Eventually I'd have to get him out of here. Lucky him.

I also thought about Lieutenant Mac. Mac was out there—camped somewhere—just not as a member of the 3rd Platoon anymore. Soon after Mac's little Q&A session with 3rd Platoon riflemen, somehow he had finagled his way out of the rifle platoon and straight to the mortars. It's no wonder he had been so curious about the mortars. I couldn't help but wonder if I had swayed him that way, during the session he and I had. What's more, I wasn't even sure the mortarmen knew that they had inherited an officer who had snuck out of the rifle squads. It didn't matter, though. In Mac's place we received a new officer, "Spud" Dunlop, who was said to have played football with the Brooklyn Dodgers before the war. Lieutenant Spud was a big guy, so nobody doubted his football prowess—and even if you did, you wouldn't express your reservations to a bruiser like him, officer or not!

"Okay, fellas, might as well dig in here," I said to my fire team, looking around the backyard.

"Say, George, where do ya think the crapper is around here?" I heard Eubanks whisper to Weisdack.

"Probably inside the house, where they all are, but . . . hey, be careful, willya?" Weisdack said back.

No sooner had I stuck my shovel in the ground than an awful smell reached up and grabbed me by the nose hairs.

"Oh shit!" I said. "Jesus Christ. Hey, Eubanks, I think I found your crapper over here."

No more than two feet from where I planned to dig was a perfectly rectangular hole—or perhaps I should say cesspool—dug into the ground, about two by three feet, and reeking to high heaven. On the three-foot side of the hole were two pads, about two feet in length, where you'd place your feet when you squatted over the hole to read. The hole was difficult to see, because the sun was just beginning to set—it was even recessed back from the farmhouse in a shaded area—yet I could still make out the brackish water down there, nearly coming up to the rim of the square.

"Well, I don't think I'll be diggin' over here. Eubanks, come put your ass over this thing. Got the new *Stars and Stripes* ya can wipe with."

"Oh, brother." Eubanks looked down the hole. "You'd think they'd have indoor plumbing or something, wouldn't ya?"

"Well, maybe," I said, "but I kinda don't think they knew we were coming."

The Japanese knew we were coming, though. That much was certain. The rising sun was just beginning to set for Japan, although, as riflemen, we only had the vaguest notion that our enemy's time was ticking down its final seconds toward perpetual twilight.

As our first night on Okinawa crept in, just as the ball in the sky began its final nod for the day, sinking below the skyline, I looked skyward and saw two planes bearing in, shining silver against the setting sun.

Now, those are some lucky guys, I thought. *Those fighter pilots are coming in for the night, and they'll be safe and sound aboard ship, and I'll be sitting right here.* I could imagine them in their flight suits, talking back and forth on their radios, about what they'd be eating for evening chow. Maybe one of them would have a pinup of Veronica Lake or June Haver taped against an instrument panel.

Yet after they banked and flew straight down, I caught a glimpse of meatballs on the underside of their wings. *Nip fighters!* Instantly, thousands of tracers lit up the sky, scratching the twilight with vertical lines. Thousands of lines, straighter than a person could draw, and suddenly I couldn't imagine the pilots anymore— let alone Nip pilots actually flying those planes—yet there they were!

The two planes dipped and disappeared from my view as they cleared below the tree line. *Kamikazes.* They were going for the ships.

My heart went out to the navy boys on those tubs, and the American pilots who dared the skies over our anchorage, flying against that sort of menace. It was insanity.

You'd think that with all the flak the navy sent up, the Nip planes would be chewed to pieces. However, many of them made it in, crippling our ships, taking hundreds of American lives back with them, and showing them off to Buddha (or whatever god it was that gave them the green light to commit suicide for empire and homeland).

Before then, I had only heard of kamikaze planes. Yet seeing them that close, especially knowing that on the ocean we had the largest armada of U.S. Navy power the war had ever seen, was a chilling experience. Even when we saw the kamikazes' handiwork firsthand, when we anchored at Ulithi, nothing came close, no matter how far away I was from the action.

At Ulithi, where we stopped briefly on our way to Okinawa, we witnessed the USS *Franklin* pass by—a death ship, a ghost ship, almost totally scuttled—as it limped silently back to the States: An aircraft carrier that had lost over seven hundred sailors to just a few Japanese kamikaze pilots. Tit for tat, in loss of lives, this kamikaze treatment was paying off for the Nips. Still, that didn't make it any less crazy. You'd see a Jap fighter overhead and immediately want to shoot it down, but the odds of knocking down a Nip plane with a peashooter were equal to standing on a beach on Okinawa and throwing a baseball all the way to New York and having Ernie Lombardi catch it. Nothing doing. In truth, a marine on the ground would have a better chance of getting wounded, with all the flak raining down around us, even as far out to sea as the ships were. The navy sent up mountains of antiaircraft fire, and all we'd have to do was wait a few minutes for the metal chunks to drift over and clobber us with shrapnel. Marines scrambled around, jumping in their foxholes, making sure they grabbed their helmets on their way down. I always kept a big box handy—the box the 10-in-1 rations came in—to use as my shield, holding it over my head as the steel peppered the earth.

As far as I know, none of us were wounded from the flak residue—the shrapnel had lost a lot of its momentum by the time it reached our company area. Nevertheless, we weren't taking any chances, despite the fact that the naval fire (a brilliant fireworks display) broke the monotony quite well.

Just about every night we'd watch the Nip planes dive at our ships. At first, it was a novelty. At last, it made us sick.

By the time we had reached the eastern side of Okinawa—the Pacific shore—the lunatics were running the asylum.

The illusion of paradise deceived us.

The ocean was a lilting shade of azure, the sandy beaches were unsullied and crystalline white, and beautiful Okinawan horses ran wild, close to the water, having been abandoned by their masters. Evidently their civilian handlers made a mad dash out of there, escaping our arrival. Not that we would have harmed the locals, but we would've certainly overturned their way of life. We hadn't seen any action to speak of since landing, and now that we had reached our primary objective, marines began stretching their legs at odd angles. We were euphoric, undisciplined, and stupid. We did everything wrong—including the officers. Everybody was guilty of something. Some of us were guilty of everything.

"Bring back that fucking horse!"

Pigs snorted and rooted around our ankles in the dust as Orley Uhls and I had our rifles pointed at two marines. In quick jerks, a dying pig's trotter lashed out its final nerve spasms against Orley's leg; a fresh gunshot wound behind the pig's ear poured a thin stream of blood into the dirt. The rest of the pigs, in the pen, like all crude animals, hadn't caught on that they could be next.

The marine closest to us, the one who'd attempted to swipe our horse, looked like he was going to say something, but Orley cut him off.

"I said. Bring. Back. The goddamn. Horse," Uhls said between gritted teeth. Orley wanted to make damn sure the two marines had heard us.

Obviously those two marines had come up from the rear somewhere. They didn't look anything like us; they didn't see what we saw, or hear what we heard, or feel what we felt. They knew nothing. The barrels of our weapons were like two pinpoints of black. They knew nothing about black pinpoints. Or how live Nips smelled. Or the anatomy of a dying pig. Or living inside of a pressure cooker.

"No, hey, I'm sorry," the second marine said as they walked back with the stolen horse. "We didn't know . . ."

We dropped our weapons. "Yeah, that's okay, guys." Orley grinned.

"Just leave the horse here," I finished.

The two marines backed slowly away, and just as soon as they felt it was safe to turn their backs on us, they swung around and quick-walked back the way the came.

"Jeez." Orley took out his Ka-Bar and gutted the pig. A fresh smell of earth and wet grass, clay, and offal came from within the pig's slit belly. "Some friggin guys, huh? Get in a war, and people forget all how to act!"

It was common to see marines riding horses around, everywhere they went. Some horses were used to carry ammunition, while other marines rigged ways to strap their rifles to the horses. The riflemen were especially adept at playing city cowboys.

There we were in full marine regalia: Dungarees, leggings, packs, and helmets, armed to the teeth, yet at the same time you could find a pack of wild marines whooping it up and racing horses down the beach. Nobody gave a damn. Some officers, like that shit-eating Lieutenant Johnson, tried to stop the races and the pandemonium—but what was he going to do? Shoot us off the horses? Horses could be shot, pigs could be shot, the Marine Corps Manual could be shot—but for God's sake, don't shoot the man behind the globe and anchor. That man had gunpowder in his veins and a powder keg for a heart. Every veteran knew that we were coming into action again. So the rule of the day was to simply enjoy life, sitting on your keister, before it was your time to get killed.

Besides, if Lieutenant Johnson ran back to the CP to report disorder among the ranks, I'm sure they'd tell him to calm his ass down, try some of the local sake, and maybe if he was lucky someone would kill a chicken, and they'd all dine well for the night.

Eventually, however, our revelry trickled to a halt. We were instructed to set up proper bivouac areas. Orders came down for us to inch farther north, patrolling on the alert, for who knew if there were Japs skulking around the upper portion of the island? What's more, not long after we reached the eastern side of Okinawa, we learned that the source of all the shelling and machine-gun fire to the south of us was the army running into stiff resistance. Very stiff resistance—and news like that had a sobering effect of its own.

The fact is, it could have been us down there, getting ripped up by the Nips, if the planners of the invasion had engineered for the marines to swing south as the army went north. The way I saw it, it was merely happenstance, as far as what the brass knew, that northern Okinawa was so lightly defended, so far, while the southern half of the island was brimming with Japanese cutthroats. After all, we remembered how tough the landing was supposed to be; and if that didn't materialize, like they warned us, then the top brass really didn't know any more than we did about strength of force and the disposition of the Japanese army.

We would find out soon enough, however, as the daily patrols grew more plentiful—and paranoia began to spread like yellow fever.

Okinawa Shima, Ryukyu Chain, April 10, 1945.

"Hey, Mace!" the company runner called to me while I sat outside eating breakfast with the boys.

"Yeah, what's goin' on?" I asked. "But keep it down, willya? You'll wake up my breakfast, and if it starts movin' I won't be able to eat it." I stuck my spoon back into the little green C ration can.

"See, now look what you made me do. I killed it. It's no good any-more."

"Well, I've got a can of peaches you can have." The company runner looked at me, exasperated. "Look, Captain Stanley wants to see you right away, okay?"

That got my attention.

I looked at Bob Whitby, and he simply shrugged his shoulders. *Beats me.* Glancing at Gene Holland, he whistled through his teeth, as if to say, *Boy, you're really in trouble now, son.*

"Okay." I sighed, placing the can of C-rats on the deck, stand-ing, then brushing my hands off on my dungaree pants. "Let's get this over with."

Whatever it was that Captain Thomas Stanley wanted with me, I was sure it was a crap detail.

Ever since I made corporal, on Pavuvu, Stanley seemed to have it in for me.

It all started with some sort of school, or a lecture, an officer was giving us on Pavuvu.

We all stood in a semicircle around the officer. *Yack, yack, yack,* that's all we heard from him; to tell the truth, most of us didn't give a shit what he was saying. A couple of other Marines and I were at the back of the class, grab-assing or whatever, and . . . *yack, yack, yack,* the officer droned on in a monotone, which was probably indicative of his own enthusiasm toward the lesson at hand.

I forgot who the other comedians were with me—it could have been Leyden and Holland. Anyway, we started up the old Tom Mix routine from *The Miracle Rider,* or some other Western that was popular when we were kids.

My two cohorts held their arms out with their fingertips touch-ing each other's, miming a pair of old swinging saloon doors. Then I would push through their arms, like a real hero, with my fingers as a pair of revolvers in my hands, guns blazing away at a group of imaginary villains. That got a few chuckles. Then I'd go through the doors again, but this time, the marines with the saloon doors for arms would swing their arms back and hit me in the backside—turning the gag into something more like a Charlie Chaplin bit.

City cowboys.

It was lowbrow humor, sure—anything to pass the time—and although the teacher for the day didn't notice, Captain Stanley was taking the whole thing in, from the entrance of his tent, only thirty yards away.

When school was over, Stumpy Stanley called me over to his tent.

"That was quite a display, Mace." Stanley glared at me, giving me the ol' evil eye. "I wouldn't say you were paying attention. What *would* you say you were doing?"

I didn't even try to offer him an excuse. It wouldn't have done any good.

"Yeah, Captain," I said. "We were grab-assing like little kids. That's all."

"Well, what we're going to do—" He paused. "Well, since you're a corporal now, I'm sure you'll be happy to be corporal of the guard for a couple of weeks. That's *two* weeks. Is that understood?"

I understood, alright. It was no big deal, corporal of the guard. That only meant I could sleep during the day, go on duty at 10:00 P.M., walk around all night talking to whoever was up, and then go off duty about 7:00 A.M. the following morning.

It's not as if there were any Nips around to worry about, so it was soft duty.

The only person I had to keep an eye out for, at night, was "Jack the Ripper."

Now, Jack the Ripper—*our* Jack the Ripper, on Pavuvu—like his original namesake of London fame, will forever remain an enigma, more powerful in myth than he ever was in life.

The rumor was, a marine was going around Pavuvu killing other marines with a knife. Of course, as far as anybody knew, a body was never produced, let alone a harvest of them. Still, they had to give this phantom psychotic marine the Jack the Ripper moniker; and although I doubt he ever existed, that didn't make him any less real.

I had a feeling, right away, that the Jack the Ripper phenomenon was a bunch of hooey. Partly because it wasn't difficult to imagine battle-stressed marines coming back from Peleliu and conjuring up something wicked lurking between the coconut trees—perhaps an overimaginative marine who had gone twisted from combat. Mostly, though, it was crap, because whatever marine decided to take a Ka-Bar in hand and give the business to his fellow troops could have chosen a better weapon to do it with! My own experience with the Ka-Bar left me with the impression that the marines would have been better off issuing us sharpened sticks, instead of the infamous blade that personified Marine Corps bloodthirstiness. The only time I ever used mine was after I returned from Peleliu, and upon spying a frog sitting in the sand, I decided I could probably hit the frog with my Ka-Bar, if I threw the knife hard and fast enough. With dead-eye vision, I held the knife a certain way and then deftly zinged it in the frog's direction. The frog simply sat there, ignoring my deadly projectile, merely regarding me (perhaps with curiosity) with his great bulbous eyes, making me feel like a fool in the process. Not only did I miss the frog, but the Ka-Bar knife was a broken object on the ground. The blade had snapped right off at the hilt, having collided with the soft sand.

So much for the Ka-Bar.

So much for Jack the Ripper, too.

It wasn't long after I had done my stint as corporal of the guard that the Jack the Ripper paranoia reached its crescendo. I was his last victim.

One night, as we were all sleeping in our mosquito-netted hammocks, a marine from another tent got up to take a leak, and as he was walking to the head, he spotted a softball lying in the company street. Knowing that I was in charge of the softball team, he must have put two and two together that the ball belonged to me, so he tossed it in the tent. As luck would have it, his pitch was a perfect strike, right over the plate, and the ball hit me square in the stomach. I let out a surprised *Oomph*—the ball took my breath away, and immediately all my tentmates rose in a clamor. Eubanks tore right through his mosquito net, and Blowtorch Willy jumped up and grabbed his .45, looking to shoot anybody or anything that looked out of place.

"What the hell was that?"

"It's Jack the Ripper! Keep your eyes peeled!"

"Mace—you alright?"

I picked the ball off my stomach, trying to clear my eyes of sleep. "Yeah, I'm okay." I held the ball up. "Hey, look, it's my ball!" I said with a wide grin.

"Oh, for Christ's sake." Blowtorch shook his head. "We thought the Ripper had gotten ahold of you, Mace."

"You kiddin'?" I asked. "Jack is gone with the last of the guys who rotated home."

Sure enough, the scuttlebutt regarding Jack the Ripper fizzled out and faded, just as soon as the Canal and Gloucester marines, like Jim McEnery, bade us farewell.

Jack wouldn't be making the Okinawa landing with us. Neither would Jimmy.

Besides, we had *real* troubles to contend with on Okinawa, in the form of murderous Japs, not killer marines. Or, like in my case on Okinawa, a captain who assuredly had troubles of his own planned for me.

Entering Stumpy's tent, I quickly noticed that Stanley wasn't alone. Standing off to my left was another officer: A thin, older marine—at least in his fifties—with graying hair, about my height, and sporting the gold oak leaves of a major on the collars of his dungaree jacket.

Immediately I snapped to attention and saluted them both.

"At ease, Mace," Stanley intoned. "Mace, this is Major Paul Douglas. He's got the idea that the Nips are cutting the communication lines between the Fifth and the Seventh. We're having the damnedest time reaching them by radio. So what I want you to do is take your fire team and escort Major Douglas. Find out what's going on, and check it out."

"Yes, sir!" I said.

"Good. Anything else, Major?" Stumpy nodded at his senior officer.

The major replied that everything was to his satisfaction. We all gave our exiting salutes, and then the major and I stepped out of the tent.

Outside, the day was bright, so Douglas and I both shielded our eyes from the sun as we talked.

"Okay, sir," I began, "so what's the plan?"

"Well, it'll be easy to follow the telephone line to the Seventh. What we'll do is track the wire to its breaking point, and if we see any signs that the Nips have cut it . . . well, then we'll make sure they don't do it again."

Douglas was right; following the line on the ground was simple. The major started off leading my fire team out of the company area, but as we moved farther off the beaten path, we found that Douglas had steadily been inching toward the rear of the column, yet still giving us a few directions here and there, so that we knew who was still in control.

The terrain itself was pretty simple, too, in that it wasn't a difficult trek, alternating between open land, spotty shrubs, and here and there a few rocky patches of turf.

As it turned out, it was the rocks that were wearing out the telephone lines—that, and probably some agitation from the weather.

Whitby looked down and pointed out this discovery. "Look there, Mace—old wire."

At various intervals we noticed the exposed copper, peering out of its conduit, frayed and cracked at different sections—some of it in really bad shape.

"Think we should tell the major?" Bob asked.

I gazed back at the major; he appeared to be idling back there, taking compass readings, or maybe bird-watching.

"Nah, Wimp," I said. "Let's not upset the applecart here. The last thing ya wanna do is upstage an officer. He's the expert, so he'll get the medal for this. Besides, if you wanted to be an electrician so bad, you shouldn't have begged for the goddamn infantry." I winked.

The joke was on us, however, when about two hours into our journey Weisdack spotted what appeared to be a small cave, recessed a little off the path from the wire we'd followed.

The cave itself was nothing like the Peleliu variety. To enter the cave you would have to stoop down, as it was only about four feet tall, and it appeared to get shallower as it made its natural run to the end, only about five feet deep.

"Whattaya think of this?" Weisdack asked me.

I squinted a little, and I could see the end of the cave, as the sunlight illuminated part of it. "Oh, nothin'. Looks like maybe a twelve-year-old kid dug this thing ou—"

Bang!

What the shit?

Major Douglas, in all his bravado, stood at the side of the cave, his .45 in hand, having just fired a round into the entrance.

Douglas looked at me. "Go in there and check it out."

Is this guy for real? I gazed around at my fire team, but they didn't know caves from an Okinawan toilet; they were simply milling around the entrance, looking to me for answers.

"Well," I said to Douglas, "pardon me, sir—but we just don't operate that way, Major. If someone throws a grenade in there, I'll go in." Now, that's what I *said* to the major, but what I was thinking about telling him was entirely different. If I didn't have respect for the officers, he would have probably received the blunt end of my opinions.

The only thing the major gave me in return was a blank expression, which told me one of two things: He understood the way riflemen did things, or he was still trying to process the information. I simply wanted him to understand—in case he ran across a more dangerous cave in his adventures—that certain steps are needed to clear a cave, or you'll be sorry.

Either way, there wasn't a grenade among us. After Sergeant Leonard Ahner blew himself up with his own grenades at the beginning of the Okinawa campaign, everyone sort of shied away from them. We even went to the great lengths of wrapping tape around the grenade's spool, as an added precaution. That way, pulling the pin wasn't enough to activate the grenade—you'd have to unwrap the tape, if you really thought a grenade was the way to go. On Okinawa, so far, we hadn't needed to use many of them, so it was a moot point . . . until you needed one but didn't have one.

Nevertheless, I knew a sure thing when I saw one, so I went in, nosed around for a second, and then came back out. "All clear, sir," I said.

"Good," Douglas replied, reholstering his .45. Everything went the way the major wanted it to, and I was there to make sure it happened.

That wasn't the last we saw of Major Paul Douglas, though.

I'll save the rest of the story for another time.

Takabanare Shima, Ryukyu Chain, mid-April 1945.

While conducting a good spring cleaning, it's imperative that you seek out every nook and cranny you can find, in order to sweep all the dirt away. Otherwise, you're only half-assing it.

That's what we're doing on the island of Takabanare. Spring cleaning. Now, whether Takabanare is a nook or merely a cranny, none of us have the foggiest; nevertheless, since there is supposedly a Nip radio on the island, communicating with Japanese headquarters, the brass made us do another shore-to-shore landing, from Okinawa to this piece-of-shit island—cleaning the dirt out. Despite our best efforts, we are half-assing it anyway. It's only us gyrenes, low-crawling on our bellies, in a perfect textbook skirmish line, feeling like a bunch of jerks as we maneuver across some islander's sweet potato field. The three native women tending the field try not to pay us any mind, but I'm sure we're making a mess out of their harvest. They simply continue working, stuffing their bags with sweet potatoes, as we feel steadily dumber for being here. We're supposed to be keeping an eye out for the enemy. What a joke!

"Mace!" Billy Leyden is beside me, crawling like an idiot, too. "Reach up there and give her the goose."

The native woman is close enough for me to goose her; her ass is sticking straight up in the air, and she keeps taking quick looks at me, as if she's expecting to get goosed, too.

"Nah," I say. "You do it, Bill."

Billy doesn't goose her either. The truth is, you can attempt to lighten the mood only so much under the burden of any strain. Besides, any joke, right now, would come out too forced and feeble, when half a world away the nation we are defending is mourning the loss of our leader.

Before we landed on Takabanare, the word came down to us that President Franklin Delano Roosevelt, the president most of us had known for all of our lives, had died in Warm Springs, Georgia, of a hemorrhage in his brain, precipitated by the polio that had plagued his life.

Sister Dorothy, be my guide.

On Takabanare, there is no Jap radio. There are still no Japs. There is only a series of unimportant little villages, under a non-American sky. Now, you ask Truman what he can do for us, on Takabanare, and we'll be all ears.

"Candy! Candy!" A little native boy comes up to me as we take a break in one of the villages; he shows me the universal sign for wanting food, with his mouth open wide and his hand going to his mouth.

"Get a load of this kid, Gene," I say. "This cute little guy is asking for candy. I wonder where he learned that shit from."

"Beats me," Holland says. "Teach him to say 'pogey bait' and he'll have every marine that passes through here givin' him all they got."

"Yeah, he sure is a cute little fella. Say, kid, come over here and I'll teach ya some English that'll really get ya by."

The small boy walks over timidly, yet he knows I'm not going to hurt him.

"Listen," I tell him. "See that guy over there?"

I point at Sergeant Wilson, Blowtorch Willy, and the kid nods eagerly that he understands.

"Hey, you're a real smart kid! Now, listen carefully, okay? You go over and tell that man exactly what I tell ya, and I'll give ya some candy, alright? Okay? I'll give ya some candy." I put my hand up to my mouth, mimicking him, showing the kid that he and I are on the same page. "Now, listen, this is what you have to say . . ."

I have to repeat it a few times for him to catch on, but eventually he has it down pat, and his eyes light up when he sees that he's met with my approval.

"Good. Now, go on . . . Candy! Candy!"

The kid walks over to Wilson, who sits on his helmet only about twenty yards away, where I can hear everything they're saying.

"Hey, little guy." Sergeant Wilson sees the kid and smiles. "You want some candy? Is that it? Candy?"

The kid simply stands there, looks up at Wilson, and with a big beautiful smile says, "Fuck you, Wilson!"

R. D.'s eyes just about bug out of his head, and I'm rolling on the ground in a fit of laughter.

"What?" Wilson asks.

"Fuck you . . . Sergeant Wilson!" the kid repeats, and Wilson laughs, too. Wilson sees me trying to hold my sides together, and immediately he puts two and two together.

"Mace, you shithead!" Wilson's eyes are watering from laughing so hard.

"Fuck you, Wilson! Fuck you, Wilson!" the kid keeps repeating, laughing the whole time. I can only imagine, when the kid's about to go to sleep at night, him lying in his bed, smiling, and softly repeating, "Fuck you, Wilson, Fuck you, Wilson," his stash of candy safely tucked away somewhere, maybe underneath what passes for a pillow in these strange Asiatic lands.

"Fuck you, Wilson."

Suddenly the sky doesn't appear to be so non-American anymore.

Okinawa Shima, Ryukyu Chain, April 20, 1945.

"Oh my God," Whitby whispers.

Oh my God is *right*. Dead civilians crowd our vision, in an open Okinawan field.

One little girl has been shot to death. Her half-lidded eyes are yellowed in the whites, the result of urine leaking into her blood-stream as she died. In the four-year-old's tiny grip is some sort of wooden toy—a top, or a spool that had been her toy in life.

Close by, a woman lies on her stomach—probably the child's mother. Her arm reaches out toward the baby girl, fingers splayed wide, as if she were trying to protect her dead child while all light faded forever in the slow ebb of death. The side of the woman's face is mashed to the ground. An almost black pool of blood has thickened below her pursed lips.

Similar scenes play out all around us as we wade through about forty dead Okinawan adults, children, old men and old women, scattered across the field.

There was nowhere for them to run.

Otherwise, without the flock of dead innocents, the surrounding countryside is beautiful. There are rolling hills and clear skies, which gently send a light breeze through the tall grass. The temperature is moderate—even chilly at night. They've issued us zipper jackets, almost the Eisenhower model, because of the change in climate. There are even trees. Real trees, standing, without being shot all to hell by constant bombardments and strafing aircraft (no, the planes *here* target moving objects).

This is nothing like Peleliu.

"Holy shit. Wouldja look at this?" PFC Eubanks looks green, his face confused. He doesn't catch on very quickly, even in the face of a couple of elderly women lying side by side, literally torn apart by high-caliber ammunition.

I look up at the soft blue sky, and it doesn't take a strong imagination to envision what happened here. I can almost make out the outline of the fighter plane, swooping in, .50 caliber guns spewing lightning, breaking into the pack of Okinawan refugees, a chisel chipping ice. Dominoes fall. The dead Okinawans lie on the ground, all with the same forward motion, shot in the back. All of them have splotches of dried crimson decorating their pajamalike tops.

Fear and surprise still tattoo their faces. Here and there, scattered among the dead are their belongings: baskets filled with clothes and crude household goods, lacquered boxes shattered by bullets and the impacts of their falls.

These were the items they cared for in life. Precious things to them then, yet now just as meaningless as a rosary around a marine's neck, or a Bible in his breast pocket.

Never, not even for a second, does it cross our minds that the Japanese did this. The Japanese have only one purpose in the air, and that is to get to our ships. There's no way a Nip pilot would fly halfway up the center of the island, all the way north, just for a little target practice, and then have to whip across the island again in order to get at our anchorage.

PFC Harry Bender, a replacement on Pavuvu, had told me that one night, shortly after we landed on Okinawa, marines had spotted something moving around beyond our perimeter. The marines opened fire. The report came back that the night's haul had been two goats and three civilians.

That about sums it up.

There had been a lot of death on Peleliu, but I had never seen anything like this. This isn't war. This is something else entirely. On the other hand, you come to expect ghastly shit like this—just not happening to civilians. These dead Okinawans are our mothers and brothers, sisters and fathers—wrapped in a different skin, yet no less important—otherwise they would have never been born.

"C'mon," I tell my fire team. "Let's head back and let Stumpy know about this."

What can the CO say? Nothing. What is he *supposed* to say? Nothing.

It is what it is.

Stumpy Stanley merely sends us back out to round up another group of Okinawan villagers and bring them back to the stockade we set up on the island.

As for the villages themselves, they are quaint but stupid looking—very foreign to the American eye, trained, as we are, to look at skyscrapers and El trains, paved roads and manhole covers. The villages are nothing but squat, thatch-roofed houses, attached four or five down a line, with a few isolated homes set off to the side—organized by local rank or station in life. The road to every village is merely a dirt path, connected to other dirt paths, which spider-web the whole island. If there were any cars on the island (there are not) they wouldn't be able to navigate the skinny roads here. Instead, the most prevalent means of transportation around the island is raw foot power. If there is any sophisticated means of communication between villages, we've never seen it, either. Which is a good thing . . .

When we arrive at the new village, there's no indication from the locals that they are aware of the slaughter of their kinsmen, just a short mile away. In fact, it's tough to know *what* the Oki-nawans think of marines, who've suddenly appeared on their soil and taken over every aspect of their lives. On the other hand, we've been told they've endured the Japanese for years now, so I guess, to them, it beats the alternative. The Nips have even taken the sons of Okinawa and conscripted them into the Japanese army. That accounts for the total lack of men our own age among the villagers. What's left of them is who we saw dead in the field: women of all ages, children, and old men, too infirm to fight. However, some Okinawans, we've heard, are sympathetic to the Japanese. That's why, no matter how docile or appeasing the Oki-nawans seem to be, we keep our guard up, in case any of them start any shenanigans. We carry our rifles at the ready. Besides, how could they give up their home and way of life to round-eyed foreigners, to be corralled like barnyard animals, and not feel some sort of intestinal emotion? Maybe the alternative is much worse than we think. Or maybe, just maybe, the Okinawans know something we don't.

The Okinawan, when the chips are down, probably doesn't care who wins the war—just as long as he is left alone, in peace.

I don't think there's a marine among us who doesn't wish just *that,* if it means getting off this island and going home, in one piece.

Some patrols, like this one, are easier than others.

The other day we were on a full company patrol, which wound its way through an abandoned Okinawan village, and my boys, in Fire Team 3, were the very last group of marines in line.

I don't know what made me do it. Perhaps a marine gets used to violence, and any respite from it just doesn't feel right. You get used to the pattern of the puzzle, the feel, the touch of it, and when one of the puzzle pieces comes up missing, you just let it go and fall in love with the new pattern.

Whatever the case, I took a tiny ball of composition C explosives, stuck it just under the thatch of the straw roof, lit it afire with a match, and walked off. About the time we got three hundred yards down the road, Whitby happened to glance over his shoulder and said to me, "Say, Mace, what the hell is that?"

I looked back in the direction he was motioning to see a great spiral of black smoke coming from the village, bubbling over the horizon, like tar in the sky.

"That?" I only gave it a second's glance. "That's beautiful country, Bob. Beautiful goddamn country."

For all I know, I burned the whole village to the ground.

I don't know what made me do it. I don't know why I didn't feel anything.

Anyway, now we have a new clan of villagers to worry about.

Weisdack is gathering them up. "Alright, you guys, c'mon, you're comin' with us. Get your shit together."

Of course, they don't understand a word he's saying—and we don't understand them, either. They babble continuously, as if they're reading from a script. *Who the hell has that much to say in one sitting?*

"Yeah, okay, sure, just . . . okay, okay, sure, you can bring that . . . and that too, sure." PFC Eubanks is obliging a very old, bent Okinawan man. Eubanks looks at me, rolls his eyes, and carries on with the old man. "Just . . . for chrissakes, hurry it up, willya?"

The whole village (what there is of it) is in a minor commotion as soon as we enter. They get the picture. All except for the children, who gawk up at us, as if we are invaders from another planet. The smallest children peek out from behind their mothers' pajama bottoms. They are cute little dumplings, all wide-eyed, with perfectly round cherubim faces. My thoughts drift back to the Nip with the moon face on Ngesebus, and how I blew up his world by blowing out his mind. Closer to the present, I think of the little girl lying in the pretty field, with a hole the size of a man's fist in the middle of her back.

My reverie is broken by a small tug on my dungaree jacket.

Before me, a middle-aged woman motions for me to enter a hut with her. Following her in, I can see the room has the same bleak look of all the other Okinawan homes. Everything is drab, with brown walls, and some sort of particle board flooring. All cheap stuff, but evidently she wants to gather up a few more of her meager belongings before we leave.

We've been on the island for close to a month already, seeing very little actual combat, so with women on the island, most of us have been looking for a little action of a different variety. We pass any broad on the road and make a circle with one index finger and thumb, then stick the other index finger through the hole, creating the universal sign for screwing. That really cracks us up.

Alone in the house with this Okinawan woman, I show her the clever little hand signal. Just joking, of course. She doesn't act shocked or anything; she merely looks at me and pats herself up and down her body. *What the hell?* She pats herself again, without saying a word. I'm about to gesture that I don't understand, but then it dawns on me. *She's saying she's too old!*

"Oh, no!" I laugh. "Hey, I was just foolin', lady." I smile at her in a way that I hope shows her I don't mean her any harm. "C'mon, let's get your stuff so we can get outta here."

Finally, once it appears we've gathered up all the locals, we begin walking them back toward the rear area, and hopefully out of harm's way.

Whitby and I are in the front of the train, yakking about something, while Weisdack and Eubanks bring up the rear, when suddenly somebody else pulls at my jacket. Yet it's not somebody else. It's the same woman who approached me earlier, and once again she's signaling me to follow her.

"Oh, brother." I lean over to Whitby. "This one's gonna cause me trouble, Wimp."

"What kinda trouble?" Bob asks.

"Ah, hell, I made a gesture to her earlier, just clownin' around, and now I've gotta follow her and see what's goin' on. Hold up here, willya?"

Whitby stops the column from moving any farther, and I follow the lady down to the ass-end of the train, just where the trickle of civilians are making their way out of the village.

"Okay, lady, this is about enough. C'mon, what the hell d'ya think you're do—?"

The two of us of stop short in front of a pair of old Okinawan men. With their gruff expressions, and their arms crossed against their chests, these guys look as if they really mean business—like cigar store Indians, if we were casting for Hollywood extras. In fact, they almost appear to be twins—a couple of ancients standing there sporting black pajamas, with practically identical dirty black fedoras. It feels as though I'm standing in front of the review board.

This is ridiculous! I'm about to lose my patience, except that the two little girls standing to the sides of the elderly men pique my curiosity. The girls can't be more than sixteen years old, if that.

It's impossible to guess their ages, however, being that the natives of Okinawa are so tiny. Whatever their ages, it doesn't take me long to ascertain that they are somehow a part of this equation.

As the lady jabbers to the wooden Indians, I catch on to what she's saying (at least I *think* I do).

"This guy here wants to get laid, and I told him I was too old. So why don't we satisfy him by giving him the girls here, and maybe he'll leave us alone."

When she stops speaking, I look back at the Okinawan centenarians, and they glare back at me. They seem so pissed I can only imagine what they're plotting against me. Kicking my balls in, roasting me over a fire, using my eyes for fish bait. I never wanted any of this. I don't see how a human being could contemplate such a heinous act. The little girls' faces wear the glaze of such serene innocence and beauty that to even entertain the thought—even for a second—of spoiling such precious gems would bring down the wrath of something far greater than two old farts in fedoras.

I wave my hands down. "Forget it! Forget it!" I try to laugh it off, placing a hand on one little girl's shoulder, patting her arm like the child she is. *These people are fuckin' bananas.*

"What was that all about?" Whitby asks as I arrive back at the front of the line.

"Wimp—you've got kids. You don't wanna know. Trust me."

"Well," Bob says as he scratches his head under his helmet, "looks like you've got some kids of your own now, Mace."

"Whattaya mean?"

Bob chuckles.

Behind me, walking just a few steps in my shadow, are the two little ones, flashing me the sweetest smiles this side of eternity. They know what I could have done. They know that they were the sacrificial lambs. Now, though, Whitby is right. "Look what the stork brought!" he says—which suits me just fine. To these little girls, I'm the greatest. They don't need to know that I've killed men.

They don't need to know that I'll do it again. To me, the little girls represent all the cleanliness in a world that was dirty enough to send us all to hell at speeds much faster than it is humanly possible to keep up with.

As for the older Okinawan women, they are a different story. Every so often one of them derails the train when she has to use the facilities. Except there aren't any toilets out here, so the Okinawan woman squats right where she's at and sprays the ground for all to see.

We can't get back to the company CP fast enough.

As we bring the last of the villagers to the stockade, one of the rear echelon flunkies spies me out and walks up to me.

"Say," he says, "my buddies and me were wondering how you guys keep all these people in control like this. That's a lot for four marines to handle, ain't it?"

"Oh, no," I say. "Ya just *talk* to them."

"No foolin'? Boy, that's great!"

"Yeah, watch this." I turn around, raise my arm, and start unloading the best nonsense language I can conjure up, and the villagers simply get up and start following me. The natives don't have a clue what the hell I just said, and neither do I; nonetheless, this rear echelon guy's jaw drops, and he turns around to his buddies. "Hey, get a load of this! This guy really knows the language!"

Yeah, I think, *this knucklehead will probably go home and tell his pals how he captured a bunch of Nips by talking them into submission. All he's really done is guarded a few cans of Spam against a horde of hungry riflemen.*

Semper Fi, stupid ass. I hope your pecker drops off from screwing all those Okinawan hookers.

At the stockade, there are groups of Okinawan women, of all ages, who make gestures and signs of sexual innuendo to any passing marine within fifty yards of them. Which pretty much means they gyrate all day long—except when they stop to pick the bugs out of each other's hair. These are prostitutes, hunkered down be-hind the wire stockade fence, leaning down one in front of the other, so her sister can sift around her scalp, picking the fleas out, or whatever vermin she's been cultivating in there.

Seeing something like that should kill any rifleman's desire to hold court with the local tail. Or at least that's what one would think—though I have a feeling, the longer we stay here, some of the more adventurous marines might take a stab at the night with a lit candle.

It happened the very next day, in fact.

I think we're beginning to sense that it won't be long before we're in the shit again—and any last jolly before you die is a jolly you won't have to regret.

The field telephone rings, and a marine picks it up.

From the other end a thin voice comes through the receiver. "Hey, is Mace around?"

The marine who picked up the phone looks over his shoulder, sees me, and then shouts over, "Hey, Mace!"

"Yeah, what?"

"C'mere, you've got a telephone call. It's the mayor of New York. Wants to know if you've got a Purple Heart on."

Yeah, sure. The mayor. Lemme see if he can get us the fuck outta here.

"Hello, this is Mace," I say into the field telephone.

"Say, Mace." The voice comes through the other end. "Boy, have I got some dirt for you." I recognize the voice of PFC Verga, one of the new guys in Leyden and Bender's platoon.

He continues, "Listen, ya might be able to do somethin' with this. It's about Leyden, right? This Okinawan dame is coming up the road—a nice-lookin' honey—and somehow Bill and this broad work out a deal. Leyden gets some tail and this sugar gets . . . I don't know what she gets in return, but anyhow, the next thing you know, Leyden has her up against the side of the hill, bangin' away at her—an' a lot of the fellas are crowded around just watchin', tryin' to sneak a peek, ya know? It was the damnedest thing!"

We laugh. This really made my day.

"So," Verga says, "since you guys go back a ways, I thought you might like to know. Ya know, give him the business about it, or somethin'."

"Oh, you bet I will!" I say. "Here, get Bill on the horn, willya? Oh, and Verga?"

"Yeah?"

"Tell him that Stumpy's on the line."

I don't have to wait long until Leyden gets on the phone. He must have run right over.

"Yes, sir!" he says.

Lowering my voice and making it sound a little gruff, I try to make sure that the South Ozone doesn't leak out, or he'll be onto me right away.

"PFC William Leyden?"

"Yes, sir!"

"Yes, PFC Leyden, I've been getting some terrible reports about you having something to do with one of these Okinawan *girls*? Is that correct, Private?"

A short pause, then "Ye—"

"And do you *know* what can happen to you?"

"Well, I don't . . . umm, I don't, what can—?" He begins to really stammer, and it takes every bit of my willpower not to crack up right away. I can just imagine the boys from the 1st Platoon crowding around Billy, eavesdropping on the conversation between Leyden and the company CO.

"Well, first of all," I tell him, "what we've got to do is take a test!"

"Yes, sir!"

"Now, I want you to take out your pecker. Do it now, son! Check it out, squeeze it off, and see if anything comes out!"

"Ye . . . yes, sir."

"And what do you see?"

"Nothing. Nothing, sir!"

"Okay, good. Now do you have any iodine there, or something like that?"

I hear a muffled, shuffling noise, telling me that he's put his hand over the receiver, and in a faraway voice I hear the confused PFC say, "Iodine?"

He comes back on the line, clear again. "Yes, sir. Iodine, sir!"

"Good! Okay, squeeze that off again, and hold the end of your pecker where that little opening is and put a drop or two of iodine in there. It might burn a little bit, but that's the best precaution."

"Yes, sir!"

"Are you doing it, Private?"

"Yes . . . yes, sir."

"You know, Private," I begin again—but I had better make this short, because I can't hold back my laughter much longer. "I did have thoughts of making you corporal, but I have to think hard again about whether I want to do this. I can't have my corporals traipsing all over the countryside fornicating with the local indigenes, now can I?"

"Yes, sir! I mean, No! No, sir!"

"Okay, that's fine, Leyden. Now, you take a look at your pecker every day, and if anything comes out of there, you go down to the aid station—and if you do? Well, I'll put that in my report, and you can forget all about that promotion. Is that understood?"

"Yes, sir!"

"That'll be all, Private." I hang up the phone, laughing so hard that I can barely catch a breath.

Soon after, I'm sitting around with my fire team, telling them what I did, when I hear the most god-awful string of curse words, followed by laughter, blasting from the direction of the 1st Platoon.

"That sonuvabitch Mace! That dumb bastard, when I find him, I'm gonna shove my foot so far up his ass! Where *is* he?"

I knew his platoon mates couldn't hold back the gag for long. Someone would give me up, sooner or later. It's a good thing Billy and I are such good buddies—though I'm sure he's already hatching a scheme to pay me back, in turn.

"Gentlemen." I rise and bow to my fire team. "I regret to inform you that I'll be indisposed for the evening, so you'll have to carry on without me. In other words, I'm making myself scarce before Bill catches up with me. So long, fellas. It's been good knowin' ya."

Okinawa Shima, Ryukyu Chain, late April 1945.

"Well, lookee here—marines back from patrol!" Private Freddy "Junior" Hudson grinned at us as we stumbled our way back into camp. "Kill any Japs while you were out there?"

I sat down on the ammo crate beside Junior, taking off my helmet, and began running my fingers through my hair. "As a matter of fact, Junior . . . we did."

Junior gaped at me for a moment, trying to decipher exactly what I was saying. Then he started laughing. "Ah, who do you think you're foolin', Mace? You can go blow smoke somewhere else! Japs, my ass!"

Why *would* Junior believe me, anyway? Nearly every day that's all we did: patrol, patrol, patrol, without a Jap in sight. By all appearances, it seemed that the Japanese had never been on the northern end of Okinawa. We knew, of course, that the army was getting their asses handed to them to the south of us, and we knew that it was only a matter of time before we, too, would head south and into the fray; nevertheless, the monotony of constant patrolling, the absence of Nip resistance, and the familiarity of the same old faces was really starting to get to eager marines like Private Freddy "Junior" Hudson. Couple that with the fact that Junior had joined the marines to avenge his brother's death on Tarawa, and any real skirmish with the Japanese that Junior wasn't a part of would've turned him green with envy.

Poor Freddy Hudson, only seventeen years old, who wasn't much to look at, and who couldn't catch a tan to save his life, got chased all over the USS *McCracken*, on our way to Okinawa, by Billy Leyden and me. We had Junior fooled into believing that Leyden and I were going to rape him, since we hadn't had a woman in so long. Off Junior ran, a shot out of a rifle, we had him scared so bad. We wouldn't have been able to catch him, even if we wanted to. Everybody got a real kick out of that one, all except for Junior, who, evidently, wouldn't be fooled again.

He was a real ace softball player, though, and Junior had the type of kid-brother personality that everybody liked.

Junior was justified in his skepticism, alright.

"Suit yourself," I told him. "Really, it was Eubanks over there who did the shootin', and Weisdack tagged along with him."

"Alright, wiseguy." Junior crossed his arms at his chest. "Then tell me what happened."

We were patrolling an area that we had been over time and again, the same boring hours, only on a different day. To our left was the same recessed area in the ground—a bowl-shaped indentation in the earth, where water had collected long ago, allowing a copse of tall trees to grow nice and pretty, amid the rolling hills in the area.

As a platoon, we passed the area like it was nothing, my fire team bringing up the rear. Weisdack was on point, followed by Eubanks, then Whitby, and then myself, as the last man in line.

I wasn't looking directly at Eubanks at the time, but evidently Eubanks glanced down into the trees and spotted something he didn't like among the foliage. The next thing I knew, Eubanks brought his BAR near his shoulder and unloaded a full magazine into the trees. Eubanks quickly looked at me, but before I could say anything, he had Weisdack following him into the thicket. Without a word, Bob caught my eyes, a nervous look. I merely shook my head and trotted over to where Whitby stood. *Damn idiots,* I thought, *running down there without even thinking.*

Only about thirty seconds passed, and out came Eubanks, panting, followed by Weisdack.

"Four." Eubanks held up four fingers, between breaths. "Got four of 'em . . . Nips down there."

Weisdack merely nodded that it was true, catching his breath as well.

"Damn." Bob's eyes darted between us. "What do ya think they were doin' down there?"

"Probably talkin' about what easy duty they had, without seein' a single marine in the area," I said. "Well, Stumpy'll wanna know about this. C'mon, we'd better get back with the platoon."

Junior still looked at me as if someone had rubber-stamped LIAR across my forehead. "So, that's what happened, huh?"

"Yep. I was about to go report it to Stumpy. You can ask any of 'em. Wimpy, George, Eubanks. We were all right there."

Suddenly Junior began nodding his head. "Yeah, yeah, okay . . . You really aren't kiddin' me this time, are ya?"

"Junior . . . I told ya—"

"Whoo!" He got up. "Wait'll I tell the fellas about *this*!"

"Hey, hey, wait up, willya?" I said. "Let me tell Stumpy about this first, Junior. In the meantime, wouldja mind asking Weisdack to come over here to see me?"

"Sure, I'll do that." He smiled. "Damn, I wish I had been there to see it!" Then Junior held out his arms, as if he were cradling an invisible machine gun, pretending to hose every Jap on the island.

I lit a cigarette and took a deep drag on it. I didn't have to wait long for Weisdack to arrive.

George sat down, looking as exhausted as he assuredly felt.

"Shame about Ernie Pyle, huh?" George asked as he took a

cigarette from his pack. "Guy getting killed like that, after all the shit he'd been through. Makes ya wonder, huh? Don't even know why he was here, when he didn't have to be."

It really was a shame about Ernie Pyle. The only newsman to truly earn his stripes in combat was killed on his first jaunt to the Pacific. We all applauded him coming, and when we found out he was killed, to be honest, some marines took it harder than the president's death. Still, it was just one of those things. Ernie probably fired more bullets with a typewriter then some marines did with a carbine, and he came over here for the same reasons all of us did: for the love of his country, and to discover what was right and just in this world, even when everything appeared to be going so wrong.

"Look at Junior." I pointed, and Weisdack's eyes followed. "Running around here like a new colt, this way and that . . . never stoppin' . . . Remember when we first got here and I told Junior, 'Everything we told you on Pavuvu about combat is not happening now . . . but it *will*'?"

"Yeah, I remember." George chuckled.

"Well . . ." I took another long drag. "It's about to happen, George."

I wanted so badly to add, *But you won't be coming with us.* Though I stopped myself short.

"Yeah?" George replied.

"Yeah. How's that back of yours, George?"

George stiffened when I inquired about his ringworm-riddled back; nonetheless, he attempted to brush me off. "Oh, it's fine. Nothing a little medicine won't cure, is all."

He knew he was lying. George knew that *I* knew he was lying. The only one sitting there with a rubber stamp across his forehead that day, was George Weisdack, from Donora, Pennsylvania.

"Listen, buddy," I began. "Did I ever tell you about Lyman Rice?"

"No." George shook his head. "I don't think so."

"A good-lookin', blond, curly-headed guy . . . a real nice marine. Got a bad case of ringworm on Pavuvu—"

"Now, wait a second!" George interrupted.

"No, no," I said. "Lemme finish my story, willya?"

George appeared put off, yet still he sat there, fidgety, like a kid in church.

"Anyway . . ." I chuckled at the thought of Lyman Rice on Pavuvu, before we invaded Peleliu. "Lyman had a Victrola on Pavuvu, right? Played some great records. Ya know, Frank Sinatra, 'Without a Song,' Fred Waring singing 'Where or When,' McCormick bellowing *The Barber of Seville*. The works, really. We had a good time. But there was this damned ringworm . . . and ya just knew that Rice was in a world of pain, though he was a real tough marine. He wouldn't let on that it was killin' him, see?"

"Yeah," Weisdack said, although he was looking away from me, staring off into the distance.

"Yeah. Well, that was Lyman Rice." I patted George on the leg. We sat in silence awhile. Eventually George looked back at me.

"So . . . well . . . whatever happened to his ringworm? Did he get it cured?"

"Oh, yeah, yeah, he got it cured. In a manner of speaking, I guess. He got killed on the Five Sisters. I don't suppose you worry about ringworm on the Five Sisters if you're dead, ya know?"

I tossed my cigarette on the ground and snuffed it out with my foot.

Life, like fire, doesn't survive without oxygen. Even Paleolithic man knew that. It's only when you add blood to the equation that it turns the whole world red with flames.

"Look, George," I said, in a very even tone, so that he didn't know what was coming. I was about to sucker-punch him from the heart. "Can I ask you for a little favor?"

"Sure, Mace. Whattaya want?"

"I want you to gather up your gear, walk past Chulis, and go down to the battalion aid station. Then I want you to get on a boat and get off this fucking island and go home, George. Go home."

George finally understood in the silence that followed.

Presently, George stood up, leaving his rifle propped against the ammo crate. He looked down at me. "Okay, Sterl. See ya stateside."

"Sure thing, George. Stateside." I smiled.

There's crying out in the darkness. I hear it and my eyes automatically squint, as if looking more intently into the nightscape will enable me to make out the sounds more clearly—to somehow get a bead on where it's coming from, or to convince myself that it's nothing, when it really is.

PFC Eubanks is at my elbow, lying right beside me, peering out into the gloom, too.

"Mace," he whispers. "You hear that?"

I can see the whites of Eubanks's eyes, big, round, scared. The crying warbles in pitch, spine-chilling, sending gooseflesh up my arms. Otherwise, the night is as quiet as a tomb.

"Yeah, I hear it." I look away from Eubanks and back out into the night.

Eubanks's voice quivers. "Sounds like . . . it sounds like . . . *Christ,* it sounds like a *baby.*"

It really does sound like a child crying out there. Or it could be a Nip trick to entice a marine to go out there and get himself killed out of the kindness of his heart.

A few minutes pass and Eubanks can't take it any longer.

"Psst . . . Mace? Say, listen . . . ya think we ought to go out there and check it out?"

"Nah, bullshit." I gaze back at Eubanks. "We stay put. Ya got that? The last thing we wanna do is go out there and kill a little friggin' kid."

So I've solved the mystery of night. It's not the darkness outside of me that frightens me. It's the darkness we carry within ourselves that's truly scary.

On Peleliu, when the sun went down, while on guard, I had conjured up a myriad of monsters, skulking in their natural habitat, shielded from view behind a curtain of shade. Some of them were real—most of them were imagined. Now, on Okinawa, I should be afraid, but I'm not.

I'm more curious about the explosions flashing off the horizon, way to the south of us, than frightened by them. White, red, and orange lightning paints thin images of a faraway war, where the army is catching hell from the Japanese on southern Okinawa.

The strobes of light are mesmeric. I'm hypnotized. Curiosity asks, *What will it feel like to be among those lights?* After all, from where I sit, they carry no more harm than the lit end of a cigarette. Logic retorts, *You'll know soon enough, Corporal.*

So it's not the unknown that will kill you, after all. It's what you *think* you know that twists your guts up in knots.

I'm sleepy. I don't know the answer.

Soon we'll head south. Combat again.

11

HOPE, LIKE DEATH

Now!

Okinawa, May 2, 1945.

Suddenly we're running across a dry rice paddy. *Thip thip thip thip!* Japanese bullets come in from the left and spin up tufts of dirt in front of us. *Christ!*

"Stay loose! Don't stop!" I yell.

We run right through the spray of Nip bullets as if we are invisible.

Like hell! The Japs can see us as plain as day, across a field like this! Forty yards of open ground. The earth heaves—a cauldron boiling over with a company of sprinting marines. All kinds of crap zips through the air. Explosions fall, left and right, but I am only vaguely aware of the din. Nip artillery and gunfire cancel each other out in a field bled of sound. That's the truth—in the middle of it all, it's life within a vacuum. No time to think. No time to feel.

Or let me put it this way before I run out of time:

This is southern Okinawa—and it's a bastard to be here.

The whole run takes only fifteen seconds, but a lot can happen in fifteen seconds, on Okinawa. It takes one-point-five seconds for

Spud Dunlop to get hit and fall like a sack of potatoes. *Tick!* In one second PFC Westbrook is eaten up by shell fragments (he's not going to make it). *Tick!* Just a few feet over, in all this shit, Lieutenant Sam Menselos falls. *Tick! Tick!* I sent Mom the wristwatch I took off of the dead Nip on Peleliu. In Queens the watch ticks off the seconds as if they mean something special, but time don't mean shit on Okinawa. Not right now, anyway. Not with Jap knee mortars coming right up our asses like clockwork.

This guy, Albert Einstein? He put together all these special figures and formulas to tell us that time is relative. He could have saved himself the trouble and spent fifteen seconds with the marines on Okinawa. Then we'd see how fuckin' smart he is.

Here's the rest of the story.

Fighting the Japanese, darting across a rice paddy like this, in the face of withering fire, is time compressed, time expanded, time destroyed, yet never time on the money. That's what I want you to understand. The story's no good if it doesn't make any sense . . . and from this moment forward, none of it makes an ounce of sense.

When I was on Peleliu, I could break down the moments and give myself hope against the gallows. On Okinawa, the moments break the person down.

By the time we hit the embankment, on the other side of the rice paddy, we're safe but we're sorry. Also cold and wet—the temperature on the island has dropped considerably, the mist in the air a prelude of the rain to come.

The whole goal of this morning's run was to go over the rise on our side of the line and attack the Nips on their side—crossing open ground in the process, and climbing over an eight-foot-tall embankment to reach the Japs.

Whatever genius hatched this plan must have been a regular Einstein.

"Dammit!" Junior yells as he runs up to the embankment. Junior, like the rest of us, attempts to slow down, lest he slam right into the slope. "Where the hell are the Japs?" He stops running.

With my back against the embankment, I crane my neck, looking over my shoulder, and then up—measuring the height of the wall that separates us from the entire Nip army.

Junior sees what I see, and I notice the slow realization cross his face.

"That's about right, Junior," I tell him.

We've only been on southern Okinawa for a day, and already it's evident what the trouble's going to be. Unlike Peleliu, where at least the enemy would come out and play, Okinawa gives off a helpless and depressing energy. A marine can't fight what a marine can't see. Out here, there's only the notion of Nips—even though we're fully aware of who's smacking us across the mouth.

The shelling begins to taper off, but that doesn't make us less jittery. Some marines simply collapse from the run, out of breath; they can't believe they made it. You almost want to check for bullet holes in your dungaree jacket. Mostly, we crouch behind the embankment, wondering what our next move's going to be. If we're supposed to scale this wall, forget it; we left the ladders on the amtracs a month ago. If we go back, then what was the point? Well, that's the infantry for you. We don't ask questions, we just do it. It is the riflemen who are always at the front of the attack, always up against some sort of obstacle or embankment, as thick as the job is hard.

The only consolation is that, protected as we are against this wall, the Nips can't see us either. Still, the Japs toss in a few shells on the rice paddy for good measure, sprinkling us with dirt, and who knows what else.

"No, no! I don't need a stretcher! Leave me alone!" I look over in the direction of the shouting and see that they are still trying to evacuate Lieutenant Menselos. I don't know how badly Menselos is wounded, but the way I figure it, either he's showing his moxie or he's playing it smart. Menselos knows that if they carry him out of here, they'll have to cross the rice paddy to do it—and crossing the rice paddy on a slow-moving stretcher would be like putting a bull's-eye between your ass cheeks. *Bang!* Anyway, I lean into Whitby and kind of joke, "Look, Wimp, if that guy don't wanna get on the fuckin' stretcher, I sure as hell will!"

Bob doesn't say anything, though. He simply gives a wan smile.

The fact is, nobody's talking—especially the new guys. They all sport the same feral look in their eyes, from being shaken in a cage and tossed in a corner. I look, and I wonder if I appeared that frightened when we hit the beach on Peleliu. Except that it doesn't matter, because whatever they're feeling, I'm probably experiencing the same thing.

Given that Okinawa has its own fears to fight, there's no way even the saltiest vet could have anticipated this. What puts a sharper point on it is that the whole experience is viewed against the relative ease we had during the month we spent on the northern part of the island.

As soon as we reached southern Okinawa on May 1, 1945—*WHAM!*—they let us have it!

One moment we were cautiously walking through the rubble, nervously scanning the bombed-out hills before us, and in the next second the ground felt like it had lifted a foot, as the artillery began to fall in. When the earth dropped again, I swear, we were scrambling around on thin air.

We made haste, but fast!

Zigzagging at a run, I passed an officer calling into his radio, "Smoke! More smoke!" *Kzzzzzkzzz!* A smattering of dirt clods bounced off the top of my helmet, in between the explosions. Marines were just about breaking their necks seeking a safe place to hide. Finally I dropped into an army-made foxhole. Other marines did the same, peeking out over the rims of their holes, and *flash!* A volcano erupted and sent so much muck into the air, there was only a giant wall of brown before our eyes. I closed my lids, and all I saw was red.

Eventually the incoming began to die down, being replaced by a thick carpet of new smoke rising over our whole area, swirling over the ground, and shrouding us in a fog. The tendrils of smoke, wafting in our midst, reminded me of the mist that always appeared in the graveyard scenes in one of those horror pictures. I never liked that kind of film, even as a kid.

They've got this whole place zeroed in. Realization hits hard. *There's* nothing *they can't hit out here.*

Now I think about Europe and how the GIs are getting blown to pieces over there.

In this case, though, the Nip volleys were only designed to shake us up—and teach us a lesson: *There's nowhere we can't touch you. You will be violated, repeatedly. You will never forget our advances.*

"Sonuvabitch! These guys aren't fucking joking!" Eubanks said.

"No, they're not," I agreed, while I watched the smoke dissipate, revealing the hillocks beyond the fog.

Meandering out of our holes, cautiously, we took in our new environs, measuring the feel of the place, ominous and oppressive. It was worse than we thought. Everything was mired in at least six feet of confusion. Not even the officers had a clue.

"What the hell's going on with this place?"

"Whatever it is, it looks like this line has been occupied for a long time."

"Well, you can bet the big-shot marines will have to do what the army couldn't, huh?"

Another marine smiled. "That's a familiar goddamn refrain, if I ever heard one."

"Hey, fellas—but at least they left us some coffee!"

It was coffee, alright, but it was even worse than the regular sludge the marines foisted on us. The coffee was in a five-gallon kerosene can, cut off at the top, and just sitting out in the open, cold and still. So we got an idea and put some composition C underneath the can to heat up the joe. Although there couldn't have been enough heat—not even in the earth's core—to make this brew go down any better. For all we knew the army guys could have pissed in it, cleaned their weapons with it, or used it to prime a carburetor. But get *this* . . . it was good stuff! You'd take a drag off of a cigarette and then a sip of the coffee, and the bitterness in the back of your mouth alone was enough to wake you up. Not that many marines needed a pick-me-up. First of all, it rained like a sonuvabitch our first night in, and after we attacked the embankment, the following day, every marine—veterans and new guys alike—was hepped up with a good case of the nerves. For good reason, too. This was a new type of war, and it bit hard beneath the flesh, cutting against the grain of the combat we had come to expect.

Even as we were being trucked down south, the sunshine turned cold and lifeless. The truck engines hummed too quietly as the weight of our new surroundings formed the manacles that would create within us the prisoners of battle, slaves to the gun.

Farther south, the scene changed slowly from green-on-green to a filthy sickness, which seemed to cover everything. Southern Okinawa looked like the black-and-white photos of Belgium during World War I—muted earth tones, scant vegetation, pitted and pocked ridges from the constant shelling—and in the many shell holes along the muted ground lay the detritus of war in its myriad forms. Empty crates of ammunition, spent shell casings, burned-out military vehicles of all types, discarded personal equipment . . .

In one spot along the road, there were the rows of army dead—covered in ponchos, lying on stretchers, most of them shoeless, their buddies having scavenged the best pairs for their own use. I looked down at my own boondockers, to check the wear, wondering if anybody would have any use for them if I got killed.

When you think like that, it's not fatalistic. Fatalism would be checking your buddy's boondockers to see if he wore the same size as you.

As far as I knew, nobody thought like that. In fact, we didn't speak much during our whole journey south. Marines were simply too busy taking it all in—and puking out what the mind couldn't stomach.

Now I know what our evening supper must feel like. It starts off nice and tasty, pleasing to the tongue, but then it gets chewed to bits by the teeth in things. That's okay, though, because once it hits the belly, it's still relatively in one piece. Then it has to wind its way through a labyrinth of guts and tripe, squeezing its way through the countless bends and turns that sap the nutrients from it—finally just to come out another piece of shit, like everything else that succumbs to the process.

Like the army guys we were relieving—the 27th Infantry Division. When they let us off the trucks, we walked the rest of the way to the front (*This place disappoints me*) as the army headed back to the rear for a well-deserved break. I had seen this exchange before, and it never deviated from exactly what it looked like—removing the dirty linen and putting out the clean. New company had arrived.

Even as we loiter against the embankment on May 2, bitterness rises in the back of my throat again, only I haven't had any army joe to put it there.

Sergeant Chase walks over.

"Say, what's the dope, Sarge?" I ask.

"Well, we're pullin' out of here, for one. The way they look at it we're stuck or somethin'."

Well, that figures.

Chase resumes, pointing across the way. "See that embankment? The one that follows that draw, back where we came from? We're gonna cross that thing, one at a time. Gotta keep our heads low—but when we get up to our side of the line, over the rise, we should be okay."

So that's the straight skinny: a "strategic withdraw." In other words, a retreat, and retreat we do. Only this time, as far as I know, we don't receive any casualties from the Japanese. The only thing that comes close is the poor marine who was right behind Whitby.

See, to get back, the only obstacle in our way was a gully, which most of us jumped over with ease. It was only a few feet deep, but because Bob was such a shrimp, he balked at making the leap. By the time the 3rd Platoon made our jaunt back, everybody had ceased with the one-at-a-time business. Each marine went as he pleased. So as Whitby was standing at the lip of the gully, contemplating the leap, another marine, running with his head down, plowed right into Bob's back. The marine's helmet gashed his nose, and Whitby went across the gully anyway.

I'm not so sure it would've taken us all day to go one at a time, despite our rush to get the hell out of there. Besides, the only thing that mattered was finding a secure way back, instead of the hard way forward. It was the upside to the alternative—and that was going down for good!

May 3!

Heavy mortar and artillery fire drops in on the 1st Platoon right after they clear the rise.

They're getting hammered, for God's sake!

I watch the earth rain upward, toward the sky, just beyond our lines.

The call goes up immediately. "Stand by with ponchos for the wounded!"

We're right behind the 2nd Platoon, waiting our turn to go over the rise . . . just like we did the day before, up and over, attack the embankment . . . and then what?

Marines run like mad, heads on backward, a classic route. The attack ends just as soon as it began. "Ponchos! Ponchos, over here!"

I spy a group of Marines struggling with a limp marine in the center of a poncho, and I sling my M-1 over my shoulder and race to help them get the poor guy to safety. *Boom boom boom boom boom!* The rapid-fire artillery is still shattering the ground, but I don't think; I merely react.

"C'mon, guys, fuckin' move it!"

I run around toward the rear of the poncho, hooking my fingers under the fabric, trying to keep the train balanced, because whoever this wounded guy is, he's giving the team fits. You waddle like a duck, trying to move a load this heavy, not letting the poncho down, not letting your buddy down—because if this guy falls, you'll cringe inside. Because once a marine falls, you don't want to let him down again.

This wounded marine . . .

Boom boom boom boom boom boom!

Oh, sweet Jesus!

The wounded marine has his dungaree jacket pulled up to his chest. His dungaree pants are pulled down, all the way to the middle of his calves. Where there isn't blood, I see the chalk white of his skin, appearing nearly transparent, so blanched I can make out a web of blue veins beneath the skin, sending blood through his heart, and out of a hole in his groin where his genitals used to be. Actually, I can't tell how big the hole is down there, because of all the blood—but his penis and testicles certainly aren't in the near vicinity.

It's Sergeant Heeb. We're carrying Sergeant John P. Heeb, from Rushville, Indiana, out on a poncho, in a swirl of chaos, and it wouldn't matter a good goddamn if he lived or died. Robbed of his manhood, he's a goner. To have survived Peleliu, only to lose your balls on Okinawa?

This island will end up emasculating every one of us.

Finally, it's quiet. Quiet enough, anyway. We settle in behind a humpback hill, which is part of the odd terrain that dots all of southern Okinawa.

They pull K Company into battalion reserve, a few hundred yards behind what they now tell us is called the Shuri Line. Pulling us back is really laughable, because it's much easier for the Nips to lob their artillery in at an arc, as opposed to the flat trajectory that looks our front lines square in the teeth. This means that the poor riflemen who think they're safe might really be in for the works.

A case in point: All hell breaks loose!

The impact of the first rounds leaves you reeling. The rest leaves you numb.

There's no use to trying to describe what being under an artillery barrage is like, nor how helpless you feel, getting trapped like this . . . but insanity? I can tell you about crazy, and it has nothing to do with bravery, or the roar of the crowd. Dumb is plain dumb, but crazy is just how it sounds.

"Hey, you dumb sonuvabitch, get down!" The ground tilts right . . . then left, and stays there. Only nobody actually yells this to the major, and even if somebody *did*, Major Paul Douglas wouldn't have heard anyone over the gleam of the oak leaves radiating from his collar, let alone the noise from the cannonade.

As if he were back in the States, relaxed in his swanky Illinois home, standing in front of his lavatory mirror, Paul Douglas strolls over to a nearby tree, debris falling all around him, while he takes out a safety razor, hangs a pocket mirror on the tree, and begins to shave his face in the middle of a Nip barrage.

Sane marines scramble and jump in foxholes, our hands over our helmets, our fingers plugging our ears, taking quick looks over the edges of the holes to watch the crazy major get drilled. Yet he never goes down—and a poor newlywed like Marion Westbrook does?

Anyway, seeing something like that—nobody would believe it back home, even if I were to tell them.

Nobody would believe a fraction of what I've seen.

Cherry-boys, in sailor's caps, tongue-wag the local villagers with tales of blood and Japanese villainy. Seventeen-year-old enlistees, still sweet with candy behind their ears, who couldn't tell you the difference between a peep-sight and a poop-hole, can recite anything you want to know about slitting Nip throats. Still the riflemen on Okinawa hear things beyond sound. We see things that were never meant to be seen, as we fade into the night.

Late at night (May 3? May 4?), we're called out of our foxholes and instructed to move out. Tiny sweat beads are cold on the backs of our necks. One foot in front of the other, single-file soldiers, traipsing around in the darkness, with no information to go on. *Zilch*.

Junior's voice is small and distinct, right behind me. He's got a cautious tone now, a whisper.

"Mace. I wish I had one of those . . . *things*, right about now. What did they call those things? Snoopy Scopes? Snooper Scopes? Is that it?"

Yeah, they are called Snooper Scopes. I nod to Junior that he's got the name right, not considering that Junior can't see me in the darkness, any more than a Snooper Scope can.

They had brought these gadgets up to the line—some type of night-vision apparatuses. The first one, as big as a football, they called a Snooper Scope. You looked through the lens in the front of it, and it lit the night up green—not necessarily giving a better field of vision, but only a different tint to the darkness. In effect, it made the vague shapes in front of us even more blurry, as opposed to the sharpness of the naked eye.

They even had a version of the scope that fit on a rifle. Though the clarity was a smidge better, if a marine sniper tried to pick off a Nip at five hundred yards, at night, it would take a lot more than a fancy scope to drill a hole through his rice-eating ass.

It would take a lot more than a marine sniper, for that matter.

I had already seen one of those snipers operate, and all he did was clean his rifle, look through his scope for a few minutes, and then resume the rifle cleaning. Over and over, he would perform this noble task, never deviating from the script; then, when he felt he had sniped enough, he'd move to another spot in the rocks, in case the rocks on the Jap side of the line had spotted him spotting them.

We walk a few more yards, and eventually I ask Junior where his squad is.

"Beats the shit outta me," he whispers. "Back on Pavuvu, maybe, playin' softball. They asked me to go out to left field, and I guess I went too far." Junior stifles a chuckle.

"Yeah, I guess," I whisper back. "Well, go link up with 'em or somethin'. Besides, I thought you were here to kill Nips."

"You seen any Nips?"

"Nope."

"I rest my case," Junior chides. "Anyway, it's too damn dark to find anybody, so I found you instead."

With that I have to fight back a laugh of my own. Junior is trying to be clever—and he *is* a clever kid. It's just that, deep down inside, perhaps I want Junior to be another Larry Mahan or Seymour Levy, but Junior isn't. Junior Hudson is just another well-meaning kid, with a joke and a smile, who found his way into this war because of a brother he'll never see again and a sense of righteous vengeance that followed suit.

I won't be the kid's dead brother.

All through the night it's more of the same. "Move out!" "Hold up!" That's all we hear for God knows how long. Eventually we're told that the Nips are going to make a landing on the coast, and we're out here to make sure they die before they hit dry land. Five hundred Japs. Maybe that many. Four hundred. Three hundred. That's probably closer to the truth. Blind man's bluff. Just knowing that we're groping around in the dark makes this a deadly game of chance. I think I see the white echoes of a battle raging, somewhere off in the distance, with the muffled toy-gun pops of machine guns and rifle fire—so far out, I don't know if it's real or just the afterimages of the crap we experienced in the last couple of days. Nevertheless, the word comes down that the 1st Regiment wiped out an outfit of Nips trying to make the landing we were sent to oppose. *Good. Better them than us.*

On the other hand, if we knew the dangers that faced us with the coming dawn, we would rather have had the safety in numbers the 1st Regiment enjoyed, instead of hanging our keisters in the breeze.

We got lost.

Just before dawn we discovered we were about sixty yards from where we were supposed to be in order to get back to the company lines. If that doesn't sound like much, imagine being under the safe canopy of night, only to have the sun creep in, lighting us up for the whole Nip army to see.

That sun is a slow bastard when you're just sitting around watching it come up, but when you've really got somewhere to be, the sun rises nearly as quick as flicking on a light switch.

"C'mon, c'mon, you guys, move! Let's go. Get up that friggin' hill!"

At a mad dash, we weaved, climbed, and crawled up a thirty-foot hillock, which appeared to be safe, having at least a few trees to shield us from the imminent light. When we reached the top, huffing and puffing, we bent over at the waist, our hands on our knees, looking out upon the flatland before us. "Jesus! How'd we get so lost?"

Gene Holland caught my gaze, and he just shook his head, as if to say, *This is really screwed up, Mace.* Or perhaps I only imagined that's what Holland was trying to convey. After all, how was I supposed to read through the red of those puffy eyes, baggy under the lids, stark against his ashen skin?

Somebody was running this show—somebody got us lost—but for the life of me I couldn't tell you who it was now that Lieutenant Dunlop had been evacuated.

Okay, okay . . . think, Mace, think!

Out there, below us and off a ways, I barely made out the company command post, secreted behind a tree-lined area, similar to the one we were perched on. The idea was, if we could make a run for it, we'd be safe. Except that it was too late. In less than thirty minutes the sun had risen in the east, and already we were bathed in sunlight. "Oh, for chrissakes!" I squinted up at the sun and my eyes felt burned through by the haloes ringing the ball in the sky.

For a moment my body merely relaxed in soft resignation to what was coming next. If I could have laughed, I would have. We anticipated the sound of the Nip shells coming in, even before they fell.

When the Jap rounds slammed into us, though, the last thing we did was resign.

Boom!

Boom, boom!

Boom!

"Shit!"

"Somebody get on the can and get us out of here!"

Already, marines were shimmying back down the opposite side of the small hill, in the hope that they'd be too far down the slope for the Nips to see them.

"Negative." The marine on the radio looked at us. "Request denied to return to company area. CP says to sit it out."

Sit it out?

Here's the conundrum: If we hadn't made the call to the CP, but instead just made a mad dash for it, not only could we have given the CP's position away, but also our own marines could have lit us up. They weren't expecting us. Moreover, if the Nips had us zeroed in, which they assuredly did, our chances of survival were better under the shelter of the small hill than on the dead ground between us and the CP.

The only option was to stay put, no movement whatsoever, and the Japs might get the idea that there was nobody atop this hill— that we escaped, or we weren't worth the ammunition. *Fat chance.* So we wiggled as far down the backside of the hill as we could. If the Nips stopped lobbing shells on us in the next few hours, we'd know it was safe to move. We'd know we were okay. *Just don't friggin' move.*

So we sat. There was nothing left to do but wait.

I took a seat, rifle cradled across my arms. I had been up all night, I was hungry and exhausted, and even the familiar marines looked like strangers to me now.

Off in the distance I saw a Sherman tank, throwing some rounds out toward the Japanese lines. Things like that were normal, everyday things you see in a combat zone. You spy something like that and you pay it no mind. The tankers were doing their job, and I was doing mine. Except, for some reason, I stayed focused on what the Sherman was doing—or, rather, I was just glazing over, and the tank just happened to be in my line of sight. There was a marine walking atop the tank, a few other guys standing around the tracks, while other marines appeared to be carrying crates of ammunition, or maybe some chow. The whole scene was a little over a hundred yards away, so I couldn't tell much, not that it mattered.

Then this airplane flew in from the right, gliding silkily in, smooth and sleek. I couldn't make out the markings, yet I felt it was one of our planes, because this one zipped in from the seaward side of the island, and Nip planes, when they're out at sea, they stay out there—shot down, or crashed on the decks of one of our ships. At any rate, what happened next was so bizarre that it bordered on the surreal.

The plane was only fifty feet above the ground when she dropped her tip-tank, dead atop the Sherman tank.

Whoosh! A flash fire engulfed the Sherman as the tiny figures by the tank began scurrying around—only they looked like they were running in slow motion, little trails of themselves flowing out behind them.

Because the scene was too far away for me to hear the sounds, while you're drowsy the effect was a little too unreal for me to make sense of it. It was a little like staring at a photograph of people you don't know, and expecting to have some sort of emotional attachment to the chemical-soaked paper.

Whatever possessed the pilot to ditch his tip-tank over the marine lines was anybody's guess. Maybe he was in trouble, but *Jesus*—what a way to do it!

When we finally got the word to make our run for the CP, it sure as hell didn't take us long to get there. What's more, we couldn't have been more pleased that we came out of that trap relatively unscathed in the process. Only just as soon as we arrived the call went up to move out.

"Hey, fellas, nice of you to join us. Now let's get your stuff together. We're goin' back on the line."

To the 3rd Squad, it felt like we never left the line.

May 6, 1945, Asato Gawa, Shuri Line.

The rain falls. It always seems to fall these days. If it's not raining, it's sprinkling. If it's not sprinkling, it's misting. If it's not wet, it's not normal.

I open a can of C rations, and the rain dances in it. My feet are puffy albinos, pink under the nails and sopping up moisture. We smoke under our ponchos, we eat under our ponchos, and we try to sleep under them, too. The front line is a poncho city—each a private shelter, erected in honor of keeping home and dry. Asylum and safekeeping, however, are just an illusion, abetted by the fact that everybody is hiding beneath one. Hiding something. We all hide something. It's better to keep your eyes open, and your paranoia sharp, or you'll die under a goddamn poncho. They'll wrap you up in the sucker and ship you off on a jeep, stacked with the other poncho-clad marines.

Yes, it's much better to see it coming, rather than being killed by what lurks in the spaces between things.

A machine gun rattles off to my left. *Tat, tat, tat tat . . . tat, tat, tat tat tat!* Instinct jerks my head in that direction to see what's going on.

The machine gun spits its fire as I watch three pajama-clad people moving up and down one of the hills in front of our lines. It doesn't make any sense, what they're doing there. Maybe they're Nips or maybe they're civilians. Who knows.

That's PFC James Allen, a machine gunner in the 1st Platoon, about fifty yards to my left, letting loose on them with his gun.

Allen is on the left-hand flank of the line, with the 1st Platoon, and I'm on the right-hand flank of our line, with the 3rd Platoon, on the sides of what amounts to a boomerang-shaped line. So that means that Allen and I secure both flanks. An evil position to be in. As the line moves farther forward, toward the bend of the boomerang—about two hundred yards to the front—the ground elevates a good fifteen feet, where they moved the company CP.

Boy, it's lonesome out here—and disconcerting as a sonuvabitch, seeing that nothing stands in the way between you and the Nips, except the crooked and chewed-up land, which has been pounded down to nothing but a muddy sludge.

Tat, tat, tat, tat tat tat tat tat!

From my foxhole, I see that Allen has a good bead on the figures in black, by the way his tracers fly from his gun. *Up, up . . .*

up! go the rounds, in measured bursts. The figures try to escape the bullets by struggling up a small hill, but Jim keeps walking them up. *Tat, tat, tat tat . . . tat, tat!* Allen must have opened fire because curiosity got the best of him, or he's privy to information that I'm not. I can just imagine his deep blue eyes, set off by his ruddy skin, an American mask behind his gun, as he walks that sucker up and finally catches one. *Spat!* The body crumples up like an ant's carcass, curled in the middle, and slides back down the hill into a pool of brackish water. The other dark figures make it over the hill and disappear.

Every once in a while that's how we see the Nips—off in the distance one moment, but in the next second they've vanished. I take aim and fire off a couple of shots at one, but when they disappear like that, it leaves me wondering if they were ever there at all. There's no telling if I killed one or even if it was just a civilian on the horizon.

I've got mud on my face, because one of those big bastards—a Nip 320 mm mortar, a "screaming Jesus"—landed about thirty yards from me and threw crap everywhere. Swiping my hands on my dungarees, I only come up with more mud on my palms, and more mud, and more . . .

The Japs send over everything they've got, periodically, to dust us over. That's not all they do to screw with us. They affect our minds, doing it in stupid ways, too.

"Corpsman!"

It's hard to believe, isn't it? I can't tell you how many marines we've lost in the last few days, but it's a lot.

A couple of flashes of green and brown run by, hot on the trail of a wounded marine.

The scenery never changes. Marines always get killed like that. Like I said . . . *stupid.*

A case in point: There's a tank, about ten feet to my right, and eight feet above me, as the ground rises. The tank has been wiped out for ages, yet some new Jap spotter sees it sitting out here and lets loose five or six rounds on it.

It's absolutely insane how loud the rounds clang off the tank. This goes on for what seems like an eternity, until an old salty vet on the Nip side of the line informs the new spotter that Charlie Chan, or whatever his name was, destroyed the tank last week.

Evidently, not all the spotters get the same memo, because the next day they are back at it again. *Clang, boom! Clang, boom! Clang!* I'm fed up with this crap.

So between this and the rain and the phantom Japs and being on the line for days on end, it really starts to grind me. I gnaw my lower lip; I beat out rhythms on the forestock of my M-1—any juke or jive, swing beat will do, recalling how Joe "the Book" back in Queens would regale the young street-corner crowd about Cab Calloway and Gene Krupa, laying out with the cocaine. Then there was that little fucking organ-grinder monkey that Johnny Blade owned. I was walking home, and the little sonuvabitch ran and jumped on my back, screeching and screaming various simian obscenities—and there I was, pulling and tugging, trying to get that monkey off my back. I thought I'd have to run all the way home with him before he finally flew off and hightailed it back to Blade's house. All of these hidden secrets in life, as I lie with my back to the rear of my foxhole, my ass in a pond of mud, while I simply adapt. A marine knows a few secrets, too. Although nobody back home would want to hear them. I adapt because there's no other choice.

You adapt but you don't.

The thing is, though, I'm breaking the cardinal rule, and I'm thinking of home.

I can smile at something like that.

That is, until I run out of things to smile about.

"Where the hell did you get that jeep, Corporal?"

I'm standing in front of a lieutenant—I have no idea who he is, or what outfit he's from. I'm simply stunned by his question.

Here I am, covered in filth, with blood on the sleeves of my dungaree jacket, I'm unshaved, my helmet is at a cant, there's mud bulging from beneath my fingernails, and the memory of sleep is solely a dream I had once upon a time.

"I brought some wounded in on the jeep, sir . . . I—"

"I didn't ask you *what* you did with the jeep, Corporal. I'm asking you *where* you got the jeep!"

There he is, his dungarees spotless, his pants neatly tucked into his leggings, his nails clipped, his teeth annoyingly white, his face so smooth I could count the pores on his chin, and beneath his cap I can see the finely trimmed sideburns of a newly minted haircut—something I've not had in a month.

"I found it abandoned in an open field, sir!" I hope he caught the bite of venom in my voice. I really hope he did. The thing is, I've never disrespected an officer before, but right now I feel like punching this turd in the throat.

After everything that happened today, perhaps I deserve that luxury.

The day started off fairly quiet. Whitby and Eubanks and I were sitting in my foxhole and talking about—of all things—we're talking about babies! Of course, Whitby has a couple of little girls whom he sometimes speaks about, and one of Bender's buddies, Garner Mott, has a new baby boy, whom he's yet to meet, baby Nicky Joe. Mott is always, *always* going on about Nicky Joe, passing the kid's photos around, smiling and laughing about what he's going to do whenever he gets home to his wife and boy. It's great.

"So, Wimpy, how much poop do ya think ol' Mott's gonna have to wipe when he gets to that baby o' his, huh?" Eubanks grins wide.

"Oh . . ." Bob rolls his eyes. "That ain't nothin' compared to washin' them dirty diapers!" Whitby gestures with his hands, and

I can see his mitts are grimy and cracked—nothing any mother would want touching her sweet infant's powdered behind. Bob shakes his head and whistles. "I'm just glad those days are behind us, with my girls." He pauses, and his smile fades a little. He's thought of something he wished he hadn't. Yet he smiles big again, putting on a brave face. "Ya know . . . but then you look around . . . and see how much they've grown, an' . . . and sometimes you just wish they were babies all over again."

We chuckle. Today the sky is as gray as always, but at least it hasn't rained yet.

"So." Eubanks claps me on the shoulder. "When you have a kid, Mace, what are ya gonna name the little fellow?"

"Me?" I raise my eyebrows. "Well, I think I'll start off by eliminating Euban—"

Snap!

I look down at my poncho and suddenly there's a hole in it that wasn't there a second ago. Eubanks and Whitby see it, too, and we're down in the foxhole, in the blink of an eye.

"Christ, Mace, you alright!?"

"Yeah." I pat around my body a couple of times and then poke my finger through the hole in the poncho. I look at the boys, and their eyes are wide. "Sonuvabitch, fellas, that was way too friggin' close."

"You're not hit?"

"Nuh-uh. No, I'm fine."

Strangely enough, though, everything is still quiet. We didn't even hear the rifle shot, only the snap of the bullet hitting the fabric. Yet just a little ways off, and getting closer, we hear voices—American voices—and one of them sounds familiar.

The three of us look out of my foxhole—perhaps appearing like a scene from *Duck Soup*—and it's just who I thought it was. Major Paul Douglas and his entourage have shown up, with six marine bodyguards and a stretcher bearer in tow.

"Major Douglas," Whitby says flatly.

I glance over to Bob. "What? You seen it, too?"

"Shavin' when all that shit was comin' down?" Bob's face appears grim. "You betcha."

"Well," I say, "the way they're headed, we'd better let them know they're comin' into a danger zone, or they'll be sorry."

The oddity about the boomerang setup is that behind the straight line between where PFC Allen is arranged with his machine gun and my position, you're safe inside the boomerang, but if you cross the line, heading into the CP, you're likely to get clobbered.

No place is truly safe out here, but from the Nips' vantage they have spots they like to zero in on, not to mention the odd-duck shell they'll throw into the soup, just to see if they can take out one of us on a stretcher.

Before we can warn the major, *bbbrrrrrrpppppppp!* A Jap machine gun opens up, sprouting mud funnels all along the line. "Shit! Get down!"

We can see Douglas and his entourage pause for a moment, appearing to be about to scramble, but they don't budge. Uncertain of what to do, the machine gun rips through them and sends a couple of marines at the end of the line spinning toward the earth.

"Goddammit!" Eubanks says between gritted teeth.

As tight as our space is, the three of us still manage to bring our weapons to our shoulders, futilely hoping for something to shoot at—at least preparing to deliver cover fire.

The Nip machine gun continues, yet it's off target, raking the mud around where Douglas and his men used to be. Evidently, the marines finally spread out far enough, where they're at safer intervals.

It feels as if the oxygen has been removed from the air. The gun stops. Our eyes dart around, scanning for any signs of close-by Nips—or any of the major's men, for that matter. I realize I've been holding my breath, and I let it out slowly. It would be foolish to run out there and try helping them. If they can somehow get up and make it closer to the inside of the boomerang, we can get them out of here. Yet the problem is further compounded by the fact that some of those marines are wounded. That makes the trick of getting them to safety closer to suicide.

"Men?" Douglas says, out of breath, but still retaining his stentorian timbre. "You men come up to my position!"

"He's gonna get these guys fucking killed," I mumble under my breath

There's a long pause. We can see Douglas, safe inside the boomerang, but we can't get a fix on his men, down the slope.

Eventually a weak voice floats in the air, location unknown. "We can't, Major, we're pinned down and have two wounded men!"

As if to accentuate this point, the Nip machine gun rattles off a few bursts, smoking the ground, close to the wavering voice. What the Japs are really doing is seeking the direction of the voices, the same as we are.

Major Douglas replies, "I order you to come up here, now! That's an order!"

Nah, nah, I think. *Don't you do it, guys. Don't even think about it.*

They don't have to think about it. The sky erupts—and that's it! Hundreds of rounds rain in!

Screeeeeeeeeeeeeeeeeeee!

These are no mere explosions; instead, the shells coming down are so intense it sounds like the film in a projector being rewound, only amplified a hundred times. *Vmmmpppp, vmmmppp, vmmmppp, vmmmppp! Sssstttt, sssstttt, sssstttt, vmmmppp!* You dare not open your mouth, lest you collect a bellyful of fire.

Then something snapped inside of me, as the world went to hell around me—something happened that isn't easily explainable.

I jumped out of my foxhole, sprinting inside of the boomerang. I don't recall why I did it, and why nobody stopped me, but out there in the midst of the falling shells, a call for a corpsman went unanswered, and I simply couldn't stand the feeling. Nothing was real. In fact, all the images in those moments were still-life photographs, captured in the eye of a cyclone: One image passed, and then another, in rapid succession. One image was of the two wounded men from Douglas's cadre. Somehow they had made it inside the shelter of the boomerang, but with the shells falling in, no place was safe. They were holding each other up the best they could. Another image of a jeep! (I make a break for the jeep!) Then "Hurricane" Hensen. Bloodied. Bishop. Bloodied. Then another marine—he might have been the corpsman for all I knew. I didn't care.

(I spotted the abandoned jeep, sitting in out in the open, and all I could think about was getting the wounded men the hell out of there. Only when I hopped into the jeep, nothing happened—it wouldn't start! *Okay, stupid ass.* In my haste, I forgot to turn on the damn ignition!)

Somehow, I manage to pull up in the jeep to pick up the wounded, despite the jeep's protests.

"Okay, let's get these guys loaded up! C'mon, give me a hand!"

A few marines rushed over and helped me lift the wounded onto the back of the jeep, although it was rough duty trying to cram that many into a vehicle designed to accommodate only four passengers. The end result was six wounded marines, some dying, stacked in the back, little toy soldiers: arms and legs sticking out here, a slightly wounded marine attempting to keep his perch there.

Frantic.

Never mind that I had no idea how to shift the gears of the jeep. Even the simplest tasks can get muddled when time comes down on you. Mud was up to the tires as the jeep's wheels spun out, fanning sludge and belching smoke from its exhaust. A few shells fell in, but my main concern was how back-heavy that thing was, weighed down with marines. *If I can fight these gears in the right direction, I'll grind this thing to hell to move this lurch-wagon forward . . . Goddammit, this piece of shit!* Every curse word under the sun . . . if I could only make this thing move! *Move, goddamn you!* We were moving, alright, but the ground on Okinawa was nothing but a quagmire of slop, deep grooves, shell holes, and furrows—anything to bog the jeep down, not to mention everything to toss the wounded out. All the time I was thinking that at any moment a Nip shell would come down on us and kill all our efforts, effortlessly.

Finally, our luck changed; we were on solid ground. Firm enough, anyway, for me to afford a few quick glances at my passengers along the way to make sure I hadn't lost one on the trip. Firm enough to actually feel a gust of wind on my face as we began gaining decent speed.

By the time we pulled up to the battalion aid station, it was all worth it.

I didn't even have to hop out of the jeep. Immediately a team of corpsmen, medical staff, and a few regular marines came out and began unloading the wounded, shouting out medical terms, orders for bandages, for drugs, for stretchers, for anything to help the wounded . . . as I merely closed my eyes, exhausted to the center of my being, though wholly absorbed in the sounds of salvation for a few broken marines I was lucky enough to escort to safety. Just think, how ironic, Hurricane Hensen and me, on a jeep ride again . . . Peleliu, 1944.

I could have fallen asleep, right where I sat, my forehead resting on the steering wheel. Besides, after everything that happened today, perhaps I deserved that luxury.

Only Lieutenant Clean Gyrene doesn't think I deserve anything, nor, evidently, does he think much of the six marines I brought to the aid station. Granted, those marines probably would have made it without the jeep, without me, or even without Major Douglas nearly getting a pair of them killed. But to give me shit over a crummy jeep that would have gotten smashed to oblivion just sitting there anyway?

"I found the jeep abandoned in an open field, sir!"

The lieutenant eyes me coolly, in a manner that speaks volumes about where he believes he resides in this world, versus the place he *knows* I do.

He doesn't even bother saluting. He merely turns around and dismisses me. "Well, leave the jeep here. It belongs to us."

No shit. I thought it was mine, asshole.

All I can do is turn around and walk away, striding past our artillery guys, slogging past the mortarmen, toward the company CP, and out onto the very flank of the western side of the boomerang, into my little foxhole, where I've been holding the line. Holding the goddamn line. On Okinawa.

The whole way back I'm fuming. I mean, I'm really eaten up. Given enough time to walk it off, though, I realize I'm lucky to be a Marine Corps rifleman. I could never talk about babies with a shitbird lieutenant like that. I could never joke about Junior's pimples, or laugh at Wimpy for trying to jump over a gully, and I'd never have the opportunity to do my part by wiping a Jap from the face of this earth, if I spent my days making life difficult at a battalion aid station. No matter how much I hated being there, at least I had a reason to stay. I had a reason for joining the marines. I had a reason for helping those boys to safety. I had a reason for being in the middle of danger, too many times to count, now— and I know that I will do it all over again, before this war runs its course. One way or another, I will.

Because reason makes all the difference in the world.

Because a war without reason is no war for all.

"Jesus, Mace." Eubanks is waiting for me back at my foxhole. "You look like hell."

"That's funny, I was about to say the same thing to you. Did you see whatever happened to Major Douglas?"

Eubanks shakes his head. "No, hell, no—I was too busy watching you tear out of here. I thought you were a goner, for sure."

I take a drag off my cigarette; it's the last one in the pack. "Whattaya mean by that?"

"Whattaya mean, what do I mean? The way them Japs were walking their mortars in right behind ya—Christ! Maybe you didn't see how close they were to ya, but boy, we sure did!"

I don't doubt what Eubanks says; nonetheless, the fact is I didn't see or hear any mortars walking up behind the jeep. I was simply too focused on getting the wounded out of there.

The truth is, I couldn't care less about what didn't happen. I'm only concerned with what did.

Here's the rest of the story. I hope you understand.

Understand the way a marine feels when he's lounging in his foxhole, and all of a sudden he looks up in the sky and spies three white streamers in the air, coming in from behind the company lines. The streamers are the tiny trails that mortar rounds give off, only they're not visible most of the time. You have to catch them just right, against the skyline—as they've traveled a long way, having lost velocity, almost suspended in the empty air, like a child's mobile above his bassinet.

The streamers are at a good distance, dipping down now, in the vicinity of the 1st Platoon. About to drop. About to drop.

The stomach turns. These mortars are some of ours.

Thump!

Thump, thump!

"Stretcher bearer! Over here!"

You lie to yourself and say they're not, but they are.

It begins to drizzle.

Children tell stories that when it rains, it is the angels crying up in heaven; sweet little angels, sweet little children. If that's really the case, then on Okinawa, the angels truly have something to cry about. It's always friggin' raining here.

Now it's raining on our own guys.

"Stretcher bearer! Over here!"

We're off the line, for a brief respite, and it's probably the only joyous day that any of us have had on southern Okinawa so far. From here on out, it will assuredly be the last.

"Can you believe that?" Leyden grins. "I just can't believe it."

Orley Uhls sits on a stump, not far away, eating something out of a C-rat can. "Ya know," he says, with his mouth stuffed with food, "this is just one step. And the next step means we get our asses out of here. Mark them words, boys." Uhls accents each of his words with a wag of his spoon, to prove his point.

Somehow, some way . . . we know it's the truth.

This morning we were listening to the radio on a tank when the word came over that Germany had surrendered to the Allied forces—that the war was over in Europe.

The news came as a shock, because not only did it seem like the war would go on forever (war had been so ingrained in us over the last few years that, sadly enough, we couldn't imagine ourselves without it), but also, the fact that we were still here, combating the Japanese forces, made a warless world a chimera that seemed to laugh in the face of our current situation.

After all, the news didn't change the position of our lines, or the texture of the mud, the tint of the sky, or the amount of ammunition each of us carried in our pouches. Nor did it change what we knew was coming—that we'd be making another assault on the Japanese soon, and more marines would surely die in the process—like PFC Garner Mott yesterday, like a few other new marines (nobody seems to remember their names).

Still, if there was an end to all of this, the news made it more real, somehow more tangible, less fantastical to the mind—if only for the reason that hope, like death, is a contagion that spreads, for better or worse.

"Say," Junior says, "maybe now we can get the Germans to come over here to lend us a hand, huh?"

A lot of marines nod in agreement. It doesn't sound like a half-bad idea. We've all heard the Germans are fierce fighters, so maybe they could supply us with just enough forces to get us over this hump.

We are being naive, of course. We're only viewing the big picture from a foxhole's view. None of us has a clue that the Nazis were committing atrocities against the Jews and Poles. To the marines standing right here, hearing the news, the German people are just like us. They look like us, they dress like us—hell, there are tons of Germans back home, and they are all good people. Uhls? That's a German name, and he's pretty good at killing Nips, so why not the rest of them?

Because we are the United States Marine Corps. We started over here, so we'll have to finish over here—even if that means invading mainland Japan. Even if that means dying to the last man. Even if that means more of Okinawa, because nothing else matters but the moment at hand, let alone what's going on in Japan . . . or Europe, or Russia, or the Philippines.

The war ending in Europe was merely the last bounce of the ball. Now it was up to the marines to put the ball in the basket.

Have you ever tried to dribble a deflated ball?

May 8, 1945.

12

WHATEVER HAPPENED TO JUNIOR HUDSON?

"*Hey! Where the hell are you going?*"

Okinawa, May 1945.

One moment Sergeant George Chase is lying beside me in the middle of a muddy road, alongside a levee—we're about to run up the road, and into the jaws of a Nip counterattack—and in the next instant he jumps up and takes off toward the rear.

"Hey!" I yell. "Where the hell are you going?"

Chase doesn't look back. He just keeps running. "I got hit in the arm!"

Bullshit! I didn't so much as hear a snap or feel his body move before he hopped up and ran. Chase was as close to me as Donald Schwantz was on Ngesebus—hip to hip.

One more glance over my shoulder and Chase has already vanished. *Screw it. I never liked you anyway, ya sonuvabitch.*

I look back up the road, and I see some marines run by in the distance, but brief blooms of Nip artillery shells obscure them from my view. The artillery appears to be walking straight in my direction, so I know I have to get moving. Get moving, or that crap will come right down on top of me.

The whole attack had been another foul-up.

The rifle platoons started off this morning with weapons at high port, thrusting into the guts of the Japanese lines, only to find ourselves scattered by Nip high explosives, about fifty yards in. The Japs didn't even have to use machine guns or small-arms fire to break the attack; the artillery did its job again, just like it had from day one. We were nothing but eggshell targets, scrambled on the inside, cracking down the center.

Thunderclaps popped the tops of our heads open and sent their currents straight to our brains—

—*shut the hell up!!!!!*

All you can do is grit your teeth and tuck your head, swerving, like a drunk, at a jagged run, as you're pelted by the mud, crud, and unidentifiable gunk that for all you know could be bits of your buddies flying by and attaching to your skin, your clothes . . . your goddamn mind! Vague human-shapes lie still on the ground as you run past, having blended into Okinawa's shade so that the living and the dead are no longer separated by breath and pulse. I went through all of this, only to find myself in the center of a churned-up road, with no idea if I was too far ahead of the attack or too far behind. I barely even recognized Sergeant Chase.

"Chase!"

Boom!

A spray of mud falls just outside of our reach. I slip and fall in the sludge, hugging the earth, only raising my head after the last particles of mud fall.

"Chase." I low-crawl next to him, nearly out of breath. "We gotta get the hell outta here. Get up the road!"

The sergeant simply gives me a sideways glance, as if I'm an annoyance. Still, that's all it takes for me to see his downturned countenance and the premature crow's-feet at the corners of his eyes. He's eaten a rotten egg. It's a rotten day.

Chase helped me realize that we were ahead of the attack after all. He got up and dashed away, leaving me stranded.

Oh, to hell with it.

My only option was to push forward. I knew that up the road the Nips were waiting. Waiting by the hundreds, perhaps. This damned sense of duty I've always had, that cursed feeling of purpose—either the Marine Corps trained me too well or they didn't train me well enough. The way I see it, if they put a rifle in my hands, I'm accountable for using it.

Though the rifle saved my skin on Peleliu, it would probably get me killed on Okinawa.

Okay, Mace. Get up. Let's go—

(pause)

Listen to me . . .

She's not here.

My eyes begin to sting from the threat of crying, so I press my palms deep into my sockets, damming up the stream where dead emotions live. I tell myself that it's only mud in my eyes . . . or the wind, slapping my face, sledding pell mell down Donnelly Hill.

Was she ever here?

Every day in combat, on Peleliu and Okinawa, every morning before I started out, I invoked her name. *Be my guide.* Every morning, except this day I never gave her a thought. Before today, I always named her. I might not have consciously summoned her spirit, but I did. *Sister Dorothy . . .*

I did.

Yet from the moment I jabbed the buttstock of my M-1 into the mud and used it to pull myself to my feet, everything went quickly—rapidly taking what was left of my light and turning it to deepest black. I became King Midas in reverse, where everything I touched turned to shit.

Let's go.

Suddenly I see myself, running from afar, and before I know it, I'm in the center of a chewed-up area of the line. *Dammit!*

Hurriedly, I dodge into a good-sized shell hole. It is still smoking, swirling and warm inside—the bowels of a newly turned grave.

As far as I can tell, I am the only target out here—and that's the last thing anybody wants to be. *Okay, do somethin'!* If my sense of direction is right, I'll have to slog through this patch of trash to get back to where we started. Maybe. Yeah, maybe. That's it.

My sole companion is the rasp of my own breathing, serrated, too fast, as I tentatively peek out of the hole, trying to get my bearings. Nothing. No marines, only the dysentery-splotched earth and the incessant buzzing of hundreds of flies, clogging the ground, too engorged and gross to fly.

There's something dead out here.

There is a stench that mingles with the odor of wet earth, and although it doesn't smell natural, in reality it's as natural as entropy, twofold. This place is a wreck of ruin. Despite the sounds of battle coming in shortwave, this plot of ground, with four shell holes in its belly, retains only the fading echoes of how loud it was earlier. It's creepy when you're separated from anything alive. A sole survivor.

It doesn't help that it begins to drizzle again, either.

Move!

A high-pitched—

No!

The high-pitched warble of an 8-inch Jap artillery round abruptly pierces my eardrums. I'm looking around frantically for the shell that's bearing down right on top of me, feeling like it's coming straight up my ass. Not metaphorically, but literally, right up my ass! I take another fast look toward the heavens, wanting to see the one that kills me, yet all I see is the falling rain. *Down!* Burying my face in the earth, I curl up, fetal positioned.

It lands two feet to my left.

Rung!

I've got my head in a church bell, and somebody is banging the hell out of it.

You hang on. You just try to hang on as the earth attempts to heave you out of her womb. I've got a screamer in my skull, and the lunatic is planning his escape.

Rolling over, in the bottom of the hole, I exhale in one great puff, as if I've been gut-punched, almost expecting smoke to spew from my mouth. It's over. I check my body for blood.

Somehow, slowly, I manage to bring myself to the rim of the shell hole again, only to see three horizons vibrating before my eyes, until finally they settle down and meld into one straight line, the way edges are meant to behave.

It was a goddamn dud.

"It was a dud," I whisper. Still, the dud struck too close, making the hair on my arms stand, electric. The scent of crisp ozone and the metallic tang of hot brass permeates the air. *Oh, Jesus Christ in heaven.* I shake my head to clear the heat from it.

Bbbrrrrrrppppppp! A Nip machine gun touches off, somewhere to my right—*too close*—so I run and launch myself out of one hole, diving into the next.

Every shell hole appears the same.

I am only hazily aware that Bob Whitby is beside me now. If I say something to him, he might simply disappear. Yet just as I'm about to speak—

Another 8-inch needle comes squealing in, a freight train, bearing down with its brakes locked, tight.

This one takes forever to get us, so I quick-look at Bob. Yes, he knows. We have an instant to decide: Stay in the hole and bank on another dud, or make for the next hole and roll the dice. Decide.

I move out, and maybe Whitby comes, too. At a trot, I crane my neck upward, attempting to work out where the shell will land.

WHAM!

We're dead.

Levy and I are on Pavuvu, our feet in the drainage gutter, snapping our fingers to Sinatra singing "I'll Be Seeing You," before we ship off to Peleliu.

There's the sensation of being lift—*Gah!*—

Thrown—

Suck in air, a wheezing sound . . . It's all in water—every word, belching out sound-bubbles. Drowning. Suck in air—great gulps of . . .

A skeleton at your shoulder. Icy fingers squeeze firmly around your neck. Leaving blue-black impressions there. A green smell. Nauseous.

Not a dud.

Can't breathe—

The sound of breaking glass . . .

I want—

Images of marines coming toward me flicker in and out. The bulb burns out.

Voices come in tinny, at first—the first recorded human voices—scratchy in character, a dull needle, skipping on a warped groove. The thing is, they claim you never hear the one that kills you, and I never heard the explosion—only a rapid-fire cluster of sensations that don't peel off as a score of corpse fingers pull me deeper into the sod. There are only the voices, wafting in clearer, unraveling, decoding, beneath a steady flatline. My mouth is filled with— *Bong, bong, bing, bong!* The bells of St. Mary's keep clanging through my bullet-headed skull. *Bong. Bong. Bong.* As a distant clock— *Tick, tick, tick, tick, clatch!* The pendulum stops swinging in midmotion. There's only the slightest impression that there are other marines helping me up now. Hell, I don't even know if Whitby was really there. No matter. Whatever happened to me, the world has gone cuckoo.

If I say anything to the other marines lending a hand, it's "Hey, I'm okay, alright? Just get your paws off me!"

It stayed loony, too, all the way through my ragged walk back to our lines—which were only about twenty-five yards away the whole time.

When I was among the boys again, I threw my helmet down and sat on it, watching my hands go from a steady shake to no motion at all. I must've been okay. *Except this damn ringing in my ears!*

"My God, Mace." Eubanks's face appeared much too close to mine for comfort as he leaned in. "We thought you guys were killed, for sure." What I really heard from Eubanks was "Erus rof, dellik rerw syug uoy thguoht ew, ym dog ecam." *Why the fuck is it always Eubanks at the scene of the crime?* My head really started to pound, so I closed my eyes, blocking out the whirring voice, only to see the image of the rough hole in the mud, only ten feet away from Bob and me, when the shell exploded, flinging us around, nothing but paper sacks in the breeze. I guess Whitby was with me after all.

When I opened my eyes again, Eubanks was lighting a cigarette for me. He put it between my lips. It was then that I realized I didn't even know his first name. The name his mother gave to him. He had always been just Eubanks to me—the young yokel with the BAR. Too bad that was the last time I ever saw him.

It was the last time I remember seeing a lot of the marines in K/3/5.

The rain begins to fall harder as I slowly make my way to a foxhole that looks like mine, although in a quagmire like this, it's hard to tell one sludgy hole in the slop from the other. Climbing under the poncho, I find it occupied by some new kid—and I mean *really* a kid, named Piazza, or something like that. I would be surprised if he's barely seventeen. It is so sad. It's sad because now they take these baby-faces—genuine Marines, mind you—who just grew their first pubic hair; and they don't know enough to stay alive in the best of times, let alone times like these, when the sky is falling and there isn't a damned thing you can do but stay and be crushed by it.

Piazza has other ideas, however. You have to hand it to him, he's a resilient kid. The rain thrums down on the poncho, loud, annoying; it might as well have been a hailstorm above the near-darkened underside of the poncho—yet this baby-face is trying to convince me otherwise. I don't want to hear this shit. Not right here. Not right now.

"Ya know," he says, "this rain, it reminds me of . . . gee, I was back home, sittin' with my girl in the car, listenin' to the rain fall on the convertible top. Just . . . ya know, holding her and thinkin', like?"

He pauses. My head feels like I have a crane in there, pulling up my brain from the base of my spine.

"Yeah," he resumes. "I told ya about my girl, Claire, right?"

I don't even know you, dumb ass.

I can tell that he's talking through a smile, "She's . . . she's amazing is what she is. Gonna get married after the war, don't ya know."

Yeah, sure, pal. What are they gonna do, stand your corpse up in a tux and wheel ya down the aisle? Fat chance.

The rain falls heavier, threatening to cave the poncho in. I don't care. It drowns out the kid's voice; it turns down the squeal in my ears. I believe I hear the roar of the crowd, even shivering as I am beneath the poncho, as if I have a case of malaria. Anyway, that's merely a product of my wild Queens imagination. Just ask Larry Mahan.

Despite it all, I manage to drift off to sleep, seeing Larry and Billy Leyden as clearly as . . .

. . . well, as clearly as a *dream*:

On Pavuvu—before Peleliu . . . before any of it—Billy Leyden and I were sitting around, and we spied Larry heading in our direction, walking at a good clip.

"Oh, brother," I said to Leyden. "Wonder what Larry's got on his mind?"

You could always count on Mahan to be up to something.

"*Dunno.*" Bill shielded his eyes from the sun. "*Maybe Larry's wonderin' the same thing, huh?*"

"*Ha! Yeah.*"

Larry arrived and just stood there, his hands on hips, waiting for one of us to ask him what's wrong. Okay, I'll bite.

"*Say, what's eating you, Mahan?*"

"*Goddammit!*" he said. "*My tent's too crowded!*"

"*So?*" I replied, thinking to myself that every marine has roughly the same number of tentmates on this island. In fact, nothing has changed since boot camp. We're in the military, for chrissakes.

"*So?*" Larry gaped at me as if I'd lost my mind. "*So? How's a fella supposed to beat off with all these guys hangin' around all the time?*"

Before I could laugh, Leyden nudged me in the ribs. Bill looked up at Larry, stone-faced. "*Well, that's easy, Larry. Listen, what ya do is . . . ya get in your rack and then pull the covers up over ya, see? Then when things start shakin', and if anyone asks what you're doin', you just tell 'em you got malaria fever. Works every time, I tell ya. Might even get you off of work parties.*"

"*Hey, ya know, that's not a bad idea.*" Mahan appeared satisfied.

"*Either that,*" I said, "*or you can climb up one of those coconut trees. But if ya fall out?*" I whistle through my teeth. "*Ya might end up breakin' somethin' you're thinkin' about usin' later.*"

When we saw Larry again he was back to his usual self. "*It worked! It worked!*" he shouted with glee.

Of course, it was only a dream of that day on Pavuvu, though. The next morning Okinawa looked exactly the same as I left it. Not that I expected anything different, but still, Okinawa made the distant memory of Pavuvu seem like . . . *Sumiko Yamaguchi . . . as sweet and quiet as a field of daffodils.*

Shaking my head clear of the morning rust, I rubbed my fingers through my hair.

Just the touch of my fingers against my scalp sent a fresh wave of delirium across my vision.

Christ, something's really gotta be wrong with me.

"Say, pal—how's it goin'?"

Sitting at the rim of my foxhole, I look up and there stands Billy Leyden, covered in his poncho. Or, rather, what used to be Billy Leyden. Billy looks like he's been on a ten-year bender. His eyes are two piss-holes in the snow.

"Oh, don't ask," I say, rolling my eyes toward the kid, Piazza, at the bottom of the foxhole, who is mercifully too occupied with stuffing his mouth to be much of a bother.

Bill stifles a snigger, squats down, and begins fishing for his cigarettes.

Cocking my thumb toward Piazza, I say, "This is what I've got over here, a fucking kid like this. Ain't that somethin'?"

"Shit, Sterl, you're startin' to sound like goddamn McEnery, for chrissakes!"

I laugh and make note of that. "Nah, you know me. It's just that they're startin' to roll these guys out on an assembly line, a parade of—"

Suddenly I remember that Billy was one of those marines. They pulled him fresh out of the ass of boot camp and shat him out all over Pavuvu and Peleliu. Only Bill, unlike Piazza, had the tendency to be a little morose over things.

After being wounded on Ngesebus, and greeting the other survivors on Pavuvu, Billy told me that he and George McNevin had listened to the wire every day to see who was killed on Peleliu—listening for my name, hoping I would make it out alright. He already knew about Levy, and that really hurt.

Yet coming over to Okinawa, aboard the USS *McCracken*, Billy came up with a different spin on things. One that was difficult for me to abide by.

Billy and I are standing on the deck of the ship, smoking, looking

out over the ocean and watching the whitecaps break and eventu-
ally vanish back into the deep blue. Periodically, small silver fish
leap out of the water in schools, glittering pretty in the sunshine.
Marine life in abundance.

Bill flicks his ashes over the railing, "Hey, Sterl, there's some-
thin' I've been meaning to talk to you about."

"Yeah?"

"Yeah, well . . . ya know, I've been thinkin'. 'Bout this whole
invasion, right? And with what happened to me on Peleliu and
all . . . if somethin' were to happen to me—"

"Hey, wait. What are ya sayin', Bill?" Automatically the tips of
my ears grow hot.

"Well, just that if I get kill—"

"Nah, Bill, screw that! I don't wanna hear any crap like that,
okay? Guys start talking shit like that and the next thing ya
know, they get themselves killed. That's the way it works. So
just quit flappin' your gums, alright? You'll be fine. We'll all be
fine."

So far so good. At least for some of us.

I glance down at the kid, Piazza, and his very presence on this
island means that he replaced somebody else; one of the old K/3/5
veterans, perhaps, who got killed or shipped home—or both.
Maybe he replaced one of the marines who still lay out there, in
no-man's-land, half decomposed, melting back into the mud from
which he came. The stretcher bearers can't retrieve their bodies, or
they, too, will get swept by machine-gun fire. So the whole place
reeks of green meat: Nips, marines, GIs, adding a new fleshy tone
to the rancid earth.

"Yeah." Billy grimaces. "This artillery bullshit is the worst.
Can't move forward, can't move back. I don't even know how we
made it this far."

I glance over my shoulder, and in the distance is a pile of rocks
they tell us is called the Castle. Shuri Castle.

"Sure," I say. "You guys in the First really took your lumps on that first day, huh?"

Billy nods in affirmation. "I heard you had some trouble of your own. Yesterday, in fact. You okay?"

"Yeah, yeah . . . I'm okay, just can't get this goddamn ringin' out of my head, that's all."

"Alright, well, let me get the hell outta here." As Billy starts to get up, I grab the end of his poncho, signaling him to stay. "Wait, Bill."

On second thought, maybe Bill doesn't look as bad as I originally thought. Perhaps what I saw was merely my own reflection, mirrored off the surface of Billy's eyes.

"Junior?" I ask. "Ya know, Freddy Hudson? Whatever happened to Junior Hudson?"

Bill looks away, his lips pursed, thin as a razor slice. "Ah shit, Mace." I begin nodding that I understand—that Bill doesn't have to finish. I already know.

Billy brings his eyes around to meet mine again. "He got all blown up, Sterl. Same as Aubrey Rogers. He just . . . Nothing left of him. I'm glad you didn't have to see it, pal."

"Sure, Bill. Thanks." I release his poncho. I don't want to say it, but I have to say it—"So long, Bill."

"Yeah, I'll be seein' ya." Billy simply gets up and walks away.

Only I never saw Billy Leyden again, during the war. Bill got his second Purple Heart on Okinawa and was evacuated a few days later.

So it happened that Junior Hudson ended up exactly like Mahan and Levy after all. It was just that I didn't imagine it that way—though I should have foreseen it. It's a sorry life when it feels better to imagine the worst. Yet it's a real sonuvabitch when you can't bring yourself to do it.

That's where the story ends.

Almost.

Two other things happened right after my visit with Leyden. Both of them—despite my inner protests, despite the fact that I wanted to get the hell off of that island—finally forced me to pay a visit to Doc Chulis, and Chulis sent me home. You see, I never quit on anything in my life. I wanted to—many times; however, a person simply can't be what it's not in him to be. Nevertheless, although I didn't know it then, the artillery round that almost killed me gave me a blistering concussion and two busted eardrums, pierced all the way through. I just hadn't been diagnosed yet. Then after what later happened with Bob Whitby? I suppose you could say that I performed my duty as a rifleman in K/3/5—and I had no regrets, no desire to say otherwise. I finished the war, and the war was finished with me.

In the end, I'd like to think that I saved more lives than I took—but when it comes to taking or saving, a far greater hand than mine holds the scales of balance, while my hand merely controlled the weight on the trigger.

Anyway, I killed.

Have mercy on their souls. Not mine.

We are getting ready to make another attack. Marines strain to push trucks from the sucking mud, putting chains on the tires and flailing around in the sludge. Fieldpieces are pulled on the backs and shoulders of dromedary marines. Draw ammo, carry crates, clean weapons, fight the flies, smoke cigarettes, try to smile, dig foxholes, bail out water, fill canteens, pick at scabs, read some letters, examine your hands—there are myriad things a rifleman does before an attack.

Oh, yeah, and one more thing . . . send Whitby home.

Whitby sat at the edge of our foxhole holding a crumpled letter in a trembling hand, his chin on his chest, his chest hitching spasmodically—raw anguish etched on a fatherly face that never did look right under a camo-covered steel helmet. It never rained so much on Okinawa as it did from Whitby's eyes.

They only wanted Bob to come home. His wife. His two little girls.

How can pigtails ever be so pretty when Daddy's in a grave on Okinawa?

How can a kiss ever be so warm when the husband's lips are blue-hued and cold?

I'm sure a thousand thoughts were screaming through Whitby's mind as I tried to comfort him—*it'll be okay, Wimp, it'll be alright*—yet Bob was done, at no fault to Bob.

Bob simply wasn't there anymore.

"Hey . . . hey, buddy." I tried for a smile. "Why don't ya go back and see Chulis, huh, pal? He'll know what to do to get ya outta here. You don't need to be here anymore, Wimp. No more, okay?"

Whitby's eyes asked me if I was telling the truth. The truth is, if ever there was a case of combat hysterics, combat fatigue, Bob was surely showing all the signs.

Swallowing hard, Bob closed his eyes for a second while wiping his runny nose with one grimy dungaree sleeve and then the other, making dark snot-streaks on the herringbone cloth. I thought I heard him give a small chuckle, but maybe not. His efforts didn't do anything to clean his face, but at least, I'm sure, it made him feel better, as he made the walk to the rear area with a face that wasn't swollen red from sorrow. I don't think any act could have saved Bob's dignity, though. To be labeled a combat fatigue case was akin to crapping out from heat exhaustion on Peleliu, but you simply can't go on when the mind and body refuse to function anymore.

Facts are facts. Wimpy got stung with the same shell that left two gaping holes through my ears. It just so happened that the round that ended Bob's combat effectiveness was fired from a pen, and not a Nip counterbattery.

That was the last time I saw Robert Whitby, too. He walked away.

That left only me and Eubanks from our fire team—and I didn't know where Eubanks was, or even if he was still alive.

It was only when Whitby was out of sight that I allowed myself to fall into the bottom of the foxhole and rest my head. My melon still felt like someone had driven a railroad spike through it. I was a real Phineas Gage. Never quite the same after nearly getting my ass hauled away. If I could have laughed, I would have laughed about survival, a game of craps, and the many spinning wheels of chance, rolling through my brain.

The only one laughing, however, was some crappy lieutenant— the same Lieutenant Johnson, in fact, who made us get off the horses when we first arrived on the island.

Exactly *when* the incident happened with Johnson, or how long it was after Whitby left, I couldn't tell you—only that it was before the attack, and it ended up being the last measure of me saying good-bye.

"Did you dig that foxhole?" The lieutenant stands above me, looking down at me in my hole. His hands are on his hips, and the fact that he carries only a .45 on his cartridge belt tells me that this guy isn't planning on fighting the Nips anytime soon.

I stick my spade in the mud. "Yes, sir."

"Nice hole," he says, looking away and out over the gray expanse of sky. When he looks back at me he has a real shit-eating grin on his face—the kind of smirk a terrible child wears while lighting a cat's tail afire. "Too bad you're gonna have to move it, *Mace.*" That last word came out disgusting and dripping with vinegar. The leering curl of his upturned lip sparked a flame in the center of my forehead, deep within the tissue where wise men dare not venture. I wanted to kill that man. He wore marine dungarees, had round eyes, an apple-pie name, and a light-skinned face; nevertheless, if he had stayed there one more second . . .

"Anyway, we're movin' out," he says, sauntering off, on his way to polish his hard-on for being so clever.

The truth is, I wouldn't have done anything to him, because the truth is . . . I was already done. It just took a head full of barbed wire and a jerk like Johnson for me to finally see the truth. I was done when the Nip artillery nearly wiped me out, only I just couldn't fathom it. Or, rather, I couldn't believe that I had something physically screwed up inside my skull. It was always the "other guy" that got wounded and evacuated. Not me—especially considering everything I had been through to date.

Chulis saw it in my pupils, though. They constricted and dilated without any external stimuli. "Mace, I need you to go back to the battalion aid station and get your noggin checked out. You're damn lucky to be alive, pal."

Instead, I hung around.

Leaning my M-1 against the wall of my foxhole, I climbed out and gazed at my surroundings one last time—watching the marines, here and there, slosh around in the muck, observing them across a panoramic view that used to be my home, too. The sky was hard, with white marbling grained across it, white clouds that didn't stand a chance any more than I did. And their faces? There were less than a handful of marines who had made the Peleliu landing—Orley Uhls, Blowtorch Willy, Hank Boyes, Roy Kelly—and fewer still who served on Cape Gloucester. The rest of them, even if I knew them once, I didn't know them then.

Even Gene Holland was gone.

Right around V-E Day, shortly after Garner Mott was killed, some guys from headquarters came down looking for Gene. When they found him, they plucked him straight from his foxhole and led him away.

It seems that Gene had a buddy in HQ, and right after we returned to Pavuvu, Gene began to work some angle to get himself out of the rifle squads. It took a while for those strings to pull, but once they did, Gene's ass was out of the bind. Gene walked away.

He ended up driving a jeep for the rest of the campaign.

He didn't even have to steal the friggin' thing to get it.

Yeah. I chuckled. Once you look around and all of the marines you previously knew have vanished, that's the sign that either you're a slow learner or there's simply nothing left to learn.

I had lived the Pacific war.

Bainbridge Naval Hospital, Port Deposit, Maryland, August 1945.

"Good morning, Corporal," she said.

The nurse stood at the foot of the hospital bed and plucked the chart from a hook attached to the bed frame. She didn't look at the young man sitting on the edge of the hospital bed. Instead, with a detached gaze that only comes with treating hundreds of battle casualties, she merely glanced over the chart as if it were her own reflection in the mirror. The young marine knew what came next: a series of questions from the nurse—the same questions, in fact, he'd heard, seemingly a thousand times over, since he had been hospitalized, a skipping record of the same old song.

These days, however, begging for a different tune, the marine found himself embellishing the answers, just to break the monotony—amusing himself in the process.

"Do you have any ringing in your ears or loss of hearing?" the nurse began.

"What was that? Come again?" The young marine held a cupped hand, palm out, to his ear.

"I *said*, do you have any ringing in your ears or loss of—" The nurse finally glanced up at the marine, her eyebrow cocked upward, not amused.

The marine grinned widely. "Nah, nah—my hearing's fine. Thank you for asking, though. But maybe someone oughta take a look at my eyes, maybe? I almost thought you were gonna crack a smile, for a second there."

She resumed, unhearing. "Any problems sleeping? Insomnia?"

"Nope, slept like a baby."

"Headaches? Blurry vision?"

"Nope."

"How about a burning sensation while urinating?"

"No thank you. I think I'll pass."

"Any bowel problems? Constipation? Loose stool? Blood in the feces?"

"Only on Peleliu."

"Excuse me?" The nurse looked up again, this time with genuine curiosity. She hadn't heard of Peleliu either, it seemed.

"I'm sorry." The marine answered her question. "No, nothing like that. You would've had to have been there."

"Okay . . . and how about any anxiety? Nervousness? Tremors in the extremities, hands, legs, muscle tics?"

"No, ma'am. Everything's in clover." He smiled again. He also knew what the last question was going to be. It was the final joke in every regular morning Q&A session. It wasn't as if the question didn't have a measure of merit to it. It did. Nevertheless, the sheer ridiculousness of the query to any marine who had been in combat— who had killed and seen his buddies killed—would have been hilarious if it weren't so sad . . .

The nurse peered once more at the chart.

PATIENT: MACE, STERLING G.

BRANCH OF SERVICE: U.S.M.C.

RANK: CPL.

D.O.B: 02/02/1924

PRIMARY DIAGNOSIS: PERFORATION OF THE EARDRUMS, BILATERAL, Acute.

SECONDARY DIAGNOSIS (IF APPLICABLE): PSYCHONEUROSES ANXIETY, Benign

She resumed. "Have you had any violent thoughts? Thoughts of harming yourself or harming others?"

For chrissakes, sister, where have you been? Don't you know there's a war on?

"Nope." I smiled quickly (maybe too quickly).

There was nothing to smile about.

Home was just another four-letter word, if your heart was nowhere near to it.

If you'd been in combat you resented a question like that, because that line of questioning made it sound like they were peering into your skull, examining for bats in the belfry.

I may have gotten my bell rung, but it didn't turn me loony like some of the poor guys in the nuthatch ward. One of those men, in particular, was a singular shade of insanity that really turned the heart into a frown.

"Jesus, wouldja look at this friggin' guy! All day like this, huh?" Private Richard La Pierre looked back at me in amazement.

"Yeah, yeah," I said. "Every time I walk by this door the same thing."

"Jesus!" Richard peeked again through the little glass window on the door.

Behind the door was a small room, with a single hospital bed pushed up against a wall. Otherwise, the room was totally bare: four walls and a single occupant—just a kid, a few years younger than us, a navy guy whom the hospital had put there for the safety of himself and others. The rumor was, the kid, like Larry Mahan, was the son of a prominent navy officer.

Dressed only in the loose-fitting hospital-issue pajamas, the kid in the room would stand on one foot, all day, and snap his fingers. With each snap, the kid would pirouette like a ballerina while letting out a hearty "Whoooohoooo!" appearing pleased with himself no end.

Richard was still shaking his head in disbelief.

I knew crazy. Screwy things happen in the world all the time. Back in basic training, there was a real obese marine (heaven only knows how they let him in the marines in the first place), Private Quinn. Quinn would cry all the time; he really had a rough time going through the rigors of Marine Corps training. He always talked about going back to Queens, and eventually the marines granted him his wish. Quinn washed out of Parris Island, went back to New York, and then, for no particular reason, killed his grandmother one day.

"Yeah," I said, taking a final glance in the window. "It's a sad case. Almost makes ya not wanna laugh, the poor kid."

Richard chuckled. Private Richard La Pierre, from Maine, was in the 6th Marine Division and, like myself, had been to Okinawa. A bad case of jungle rot on his feet got him evacuated, but not until after he saw some of the bitterest fighting Okinawa had to offer.

"Whoooohoooo!"

"What the hell ya think happened to this fella?" Richard asked as we walked back to our ward.

"Beats me. Kid like that gets on one of them tubs, too many days at sea . . . gets in with the crowd down in the boiler room . . . the next thing ya know the boat starts swayin' back and forth like . . ."

"Yeah." Richard laughed. "Then the fellas cross the equator and never come back!"

"Sure," I said. "On the LST, going to Peleliu, some jg lieutenant, or an ensign, or whatever . . . on the boat, right? Everyone knew it. This ensign would follow marines around like they shit marble. Nobody said nothin' about it. Maybe on the sly, is all. Sure, he was a limp noodle. Something fruity like that, anyway."

"Ya don't say, huh?"

"Yeah, c'mon, *you* know. The same shit. Me and my buddy Tommy Colonna was at Camp Lejeune, on leave, right? Couldn't find a hotel, so we rent a room at somebody's house. We're hitting the rack, and the next thing ya know some GI comes in the room, starts making these . . . I dunno, sexual overtures, or whatever he's got planned for us. Tommy tells this soldier, 'Hey, get the fuck outta here, or I'll put my foot straight up your ass.' Just like that."

"Geez, those friggin' guys," La Pierre said.

"Hey, ya know, whatever turns 'em on—but they sure as hell weren't fuckin' wacko, like this poor kid."

Bainbridge Naval Hospital, Port Deposit, Maryland, August 14, 1945.

If you've seen enough combat, the chances are you've seen it all.

Even if you try to blank out all thoughts—even if you think you are watching the scenes of war impassively—the eye still catches it all, from the subtle nuances to the gross exaggerations of everything before you. You see a single drop of blood on a leaf. It's so bright against the chlorophyll green, but you don't give it a thought. Instead, the mind internalizes it, waiting for the opportunity to pour itself out in the form of tears, anger, shame, or triumph—those, or a whole range of emotions that haven't been named yet.

Because, no matter how much combat you've seen, when the end is nigh, it's difficult to believe that you've reached the closing chapter, the last page, the final sentence . . . the concluding period. We look into the faces of the dying and see myriad expressions— the greatest of which are the quick lapses into disbelief right before the final breath hitches and then evaporates into the air. In the faces of the dead, there is often a ghost of a smile that lingers on the corners of their lips, and we tell ourselves they look so peaceful. Yet at the same time we try to choke down the more serrated thought, *What the fuck could he be so happy about, dead at twenty-one?*

The poor guys never knew it was the end, even when the end was all there was to know.

So when the end came for *me*—like any combat veteran who had seen it all—I didn't know it, nor did I believe it. For how is any hardened marine to know that his last battle is not one fought over a piece of turf; instead, it is one that is fought with memories and misgivings.

"Say, Mace!"

"Huh?" I looked back at Richard La Pierre.

He laughed. "What were ya doin', fallin' asleep on me?"

"Nah," I said. "I was thinking about going down to the mess hall an' seein' if soup's on." I was lying. Richard caught me deep in thought, and whatever I was thinking La Pierre snapped me out of it.

Richard nodded. "Yeah, that's what I was sayin'. C'mon, then. Sittin' around like this will drive ya nutty, like that poor friggin' kid, ya know?"

Sitting in the hospital ward was just a part of the same old routine. La Pierre's bed was right next to mine, so it was convenient for us to simply sit on the sides of our beds and while away the time with countless BS sessions. It was something very akin to reading an outdated newspaper, over and over again, because it is the only one you have. Eventually the articles become so familiar that you only read about a quarter of the words, because you know all of the stories by heart—just like I had only heard about a quarter of what La Pierre was saying before I drifted off into places unknown.

Really, you just followed the routine. After sitting a while, you go outside and smoke a few butts, you go back inside and sit, then go back outside and smoke. You do all of this in between meals; often, like right now, food sounded like the best plan, though you'd have to beat the navy chowhounds to the punch. The navy boys were used to good food, so the swabs were always the front of the line. They overpopulated us marines by at least four to one. At that moment, the ward was brimming with navy guys, loitering around, like me and Richard.

Just as Richard and I were about to get up, however, a small commotion was heard at the nurse's desk, at the center of the ward.

I looked over my shoulder, in the direction of the nurse's desk, but I couldn't make out too much. A young nurse, perhaps a little younger than me, had both hands clasped over her mouth, and I heard a tiny gasp (yet I couldn't tell if it the sound had come from her).

"Whattaya think that's all about?" I turned back around and asked Richard.

"Ya got me," he said, craning his neck, trying to look around me. "Maybe that young one dropped a bedpan?"

"Nah, I don't—"

Then a cheer came from the same direction. The same kind you're used to hearing on the Fourth of July.

"Okay, what is *this*?" La Pierre said as he stood.

In a rush, some of the swabbies made their way to the nurse's desk.

"THE WAR IS OVER!" somebody shouted. Just like that.

I barely noticed Richard La Pierre plop back down on his bed, his hands in his lap.

The war is what?

It seemed like everybody began talking at once.

"Hey, looks like the war is over!"

"Yeah, the doctor just came down and told us the news!"

"Wait, wait! *When* did this happen? Really?"

"A bomb! They said it was a bomb they dropped on Japan! Can you believe that?!"

The navy boys hugged one another and smiled. There was laughter aplenty. But I couldn't get up. It was as if I were a part of the mattress, the bedding, the flooring, the earth.

Tears of joy were shed as some of the navy guys that weren't too infirm to dance started to Lindy Hop in the center aisle.

As the world suddenly slowed and tuned in to a lower frequency—a vibration nearly too deep to hear—I felt my head turn involuntarily in slow motion toward Richard (so slow that the individual blinks of his eyes seemed to take an eternity to complete). I saw four years fly by, in the wink of an eye, with an exclamation mark floating free, in space, without a final sentence to attach itself to.

I felt nothing. I only saw the concerns of our buried people, who didn't know the end any more than I did.

There were rifles going off, without sounds. There were hearts beating, without blood. There was a war going on, and it was over.

The war was finally over . . . and it felt so damn good . . . but it didn't feel like anything without the ones who made the end possible.

Brooklyn, New York, August 21, 1945.

Just inside the entrance of the apartment building, within a small vestibule, was a row of names and a series of buzzers, affixed to the wall, used to call up to the apartments on the upper floors. Running my finger down the list of names, I made note that I was in the right place: 486 Brooklyn Avenue. For a couple of seconds my finger hovered over the button, unsure of whether I should go through with it. Without another thought, though, I pressed the button and closed my eyes, taking a deep breath and holding it in.

I was already uncomfortable.

Just a few minutes before I arrived at the tenement, I strolled down Brooklyn Avenue, and as I got closer to the corner apartments, I began receiving odd stares from the locals. I was a walking circus. The children playing in the street, the people sitting on their stoops, and a couple of elderly people walking down the sidewalk, all paused to look at the marine, dressed as I was in my uniform. They didn't ogle me simply because I was a marine, though. Servicemen were commonplace in any part of the United States. In truth, as I walked down the street, looking at the addresses on the buildings, it was apparent to them who I was—or, at least, what I was doing there and who I was looking for.

In those days, in those close-knit city blocks, everybody knew everybody's business. Neighbors became extended family members, and local gossip was better than cancer.

Mrs. Abbot used to have a star hanging in her kitchen window. Now all she has is a telegram, folded in the family Bible. Mr. Katz's boy used to write home every day, but something happened to his son's hands at Salerno. His son is learning to write his name now with a pencil held between his teeth.

Standing in the foyer, I opened my eyes again, looking out the glass-fronted door, at how the light bent strangely against the weather-beaten panes. Oddly enough, this was the same light from the same sun I had witnessed twisting its rays below the Five Sisters, a world and a lifetime away.

"Hello?" A small voice came from an even smaller speaker, below the row of buzzers.

My heart nearly jumped in my neck, startled, yet somehow I managed to clear my throat. "Sterling Mace," I said. "I—"

Before I could say anything else, there was a buzz and a sharp click within the door's unlocking mechanism, allowing me to enter the apartment building.

Inside it was the same old Brooklyn tenement, almost comforting: plaster walls, thick painted doors, nothing too shabby, yet nothing to differentiate this building from the dozens just like it that lined every one of these crowded streets.

I rode the elevator up and found the unit number. I knocked.

The door opened, and before me stood a very nondescript, middle-aged Jewish woman—her eyes glossy and tinted a light pink, the telltale sign of tears being held back in a battle that was soon to be lost.

"Sterling?" Her eyes didn't leave mine. I felt compelled to return her stare, but I had to break off—I couldn't stand her gaze. Immediately my sight drifted over her shoulder and to the wall inside the living room of her small apartment. On the wall was the largest portrait I had ever seen. It was huge, at least three by five feet, well framed, adorned with a perfectly painted image of the head and shoulders of a smiling teenager—the type of smile that said he was now ready for the rest of his life.

I knew that smile well.

The woman saw that I was looking at the picture, and she took a quick glance at the painting herself. When she returned my gaze, her face wore a smile—one that appeared eerily like that of the young man on the wall.

Cordially, I took off my cap. "Mrs. Levy?"

"Yes, Sterling. Please . . . come in."

The heartbreaking part is that I'm twenty-one years old and I can look a man straight in the eyes and then kill him deader than hell, but I can barely brave the face of a grieving mother who lost her son to a place that most people have never heard of. Or dreamed of.

In a dreamlike state I step into the home where Seymour Levy grew up. Sy had spent most of his life here. He knew the hallways and bedrooms, the tables and chairs, the smell of his mother's cooking. The feel of his bed. Softly, he spoke the words of Rudyard Kipling, late at night, sitting in his room under the cast of a dim bedstand light. I'm sure Sy pored over the stories—*Gunga Din* and *The Jungle Book*—over and over, until he could recite every word by heart.

The sum of a life is measured *how*? By the quantity of years or by the remembrances entrusted to others?

In Sy's case, my memories of the kid made him whole. To his mother, however, his legacy simply meant he was gone.

It could have easily been my mother, standing here with a

stranger in her home—living out the last minutes of her son's life through the recollections of those who knew him till the end. That's a sobering thought, and it doesn't make one bit of difference that my mom had already lost a baby once, while Seymour Levy was an only child.

Hurt is hurt, and that's a fact, but the vacuum left in a mother's womb must be the darkest place imaginable, no matter how bright the cause for which she gave.

Just inside the door, Levy's mother gives me a hug, holding me there for a few moments before releasing me. Yet even as she lets go of the embrace she still grasps me by my shoulders, at arm's length—her eyes taking in the shape of my face, my uniform, the way that I stand.

For the first time she gets a look at the missing link in Sy's personal chain of events. One of the last people to see her boy alive.

"Here." She waves a hand to shoo away any maudlin sentiments (as if they were that easy to dismiss) and walks toward the kitchen area. "Come. Have a seat. I'm sorry the place is such a mess. I just want to thank you for stopping by, Sterling. You don't know *how* much it means to me and my husband, having one of Seymour's marine friends over. We just don't know much about what happened that day."

"It's not a problem, Mrs. Levy. Seymour was a good friend of mine." Instead of sitting where she indicated, I stop in front of the huge portrait, admiring the likeness, the nice frame, recalling the way Sy and I used to smile and give each other a thumbs-up before heading into combat.

A heart beats somewhere in the portrait, but I don't know whether it's mine or his. It's a tough thing to articulate. It's a hell of a feeling to break down.

"Sterling?" Suddenly Levy's mother is standing right beside me. She startled me; I didn't hear her walk up. "Would you like anything? Some tea? Water? I've got sandwiches."

"No. No thank you, Mrs. Levy. I'm fine, thank you." She had caught me daydreaming—remembering back to when Levy and I first arrived on Pavuvu together. Sy and I had just arrived at K Company's street and begun settling into a temporary tent when Levy gave us a big surprise.

Sy put his seabag down on a cot and looked around the quarters. "Well, if we gotta stay here all night, we're gonna need some light."

"Nah," I said. "They ain't gonna keep us here for long." Looking around some more, I saw the tent was pretty bare; at least it wasn't crowded. "This place ain't so bad, ya know, Sy? Sy?"

I heard the click of a Zippo and then—whoosh!

"Shit!" Levy yelled. There was fire all over the deck . . . and spreading!

I jumped up out of my cot. "Sy, what the hell'd ya do!?" I could see the broken glass on the floor, and the liquid fire snaking around like lava. I knew then that Seymour had improvised one of those lamps we had all seen in the veteran marines' tents. It was basically a Coke bottle filled with gasoline, with a rag serving as a wick, but in a green marine's hand it was a firebomb—a Molotov cocktail!

Levy was in a panic, attempting to stamp the fire out with his boondockers.

"C'mon, Sy!" I yelled and grabbed him by the dungaree jacket. "Let's beat it! This place is goin' down!"

We ran outside the tent, and already marines were dashing up the street with buckets of water.

Every so often there were buckets placed outside of tents, going up and down the street. At the end of the street was a barrel filled with water, for cases just like this. The thing was, these canvas tents were old and rotted, very dry under the sun, so all it took was a little spark and they'd go up like bonfires.

Eventually the bucket brigade had the fire under control, so, slipping away a good distance from the scene of the crime, I pulled

Levy aside. "Hey, look, Sy, if ya didn't like the place, all ya had to do was say so." I laughed

Levy smirked. "Yeah, well, what the hell they gonna do to me, huh? Put me in the marines?"

"Good point," I considered.

Levy's mom and I sit at a small table with a floral cloth draped over it, just inside the dining room window. I notice her hands are fidgety, nervous, as she smoothes out the already smooth tablecloth.

Propping her chin on her fist, she looks out the window, contemplative, while the sun turns her simple brown eyes into honey-colored pools.

When she looks back at me, her irises change to a darker hue, an earthy tone, without the benefit of the sunlight to soften them.

"Sterling? Did Seymour ever tell you how I felt about him joining the marines?"

"Well . . . maybe . . . something about—"

"That I didn't want him to join? I know. I know that Seymour and I didn't part on the best of terms. He was just so . . . so adamant about joining, you know? That *boy*. Once he made up his mind about something . . . that was *it*. Even as a child Seymour was like that. Ever the curious little man!" She chuckles and bites her lower lip, in order to take the pain away from where she's feeling it the most. The tears are just beginning to pool in her lower eyelids.

"And just think," she resumes. "I could have given him my blessing—but I *didn't*. It's as if I knew what was going to happen. He even died on the eve of a Jewish holiday."

There is a long pause. She produces a handkerchief and begins daubing the tears from her cheeks. I realize that the hanky had been wadded up in her hand this whole time, having already been used copiously, long before I arrived.

"What happened out there, Sterling?" she asks. "How did my Seymour die?"

Looking down at the tablecloth, I see orchids and wildflowers, marigolds and roses . . . not the shit-stained side of a cliff, with its bouquet of decomposed flesh and leaves of soiled toilet paper. I see Levy laughing at something I said on our voyage over to Pavuvu, and not the young man who regretted coming back to Peleliu after cashing out his million-dollar wound and giving it all to stupidity.

"Seymour died, Mrs. Levy," I say, hoping she can see the sincerity in my face; she can hear it in my voice. "He died very quickly. *Instantly*, even. I'm really sure . . . that is, I don't think it was possible for him to feel any pain, when it happened."

Although that wasn't the question she asked, was it?

"You were there? You were *right* there?"

"Only a few yards away."

Her mouth is moving, ever so slightly, but no sound is coming out—she's just letting the rivulets flow.

"Only a few yards away?" she pleads.

"Yes, ma'am. He wouldn't have even known what happened, it was so quick. The way anybody would want it to be."

"But . . ." She reaches across the table and grabs my hands, her eyes darting back and forth, desperate. "Was it worth it?"

"I don't understand. Was *what* worth it, Mrs. Levy?"

"What you boys did over there. Why Seymour didn't come back home. Was it worth it?"

"Ma'am . . ." I try to give her hands a reassuring squeeze. "I . . . I'm not sure what you're asking me, Mrs. Levy."

"Was it *worth* my boy not making it back *home*?"

I lean back in the chair, leaving her hands on the table among the pretty flowers. I want to be angry at the question—not at her, but at the question itself. I don't even know how I made it back, let alone how somebody else didn't. Yet one thing is certain: I know from experience that not knowing something is sometimes worse than knowing all the little details that you'd rather forget.

What am I supposed to say to something like that?

"Mrs. Levy," I begin, "I was just a marine. That's all. Just like Seymour . . . like a bunch of us, we were only doing our jobs. Sure, questions like that . . . questions like that, they're not questions that anybody thinks about, and they're not something that anybody can answer. But . . . you're asking me if it was worth it? Well . . . I think . . . I think that if Seymour thought it was right to join the Marine Corps . . . if *he* thought it was worth it? Then, Mrs. Levy . . . I promise you it was worth every last bit of it."

I finish speaking, and Mrs. Levy's hands are over her mouth, slack-jawed, still devoid of sound. However, I can make out what she's attempting to say, seen through the fingers that bar her lips.

Yes, she appears to say. *Yes, I understand. Yes and yes.*

Yes is a belief that even Larry Mahan couldn't refute.

Later that evening, when I walked out of Sy's home, I didn't feel any different. Nothing there had purged my soul of pain. There was no balm for a bleeding host.

I looked up toward the sky, however, expecting to see a trillion bright beacons in the blanket of night, just like the night I lay on the deck of the *Sea Runner,* having survived Peleliu.

This is it.

Instead, the streetlights choked out the stars, effortlessly. Yet I knew the stars were there—and that's all that mattered. Constellations of ghosts. That's all I had to show for my struggles on Peleliu, Ngesebus, and Okinawa. Constellations of ghosts.

So as I stood there, gazing toward the heavens, the only solace I had was that I had made it home—even as unreal as it seemed. I was back in New York, alive . . . and maybe, just maybe, I had a little help making it back all the way.

It must have been a glorious day in heaven the day that Sister Dorothy finally laid down her weapon, never again having to concern herself with the earthly crowd.

Sleeping on a cloud.

EPILOGUE

THE UNIFORM IS FOLDED AND put away. Everything is over: the war, my current obligations to a grateful nation—it's all over. I'm free of everything except for my memories.

That's the toughest part.

I open the front door, walk out to the street, and look up toward the boulevard. Three years ago I walked up that street with my little cardboard suitcase full of civilian clothes, never knowing that when I reached the Marine Corps they would throw the suitcase and all its contents straight in the garbage.

George McNevin comes over to eat supper with my family. My mom remarks to George that she'd like to have him over every night, because with George over, that's the most I've eaten since I've been home. George quits chewing for a second and looks at my mom. I put my spoon down.

Funny.

I don't dream anymore. Not even nightmares.

I'm just having a hard time understanding how I got here. Adjusting. Making room inside myself for life after wartime. I don't fit.

On the street corner you can still find some of the same wiseguys who used to hang out there every Saturday, before the war. They act as if the boys who were killed in Europe are still there, shooting the same shit. Of course, they're not. I'm not there, either. I'm in uniform, and they ask me where I've been. I tell them. Either they don't understand or they don't want to. They've been to North Africa, Sicily, and France. I've been to . . . *places*. Places they've never heard of.

Pitkin Avenue, in Canarsie, East New York. I go down to the shops, with my mustering-out pay, and pick out a brown zoot suit, with a one-button roll and pegged pants. My hat is a dark brown fedora with a wide three-inch brim. A familiar marine sees me on the corner in that getup, and I can't stand the way he looks at me.

So we look for jobs, only they've got this new government program: the 52-20 Club, which pays out twenty dollars a week for fifty-two weeks, until we can get back on our feet.

A young newly discharged marine walks up to a desk, and the government man behind the desk asks the marine what's his occupation.

"I kill Japanese," the young marine says. Only he doesn't really say that. Instead, he says, "I'm an exterminator."

"Okay." The government man jots down the note. "So, have you had any luck finding a job killing Japanese?" That's not what the man behind the desk actually says, either. What the man says is, "Exterminators . . . even in a big city like this, everybody's got pests, but not everyone can afford to get rid of them."

"No," the young marine concedes. "I mean, yes. People in my line of work aren't in very high demand these days." He pauses. "Especially now that the war's over."

The government checks keep coming in the mail. We blow our cash on crap games and liquor, doing everything we can to forget.

On Okinawa.

At the aid station.

"Boy, you must have really been out of it, buddy." A marine in the cot next to me is propped up on his elbow. "I thought you were dead."

"Whattaya mean?" I ask. My words come out in a coarse whisper.

He chuckles. "You were just laying there. Not movin' an inch. An' this band came by—some Salvation Army quartet or somethin', and they were playin' right at the foot of your cot. I mean *right* at the foot! And you didn't move a muscle. As far as I knew, they were playin' for a dead man!"

I try for a smile, but I come up short. I feel like the shit that even shit turns its nose up at.

The last thing I remember is a doctor sitting at the side of my cot administering a shot of sodium pentothal. I've got some choice words to say about the new officers on Okinawa. They're not like the ones we had on Peleliu.

Before that, I recall getting on a stretcher, at the aid station, and some marine comes by and attaches a manila tag to my blouse. On the tag he scribbles COMBAT FATIGUE. I don't like the sound of that, so I flip the tag over, and sure enough another marine comes by and writes PSYCHONEUROSES ANXIETY. I like that better. It sounds more clinical.

I'm married in 1946. Her name is Joyce Sellers. She has beautiful auburn hair. We have three beautiful children, Skip Mace and two lovely girls, Deborah Marie and Jody Eliza. My family is my life.

So, what's next? It's just life. There's not a day that goes by when I don't think about the war.

It's the Jean Morgan School of Commercial Art, under the GI Bill. It's a job at Republic Aviation for eight years. It's—

Off Okinawa. Aboard the USS *Bowie*. Going home.

Before we can depart Okinawa's anchorage, the cry goes up: *Man battle stations!* Kamikaze planes loop and dive; the night is lit up by tracers and antiaircraft fire. There's the real threat of dying aboard this ship, after having survived everything the Nips threw at me on Peleliu and Okinawa. It's enough to send me into a tailspin.

Over there's Major Paul Douglas, standing on the ship's deck, doing his best Francis Scott Key, under the bombs bursting in air. He's trying to gather a platoon of walking wounded to go back to Okinawa.

"See that guy?" I tell an old black army private who's been evacuated for tuberculosis. "Don't you go *near* that sonuvabitch!"

It's twenty-seven years of working for the Long Island Parks and Recreation Administration, eighteen of which I manage the Jones Beach Theater in New York, where Guy Lombardo is a staple attraction. Life is good.

I think about the war.

Going to the very first 1st Marine Division reunion in 1947, at the Hotel Astor in Manhattan, I don't recognize a single marine without his helmet and filthy dungarees. A waste.

Billy Leyden and Jim McEnery start a New York chapter of the 1st Marine Division, and they fight over who's going to be the president of the club. I'm the secretary. You put a drink in Sterling Mace's hand, and I'm going to drink it. That's all there is to it—and I don't have to remind you what Groucho Marx said about being a member of a club.

I see those faces every day.

But what does it all mean? Surely you can't sum up a man's entire life in the few sentences of a book, no matter how large the book is. The life is in the margins.

Or maybe you can.

Mrs. Levy asked me if it was worth it.

Now, I don't concern myself with politics much, nor do I spend my time examining the socioeconomic picture of the world at large.

The fact is, the United States has been in other wars since World War II, though none of them has had the global impact of the war in which I fought.

Mrs. Levy, was it worth it?

That's a difficult question to answer.

Or maybe it isn't.

If Mrs. Levy were alive today, smoothing her floral tablecloth, I might, at eighty-eight, lounging in my kitchen, alongside my African gray parrot, have a better answer for her—but only in hindsight, mind you. It's been sixty-five years since our last meeting, and the majority of those years she never witnessed for herself.

"Mrs. Levy," I would say, "it really *was* worth it."

"Was it, Sterling?"

"Yes, ma'am." I'd smile. "The simple answer is, if you were alive for me to tell you . . . What we did over there? There never *has* been another World War."

A little girl died in South Ozone Park one day . . .

Appendix A

A ROLL OF HONOR

Veterans with K/3/5 who gave their lives by the end of Okinawa

PELELIU

James P. Alley

Gilbert Amdur

John F. Barrett

William B. Bauerschmidt

Thomas R. Baxter

Donald W. Beamer

David W. Beard

Arthur W. Cook

Raymond L. Grawet

Andrew A. Haldane

James P. Hogg

Alfred D. Jones

Edward M. Jones

Seymour Levy

Charles R. McClary

Joseph R. Mercer

William S. Middlebrook

Alden J. Moore

Clarence R. Morgan

Robert B. Oswalt
Ralph H. Porrett
Tony J. Putorti
Walter C. Reynolds
Lyman D. Rice
Thomas P. Rigney
Henry J. Ryzner
Lewis L. Schafer
Walter B. Stay
John W. J. Steele
John E. Teskevich
Lyle Van Norman
Charles S. Williams

OKINAWA

Leonard Ahner
Stanley W. Arthur
Roy W. Bowman
Wilburn L. Beasley
Will G. Bird
Kenneth N. Boaz
Joseph S. Cook
Robert C. Doran
Harold Downs
Alexander E. Doyle
Josh O. Haney
Gordon E. Hanke
Raymond Hargadon
James W. Hargroder
John P. Heeb
Frederick Hudson
Samuel Y. Knight

Joseph E. Lambert

James W. Mercer

Garner W. Mott

Howard B. Nease

George D. Pick

Aubrey J. Rogers

Gordon L. Sessions

Archie P. Steele

Cecil C. Stout

Philip J. Stupfel

Lewis E. Verga

Marion B. Vermeer

Marion A. Westbrook

Jay W. Whitacker

Donald Wilkening

Marshall B. Williams

Richard L. Williams

John Wishnewski Jr.

Robert G. Woods

The above survived neither death, injury, nor illness and were not present by the end of the battles. The honor is all yours. Mine is the honor to have served with you.